# Chemical Demilitarization

# Chemical Demilitarization

## Public Policy Aspects

*Al Mauroni*

Westport, Connecticut
London

**Library of Congress Cataloging-in-Publication Data**

Mauroni, Albert J., 1962–
    Chemical demilitarization : public policy aspects / Al Mauroni.
        p.    cm.
    Includes bibliographical references and index.
    ISBN 0–275–97796–X (alk. paper)
    1. Chemical weapons disposal—Government policy—United States.    I. Title.
UG447.M34523    2003
    363.72'87—dc21          2002190906

British Library Cataloguing in Publication Data is available.

Library of Congress Catalog Card Number: 2002190906
ISBN: 0–275–97796–X

First published in 2003

Praeger Publishers, 88 Post Road West, Westport, CT 06881
An imprint of Greenwood Publishing Group, Inc.
www.praeger.com

Printed in the United States of America

The paper used in this book complies with the
Permanent Paper Standard issued by the National
Information Standards Organization (Z39.48–1984).

10  9  8  7  6  5  4  3  2  1

Dedicated to Roseann, my editor, coauthor, and greatest supporter

# Contents

viii    Contents

# Tables and Figures

**TABLES**

**FIGURES**

*Photo essay follows page 100.*

# Preface

One of the more controversial aspects of the Army's chemical warfare history is its development, stockpiling, and disposal of its chemical weapons. It has always amazed me how the Army leadership has dragged out a program that, at first glance, appears to be a rather simple and executable objective of eliminating the nation's aging chemical weapons into a $24 billion, 25-year disposal effort. Then I thought, Maybe this is like repairing the Pentagon—built from the ground up in a few years and refurbished over a 15-year period. Some things just don't get the priorities that one might expect.

As I became professionally involved in the chemical demilitarization program, I was fascinated by the degree of control that citizen advisory committees had over the Army's subject-matter experts. The Army seemed to go to extraordinary lengths to appease a few vocal citizens, not all of whom even lived near a stockpile site. When I saw the number of congressional public laws directing specific actions within the program, I began to understand more about the process of how the Army has reacted to Congressional prodding, which in turn was brought about by public clamor. Yet, as a former Chemical Corps officer and chemist by education, I could not comprehend what made this program so complex or what explained its large life-cycle costs. So much effort for such a little problem.

Of course, it isn't that simple; when the military gets involved in a public controversy, the execution of the matter is never simple. There is a long history of events and discussions that have led to the Army's heavy investment in this program, costs that the Army leadership would have probably rather seen expended in other, more productive areas. I wanted to understand more of this past to understand how the Army got itself into this position, how Congress got involved, how its were interests developed, and how the public became so distrustful of the Army's efforts. The answer was in public policy analysis.

In truth, I am not schooled in public policy, and I was associated with the Army's chemical demilitarization program for only a very short while, assisting its public outreach efforts. So why am I writing this book? Probably because no one else will, and because I strongly feel that there are parallels to other Army Chemical Corps efforts (its vaccination program, the federal response to chemical and biological [CB] terrorism, and Gulf War illness investigations, to name a few). I needed to learn how the chemical demilitarization program evolved, and the answer was in Colonel (ret.) John Boyd's observations on destruction and creation: "One cannot determine the character or nature of a system within itself. Attempts to do so lead to confusion and disorder."[1]

That certainly has been the case to date. The history, complexity of issues, and number of actors in the chemical demilitarization program make it a staggering topic to address, yet, if one strips away the technical discussions, it becomes very simply the government's attempt to dispose of its aging chemical weapons while addressing public concerns. This is a public policy concern at its most basic roots, yet the Army and the Department of Defense (DOD) have not treated it as such. My hope is that, in addition to learning a great deal about the chemical demilitarization program, we can take note of the positive and negative aspects of executing a military program in light of genuine public concerns.

There are at least three distinct bands of evolution in the chemical demilitarization program's life cycle. There is the Army-funded chemical demilitarization program running from 1972 to 1984, when it managed an executable, safe, and cost-effective program to dispose of its obsolete and leaking chemical munitions. There is the broader DOD-funded chemical demilitarization program that initiated the effort to dispose of the entire U.S. chemical weapons stockpile to make room for binary chemical munitions, running from 1985 to 1990. Finally, there is the current DOD chemical demilitarization program, which, deprived of the need to make room for the binaries, now supports the U.S. government's arms control agenda. The decisions and progress of the program have been made on the grander backdrop of these three periods, and they cannot be viewed separately if one intends to understand this area.

I would like to acknowledge the following people and agencies; without their assistance this book would have been impossible to develop: Dr. Ted Prociv, Ms. Amie Hoeber, Major General John Doesburg, Major General (ret.) Sam Bass, Major General (ret.) Bob Orton, Brigadier General (ret.) David Nydam, Brigadier General (ret.) Walt Busbee, Brigadier General (ret.) Pete Hidalgo, Colonel (ret.) Gene "Doc" Bishop, Colonel (ret.) Chuck Kelly, Colonel (ret.) Walt Polley, Lieutenant Colonel Ben Hagar, Lieutenant Colonel John Megnia, Lieutenant Colonel Tom Woloszyn, Major Bill Huber and the great employees at the public outreach and information offices of the Program Manager for Chemical Demilitarization and the U.S. Army Environmental Center.

Special thanks to my editor Heather Ruland-Staines at Praeger Publishers for continuing to support me and thanks to a great copy editor, Deborah Whitford, who has greatly improved my work. My wife Roseann, my companion, adviser, best friend, has played an immeasurable role in assisting me to complete this book. As Ellen Goodman, author and columnist, noted, "you can fire your secretary, divorce your spouse, abandon your children, but they remain your coauthors forever." Also, my deep appreciation for the long-time support of Burton Wright III, the U.S. Army Chemical School's command historian and a prolific writer, who passed away on February 8, 2002, in Springfield, Missouri.

# Abbreviations

| | |
|---|---|
| ABCDF | Aberdeen Chemical Agent Disposal Facility |
| ACAMS | Automated Continuous Agent Monitoring System |
| ACAT | Acquisition Category |
| ACWA | Assembled Chemical Weapons Assessment |
| AMC | Army Materiel Command |
| ANCDF | Anniston Chemical Agent Disposal Facility |
| ASA(ALT) | Assistant Secretary of the Army for Acquisition, Logistics, and Technology |
| ASA(I&L) | Assistant Secretary of the Army for Installations and Logistics |
| ASA(IL&E) | Assistant Secretary of the Army for Installations, Logistics, and Environment |
| ASA(RDA) | Assistant Secretary of the Army for Research, Development, and Acquisition |
| ATAP | Alternative Technologies and Approaches Project |
| ATSD(NCB) | Assistant to the Secretary of Defense for Nuclear and Chemical and Biological Programs |
| AVIP | Anthrax Vaccination Immunization Program |
| BGCDF | Blue Grass Chemical Agent Disposal Facility |
| BWC | Biological Weapons and Toxins Convention |
| CAC | Citizen Advisory Committee |
| CAIS | Chemical Agent Identification Sets |
| CAMDS | Chemical Agent Materiel Disposal System |
| CB | Chemical and Biological |
| CBDCOM | Chemical and Biological Defense Command |
| CBW | Chemical and Biological Warfare |
| CDTF | Chemical Demilitarization Training Facility |
| CHASE | Cut Holes and Sink Em |
| CMDA | Chemical Materiel Destruction Agency |
| CONUS | Continental United States |
| CRDA | Chemical Demilitarization and Remediation Activity |
| CRDEC | Chemical Research, Development, and Engineering Center |

| | |
|---|---|
| CSDP | Chemical Stockpile Disposal Program |
| CSEPP | Chemical Stockpile Emergency Preparedness Program |
| CTR | Cooperative Threat Reduction |
| CW | Chemical Warfare |
| CWC | Chemical Weapons Convention |
| CWRC | Chemical Warfare Review Commission |
| CWS | Chemical Warfare Service |
| CWWG | Chemical Weapons Working Group |
| DAAMS | Depot Area Air Monitoring System |
| DATS | Drill and Transfer System |
| DCSOPS | Deputy Chief of Staff for Operations and Plans |
| DDR&E | Deputy Director for Research and Engineering |
| DOD | Department of Defense |
| DOE | Department of Energy |
| DOJ | Department of Justice |
| DRI | Defense Reform Initiative |
| EIS | Environmental Impact Statement |
| EPA | Environmental Protection Agency |
| FEMA | Federal Emergency Management Agency |
| GAO | General Accounting Office |
| HHS | Health and Human Services |
| HQ DA | Headquarters, Department of the Army |
| IRZ | Immediate Response Zone |
| JACADS | Johnston Atoll Chemical Agent Disposal System |
| JI | Johnston Island |
| MCA | Military Construction–Army |
| MCE | Maximum Critical Event |
| MLRS | Multiple Launch Rocket System |
| NAS | National Academy of Sciences |
| NATO | North Atlantic Treaty Organization |
| NBC | Nuclear, Biological, and Chemical |
| NECDF | Newport Chemical Agent Disposal Facility |
| NOAEL | No Observed Adverse Effect Level |
| NRC | National Research Council |
| NSCM | Nonstockpile Chemical Materiels |
| O&M | Operations and Maintenance funds |
| OPCW | Organization for the Prohibition of Chemical Weapons |
| OSD | Office of the Secretary of Defense |
| OVT | Operational Verification Testing |
| PAZ | Protective Action Zone |
| PBCDF | Pine Bluff Chemical Agent Disposal Facility |
| PEIS | Programmatic Environmental Impact Statement |
| PEO | Program Executive Officer |

| | |
|---|---|
| PICs | Products of Incomplete Combustion |
| PMCD | Program Manager for Chemical Demilitarization |
| PROC | Procurement funds |
| PUCDF | Pueblo Chemical Agent Disposal Facility |
| R&D | Research and Development funds |
| RCRA | Resource Conservation and Recovery Act |
| RDT&E | Research, Development, Test and Evaluation |
| RMA | Rocky Mountain Arsenal |
| SALT | Strategic Arms Limitation Talks |
| SBCCOM | Soldier and Biological-Chemical Command |
| TOCDF | Tooele Chemical Agent Disposal Facility |
| TSCA | Toxic Substances Control Act |
| USATHAMA | U.S. Army Toxic and Hazardous Materials Agency |
| USD(AT&L) | Under Secretary of Defense for Acquisition, Technology, and Logistics |
| UMCDF | Umatilla Chemical Agent Disposal Facility |
| WMD CST | Weapons of Mass Destruction Civil Support Team |

# 1

## No More Chemical Arms

The Army's chemical demilitarization program has had its share and more of public controversy. The Army leadership has struggled for years over perceptions of its inability to adequately address the public's concerns in this area, facing concerns about whether it can successfully and safely dispose of the nation's chemical weapons stockpiles and why costs continue to climb and the schedule slips year after year. Properly managing the program seems to take a backseat to reacting to the latest crisis. Consider these fairly recent news events.

In the middle of October 2000, workers at Rocky Mountain Arsenal discovered six M139 bomblets, grapefruit-sized aluminum spheres designed to hold nerve agents within an "Honest John" guided missile warhead, in a scrap yard on the Army post. Each bomblet could hold a little over a pound of GB nerve agent, and given the age (more than 40 years old) and condition of the bomblets, the workers were unsure as to its stability. Within a day, the Army's Technical Escort Unit was on the scene to assess and stabilize the situation and awaited the Army's Materiel Assessment Review Board's approval to initiate disposal operations. The nearest community to the arsenal was Commerce City, Colorado, more than two miles away. The Army's initial recommendation was to destroy the bomblets in place (rather than risk transporting them) by placing five pounds of explosive around each munition and detonating the explosive. The charge would destroy much of the chemical agent, and the remaining vapors would safely dissipate in the open air. In fact, the Army had a formal agreement with the state of Colorado and the Environmental Protection Agency (EPA) to destroy explosively configured items with open detonations, in what is a pretty routine and accepted process.

The news of this finding was not immediately released to the public, a point that the very sensitive Colorado press found very suspicious and unneighborly when it heard about the Army's recommended disposal plan. It was not the Commerce City folks living 2 miles away as much as the 2.5 million citizens of Denver, Colorado, 10 miles away who were alarmed by the suggestion that the Army might release nerve agents into the air. The fact that the laws of physics would ensure that the volume of agent escaping explosive destruction would be dispersed into harmless concentrations within a half mile, prior to its even leaving Rocky Mountain Arsenal's boundaries, was somehow ignored or overlooked by the State regulators, who directed the Army not to move or destroy the bomblets without explicit State permission. Just a few months earlier, there had been a nerve gas leak at the chemical disposal facility at Tooele Army Depot; while no one had been exposed to any noticeable effects, the event had sensitized Colorado citizens to the chemical hazard that they lived with every day. In response, the Army held a series of public meetings and worked with state officials to identify how they could minimize any dangers.

After a month of discussions with state and federal health officials, the Army proposed deploying an explosive destruction system to contain the blast of opening the bomblets and to capture any escaping chemical agent. In addition, a collective protection shelter would be built over the scrap yard and the destruction system. By January 28, 2001, the Army had its equipment set up and was prepared to go. A soldier dressed in a Level A hazardous material suit, using a wand with a capture device at its end, gingerly picked up the bomblet, placed it into the destruction system, and detonated the device. After draining the chemical agent, the bomblet's metal shell and other residue were decontaminated. This process was repeated for the remaining bomblets.

The townspeople selected to watch the process by remote video camera with General John Coburn (commanding general, U.S. Army Materiel Command [AMC]) and Major General John Doesburg (commanding general, U.S. Army Soldier and Biological-Chemical Command [SBCCOM]) were impressed by the efficiency and safety of the entire process. The fact that the process would have been as safe and efficient and far less costly if the Army had stood by its open-air detonation process that it first considered was not mentioned by the press, Colorado politicians or Army spokespersons. Thus, a two-week project that would have costed $25,000 for a routine disposal of these small nerve agent-filled bomblets turned into a eight-month ordeal costing nearly $8.5 million.

In the summer of 2001, citizens of Calhoun County, Alabama, were told that the $1 billion facility titled the Anniston Chemical Agent Disposal Facility was ready to begin its systemization testing, which would initiate several burns of chemical agents to test out its installed equipment. The facility had been under construction for more than three years, and the local community had been living with 2,250 tons of chemical weapons for decades. The state and county had been the recipients of federal emergency response funds for more than 10 years, receiving more than $100 million, almost a third of all the federal funds going to the emergency response programs around the eight chemical weapons stockpiles in the United States. Yet, for some reason, the governor and a number of concerned citizens were not ready to say good-bye to these weapons.

About three dozen protesters were at the gates of Anniston Army Depot on the day of the ribbon-cutting ceremony on June 9, 2001, formally opening the facility for operations. The state governor insisted that he would not allow the facility to begin full operations, citing the Army's failure to fully develop its emergency response program. Although the emergency response program was meant to address the safety of storing chemical munitions at the stockpile and not the incineration operations, the governor took this opportunity to force the Army and Federal Emergency Management Agency's (FEMA) hand on addressing his demands for additional time and resources. If need be, he would file a lawsuit to stop the operations (in fact, he subsequently did file such a lawsuit, several times over a two-year period).[1]

Calhoun County officials took their case to Washington, soliciting support from the National Academy of Sciences and requesting that their congressional representatives petition Defense Secretary Donald Rumsfeld to stop the program until "maximum protection," as they defined it, could be ensured at the disposal facility. FEMA had over $40 million in emergency response funds that were not yet committed and that the Alabamians wanted for their use. Part of the disagreement was with FEMA's interpretation of necessary protection measures. FEMA had recommended using shelter-in-place kits, while the county officials had developed only evacuation routes. The Calhoun County commissioners and the state EMA had dismissed the use of shelter-in-place juts by deriding their use as "duct tape and plastic." In addition, the county wanted personal protective hoods for all the citizens around the disposal facility, a measure that the Army and FEMA both disagreed with due to some deaths that had occurred in Israel when untrained citizens attempted to use the disposable masks. Ultimately, the local politicians and hysteria prevailed over FEMA and sound risk management.

Senator Richard Shelby (R-AL) and Senator Mitch McConnell (R-KY) both began calls for congressional hearings into the Army's chemical demilitarization program. The $15 billion program had often been a target of General Accounting Office (GAO) investigations, public demonstrations, and national and local media scrutiny. The fact that 2002 was an election year for the state and for congressional officials had absolutely nothing to do with their calls for investigations into a defense program that had run for 15 years, destroying millions of pounds of chemical agent materiel without a single casualty or major incident. This history included workers within the disposal facilities and local citizens from the surrounding communities at Tooele Army Depot's disposal facility and the pilot disposal facility at Johnston Island.

In early August 2001, Major General Craig Whelden, the deputy commanding general of U.S. Army Pacific, formally closed the U.S. Army Chemical Activity Pacific on Johnston Island, ending its stewardship of a chemical weapons stockpile that amounted to about 6.6 percent of the nation's offensive chemical weapons capability. Johnston Island, a man-made island of an atoll located about 800 miles from Hawaii, had stored the chemical munitions for nearly 30 years. The Johnston Atoll Chemical Agent Disposal System had been in operation for more than 10 years, destroying over 400,000 rockets, artillery and mortar projectiles, aerial bombs, ton containers, and land mines, without a single serious incident and without any noticeable impact on the environment.

Following the September 11, 2001, terrorist incident, Senator Evan Bayh (R-IN) and a group of congressional legislators requested that President George W. Bush enact a higher state of security over the chemical stockpile sites, including additional troops on the grounds and establishing a no-fly zone. The stockpile sites had been assessed for terrorist threats and the remote chance that a plane might crash into the site in the past, but the thought was that the civilian security force, the alarms, cameras, emergency response capabilities, and heavily fortified bunkers minimized that risk. September 11 changed all those perceptions. General John Coburn ordered increased physical security measures around its eight chemical stockpile sites, taking steps similar in nature to those taken by states to increase security around their nuclear power plants.

In November 2001, the Army proposed accelerating the disposal effort at Aberdeen Proving Ground, a neutralization pilot program, to complete partial destruction of the mustard agent by the end of 2002. After all, if the mustard agent was not there, there would be no security risk. This action would require more than $200 million and would only break the agent into its subcomponents. To meet Chemical Weapons Convention (CWC) requirements, the sub-components would have to be further treated to ensure that no one could reformulate the agent. But, at the least, the threat of a mustard agent incident could be eliminated three years ahead of time.[2] Why the Army had not previously proposed to accelerate the disposal of this stockpile ahead of its planned schedule was a slightly more complex and political issue.

There would be a similar accelerated effort proposed to take place at Newport Chemical Depot, where tons of VX nerve agent sat in large steel containers. They would also undergo a neutralization technique, and the Army could accelerate its program to complete a partial destruction of the nerve agent by the end of 2003. This was also a pilot program, meaning that the disposal technologies had never been attempted on a large scale (Parsons, the contractor, had already experienced complications). The neutralization technologies had been proven on smaller scales in a laboratory, but not at this level. The disposal process would be more expensive than the incineration technology conducted at Tooele and Johnston Island (and planned for Anniston, Pine Bluff, and Umatilla), and the waste stream management would be more complex, since neutralization would cause at least five times the waste product as incineration. The citizens had swapped an incinerator for a chemical processing factory, but alternative technology was what the citizens wanted, wasn't it?

Welcome to the U.S. Army's chemical demilitarization program.

The Army demilitarizes tens of thousands of conventional munitions every year without incident, but the issue of demilitarizing chemical munitions and agents causes normally rational citizens and politicians to turn red-faced, raise their voices, and pound their hands on podiums to focus attention on this particular area. There are many reasons that this special attention takes place, and for the most part, these reasons are not associated with any overwhelming scientific or technical challenges that the U.S. government faces. The U.S. chemical demilitarization program does not require a complex effort to understand, but it has been a monumental challenge to execute. Many unfounded criticisms that citizen activists voice about the program contribute to the difficulty of executing the chemical demilitarization program, to include causing misperceptions on the part of individuals in Congress and in governor positions and even Army and FEMA leadership, who should know better.

Most of the issues churned up in the controversy are related to interpretations of applications of technology, the fundamental argument being that the Army cannot be trusted to safely and efficiently operate an incinerator without (1) allowing chemical warfare (CW) agents to leak out of their munitions during the disassembly process; (2) allowing dangerous products of incomplete combustion such as furans or dioxins to escape out of the smokestacks; (3) covering up its mistakes and lying to the public about the actual risks involved; or (4) all of the above. Many critics are convinced that the deadline to destroy the U.S. chemical stockpile is artificial (as it was, in part, shaped by the CWC and approved by Congress as opposed to being based on the relative danger of an aging stockpile) and that a better technology is just around the corner. All the Army has to do is safely store the munitions until these technologies can be applied. A "better technology" is defined as one that destroys CW agents and munitions without any (zero) risk to people or the environment and without any emissions into the open air; to these critics, costs to the taxpayers, measures of relative safety, and overall program efficiency are irrelevant.

I am not suggesting that the critics' approach is necessarily wrong, just that it ensures that Congress and the GAO will continue to criticize the program as it mounts a defense bill of more than $20 billion dedicated over a 20-year-plus program life cycle. Developing, testing, and implementing new, unproven "alternative" technologies, while continuing to store the CW materiel and weapons, only increase the cost and time to complete the program. This book will not debate the fine points of various alternative technologies; if you want that discussion, review the findings of the National Academy of Sciences (NAS), which has done a superb, unbiased evaluation of what is available out there today and what is achievable.

This book does evaluate how the Army has executed the chemical demilitarization program over the decades, with an eye toward identifying the specific challenges and policy issues that have made this effort so difficult. For instance, consider these viewpoints from the program's critics:

- The Army runs the chemical demilitarization program to comply with arms control agreements, and there is no consequence to extending an international treaty schedule.

- The Army disregards public safety issues of the stockpile sites and twists the facts to support its disposal strategy. It doesn't care about the nearby residents.
- The Army doesn't understand all the risks and issues surrounding incineration because it hasn't studied the technology long enough—evidence its inability to stay on schedule and on budget on an agenda that it set.
- The Army has not objectively evaluated available technologies and refuses to consider waiting until alternative technologies mature. Other technologies could provide the same result with safer methods.
- The Army cannot promise the citizens surrounding the eight chemical stockpile sites that they are completely safe from risk. The amount of chemical agents at one stockpile site, if released, could kill over 80,000 people!
- The Army's demilitarization studies, such as the one on M55 rocket leakers, are developed to meet its own interests (justifying the need to incinerate the stockpiles sooner rather than wait for new technologies).
- The Army denied that exposure to Agent Orange was harmful, that the Dugway Proving Ground sheep kill in 1968 was not a result of the accidental release of nerve agents, and that Gulf War illnesses were not caused by chemical or biological warfare agents. Why trust them now?
- The Army hired public relations consultants in an attempt to spin propaganda against vocal critics of the chemical demilitarization program.

These stories grow year to year, fueled by congressional candidates looking for an issue, citizen groups using advocacy science to attack the Army in court, and constant scrutiny from the press looking for a hot story. They all may mean well, but they distort the truth. The Army has had a difficult time executing this program due to a number of complex issues, including the lack of a consistent message over the decades, the lack of senior-level commitment within the Army leadership, and most importantly, the lack of effective communication with the public and congressional committees. The Army's greatest failure is that it has never recognized that the chemical demilitarization program is a public policy issue, and it has failed to craft an appropriate strategy to address it as such. Its second greatest failure is that the Army in general does a poor job communicating its important issues to the public and Congress and, specifically, does not communicate issues related to chemical and biological warfare well. Yet the Army still wants to execute this troubled program it started decades ago.

Many people are surprised to here that the Army initially proposed completing this effort with $1.7 billion and in less than 10 years, starting in 1985. At that time, this seemed a reasonable estimate by engineering cost models, as no one at that time had any practical experience in running a chemical disposal facility. By 2000, the program has grown to a $15 billion effort taking more than 20 years to complete. Recent estimates in October 2001 revised the life-cycle cost estimate, increasing the program by another $9 billion (to $24 billion), and the program could take more than 25 years to complete. Has something gone terribly wrong here? To examine this issue, we have to go back beyond the start of this program.

## DEALING WITH PUBLIC PERCEPTIONS

Rocky Mountain Arsenal was one of the three main arsenals created for the Chemical Warfare Service in 1942 to produce chemical weapons. The Army purchased over 19,000 acres 10 miles from Denver on May 2, 1942, and spent six months and more than $50 million to create a chemical weapons manufacturing capability. In addition to mustard agent and lewisite, Rocky Mountain Arsenal (RMA) produced incendiary munitions. Most of these munitions were shipped overseas to build up stockpiles in the event that the United States desired an option to retaliate against German and Japanese use of chemical weapons in kind. This military policy was entirely in line with the Geneva Protocol of 1925, which the U.S. government had signed but not ratified.[3]

RMA was inactivated in 1947 but opened again in response to the Korean conflict. This time, the arsenal produced white phosphorous munitions, incendiary cluster bombs, and mustard agent artillery projectiles. The Army had built a production plant between 1951 and 1953 to initiate its production of sarin nerve agent, based on the collaborative research of former German and Edgewood Arsenal scientists. Between 1953 and 1957, RMA became the major source of the U.S. military's nerve agent munitions.

RMA's design had consciously included a two-mile buffer around its perimeter for both security and safety concerns. The standard waste management plan at the time was to use unlined settling basins for disposal of most noncaustic liquids by evaporation and seepage. Waste products from the production lines included arsenic trichloride, acetylene, and thionyl chloride. Waste streams from the chlorine plant were much more caustic and required a different approach than for these other wastes. Caustic ponds were reported to have caused groundwater contamination several miles from the point of origin. Construction crews developed a lined evaporation basin for these wastes, depositing clay soils up to 18 inches thick and compacting them to prevent seepage.

This uneven use of engineering practices resulted in problems in the early 1950s as area farmers down-gradient from the arsenal reported serious crop damage as they used the groundwater to supplement their surface water irrigation techniques. An investigation in 1954 revealed no suspected pollutants from the arsenal but did reveal harmful concentrations of sodium chlorides (salt) migrating from RMA's direction. While there was no direct evidence pointing to RMA, the Army constructed a new lined basin in 1956 called "Basin F." This pond had a maximum capacity of 243 million gallons and had a sealed 3/8-inch-thick asphalt liner. Vitrified clay pipes with chemically sealed joints carried all liquid wastes to this basin. It was this 93-acre evaporation pond that caught the public's attention as "the most contaminated spot on earth," as one of its former commanders stated in the 1970s (a quote often repeated by environmentalists and the mass media). While it is not hard to see how a large pond of waste streams from a chemical plant can be labeled as a very contaminated piece of terrain, it is also true that waste products from this lined pond did not seep into the surrounding community's water.[4] One should not necessarily equate the most contaminated spot on earth with the most hazardous threat to people or the environment, as this hazard has never been tied to any health impacts in the nearby community.

While the Army had stopped producing GB nerve agent at RMA in 1957, it continued to seek other sources of funding to keep the post open. In an effort to foster economic growth in the area after World War II, the U.S. government encouraged private industry to lease facilities at RMA. Under this lease program, Julius Hyman and Company began producing pesticides on the arsenal in 1946. In 1952, Shell Chemical Company (later, Shell Oil Company) acquired Julius Hyman and Company and continued to produce agricultural pesticides at RMA until 1982. The Air Force requested permission to build a nuclear power plant at the arsenal to develop nuclear-powered rockets, in response to the Soviet Sputnik launch in October 1957. In the mid-1960s, RMA facilities were mixing a propellant for Titan II missiles called Aerozine 50 for the space program.

Concerns about off-post groundwater contamination caused the Army to seek other forms of waste management. In an effort to get away from the use of basins altogether, RMA constructed a deep-well injection system by drilling 12,045 feet into impermeable rock. The intent was to deposit all chemical wastes, including the 165 million gallons in Basin F, into this well. Geological inspections of the rock formations in the area demonstrated that it would keep the waste from contaminating the groundwater.

To the public, especially decades later, this process might not sound extremely safe or even sane. Just dump the liquid chemical waste down a deep hole? Yet, drawing on oil drilling practices that had been used for years prior to 1960, chemical manufacturers employ this technique safely and continue to do this today with EPA approval. The process requires a preliminary geographical investigation to identify a suitable rock formation that would hold the intended volume of wastes, as well as prevent contamination of usable water supplies or freshwater aquifers. Wastes that are particularly suitable for this approach include oils, lubricants, ammonia, certain organic and inorganic acids, detergents and surfactants, solvents, herbicides, pesticides, biocides, and other aqueous wastes. Some companies today continue to develop and manage deep-well injection systems both within the United States and in other countries.[5]

RMA checked its deep-well injection system after it was completed, with the injection of 568,000 gallons of city water. After all tests were completed, it pumped fluids from Basin F and a pretreatment plant near the basin into the well. The fluids had very little chance of reaching the surface or infiltrating the groundwater supply, as the injection point had 11,900 feet of rock above it and was sealed at the top. RMA ended up pumping approximately 165 million gallons of waste into the well up to 1966, when the Army stopped the operation.

A series of small earthquakes in the Denver region over four years had the public concerned. Experts from the National Center for Earthquake Research postulated that the liquid waste from RMA's well might have lubricated the rock shelves to the degree that they were shifting, causing these earthquakes. Despite the geographical survey conducted prior to the drilling that was intended to ensure that the liquids did not migrate anywhere, the Army leadership decided to err on the side of caution and cease operations. Two years later, in the summer of 1968, RMA started pumping the fluids out of the well and back into Basin F.[6]

The timing to decommission the well was not the best, occurring within the same year as the alleged Dugway Proving Ground "sheep kill" incident and just prior to Operation CHASE (Cut Holes and Sink Em) hitting the news.[7] In an effort to appease the worried citizens and Congressional representatives of Colorado, the Army began moving chemical munitions of all types and classes by rail to join the chemical stockpiles at Tooele, Umatilla, and Anniston Army Depots.[8] Obsolete and leaking munitions were kept at RMA and not transported. They would still need to be destroyed, either by on-site disposal or by burial at sea.

The NAS report of 1969 recommended that the Army avoid ocean placement (a euphemism for sea dumping) and examine methods for on-site disposal of chemical munitions and agents, with an emphasis on public health and environmental protection. The Army's experience at the time offered two potential alternatives to ocean placement: chemical neutralization of GB nerve agent and incineration of mustard agents. The Army agreed with the NAS recommendations and established an office in 1972, headed by a Program Manager for Demilitarization of Chemical Materiel, to develop and execute demilitarization options for obsolete and leaking munitions.[9]

Between 1969 and 1985, the Army destroyed nearly 15 million pounds of chemical agents by either chemical neutralization or incineration at Rocky Mountain Arsenal. When Congress supported the Army's binary weapons program in 1985, it came with the provision that all of the aging unitary munitions would be destroyed. The Army's 15 years of experience led them to plan and design an incineration facility at Johnston Island, chosen as the pilot plant for the demilitarization program. Construction of the first disposal facility on that remote island started in 1987, while the Army continued studies on how to best dispose of the chemical agents and munitions at the other eight continental U.S. (CONUS) locations. Initially, the Army had planned to complete its operations by 1995. This was not to be the case, however.

In 1990, President Bush announced that the United States and the Soviet Union had agreed to destroy all its munitions except for 5,000 tons. Between 1990 and 1993, the Army had to prove that its Johnston Atoll Chemical Agent Disposal System could safely destroy all munitions at that site before Congress would appropriate funds to build the other seven disposal facilities. On January 13, 1993, the CWC was signed, creating a legal commitment that the United States would dispose of its entire chemical stockpile. The Senate's ratification in April 1997 committed the United States to dispose of all stocks by a deadline of 2007.

The period between 1985 and today is most interesting to discuss, as this is the period when the Army had to work with Congress and the public to build on-site disposal facilities in eight states and dispose of the remaining CW agents. The interaction between the Army, Congress, other government agencies, state officials, the press, and, of course, the public took on a life of its own. Congress passed special legislation on chemical demilitarization in every annual National Defense Authorization Act between 1985 and 2002 (and will probably continue to do so until the program is complete). The national and local press considers the issue of the chemical demilitarization program as high-interest topics, never neglecting to mention the Army's checkered past in the sharpest of criticisms. People living near the stockpile sites are often confused between the Army's insistence that everything is under control and the various critics, noting how dangerous the disposal operations can be. Meanwhile, the GAO continues to track the costs of operating these disposal facilities, dryly noting the increasing program costs and slipping deadlines. Certainly, the Army's chemical demilitarization program is a superb candidate for examination as a public policy issue.

## PUBLIC POLICY ISSUES

The term "policy" is rather open-ended. Decision makers tend to use the word "policy" when they talk about goals, programs, or decisions. Consider the DOD's biological warfare vaccine policy, often articulated as the most recent decision affecting the execution of the Anthrax Vaccination Immunization Program (AVIP). One favored definition of policy is "a 'standing decision' characterized by behavioral consistency and repetitiveness on the part of both those who make it and those who abide by it."[10] Legislation, executive orders, regulations, and laws merely make up the ingredients of programs, decisions, goals, and intentions, which in turn are the components of policy.

Public policy is often developed to address controversial public problems or issue areas, specifically, human needs that cannot be met privately and that require government intervention. Not all problems are public, nor are all issues addressed by the government.[11] Without getting in too deep in defining what public policy is or is not, in general, we can see public policy emerge when the government identifies a public problem or issue area that requires action by various government agencies; when the government implements a program to address these issues; and when various agencies evaluate the program and recommend changes to ensure that the policy is appropriately implemented. A more simple explanation is that public policy is what the government chooses to do and chooses not to do.[12] Traditional examples of public policy reside in the areas of agriculture (e.g., government subsidies to farmers), education (e.g., government oversight of public schools, private vouchers), medicine (e.g., Medicare, abortion rights), transportation (e.g., federal infrastructure, offshore pollution), and justice (e.g., police behaviors, judicial punishments).

In the military area, policy has usually been limited to strategic issues of developing a fighting force that can defend U.S. interests. Broader topics could include issues such as the role of the military in a post–Cold War era, the "guns or butter" budget analysis, the closure of military bases and its impact on the local economy, or the impact of social issues within the military (the role of women and homosexuals in the military ranks). Outside of developing strategies and force structures to execute these strategies, it is very rare that the military has to address controversial public issues, and when the armed forces have, they are often addressed and resolved by an agency inside the Office of the Secretary of Defense (OSD) rather than one of the four services. The four services interface with congressional committees, their chairs, and those members whose decisions can influence how the military executes its programs. The Army does not do as well as the other three services in this regard, although its determination to obey and execute congressional direction is second to none.

Steven Scroggs is a retired Army lieutenant colonel who worked in the Army Legislative Liaison office from 1992 to 1996. In his book *Army Relations with Congress*, he relates the story of how the Marine Corps obtained 84 M1A1 Abrams tanks from the Army by basically outmaneuvering the Army where it really mattered—in Congress. Despite strongly worded positions from the Army, the Joint Chiefs of Staff, and OSD against the transfer, Congress supported the Marine Corps legislative team's arguments. The Marines had obtained congressional support by a variety of methods, including establishing good relations with congressional members and using their general officers to communicate the message. Scroggs argues that the following patterns doomed the Army's position:[13]

- While the Army is seen as the most honest, straightforward, and credible service on the hill, its outreach efforts to Congress are the least apparent and sophisticated.
- Dealing with Congress is seen as a burden to bear rather than an opportunity to engage; the Army doesn't understand the role that Congress plays.
- The Army is more reactive and less proactive as compared to the other services in representing its institutional interests and concerns to Congress.
- Army senior general officers are the least represented, engaged, and effective on Capitol Hill.
- The Army is least effective in selecting and communicating its priorities and larger message: Why an Army, and why this size?
- Army legislative liaison personnel seem to be on their final assignment (limits long-term understanding and trust with congressional members and staff).

Scroggs notes that while Congressional members welcome the opportunity to better understand the military and its interests, the Army in particular dislikes the appearance of lobbying Congress on issues. While military members are restrained from lobbying Congress, there is a significant difference from liaising with congressional members and staff. Also, the Army does not use its general officers, especially senior leadership, to liaison with Congress as the other services do. This lack of outreach impairs the Army as it attempts to execute its missions. The Army culture tends to support working within its own support structure with what resources it has been allocated by Congress, rather than asking for what it needs to execute its special interests and mission.

Now, the question is, Is this also true for the Army's deliberation and execution of CW issues? I would argue Absolutely yes; it is applicable. The Army is expected to be the DOD executive agent in CW issues, yet the Army leadership rarely attempts to bring its case to Congress on critical issues.[14] For instance, in the 1968 Dugway Proving Ground sheep incident, the Army leadership reaction was to make the problem go away by paying off the ranchers and did not attempt to work the issue with Congress or the Utah state officials.[15] As a result, the DOD CB defense program lost its ability to conduct open-air chemical agent tests in 1969, which continues to affect the military today as it tries to understand how chemical weapons work when exploded in the environment (such as the post–Persian Gulf War Khamisiyah depot/pit demolition incidents).

When General Creighton Abrams, as the Chief of Staff of the Army, recommended disestablishing the Chemical Corps in 1972, he took the action based on his own extensive field experience and his staff's plans to reorganize the Army's force structure following the Vietnam conflict. When members of Congress received Abrams' recommendation to disestablish the Chemical Corps, they did not feel comfortable seeing the Chemical Corps dissolved, but this was not because any military leaders tried to influence them. Rather, this was due to discoveries of Soviet chemical defense equipment in the Middle East conflict and concerns about Soviet capabilities in future European conflicts. In 1976, the Secretary of the Army returned the Chemical Corps to its full charter, but it took several years longer to rebuild the military's CB defense capabilities. This reversal was a fortunate event for the Chemical Corps but reflects the disconnect between the Army leadership, the Chemical Corps, and Congress on issues related to chemical warfare. Both the RMA history and the Chemical Corps disestablishment incident show how the Army tries to deal with CW issues internally, rather than working with other bodies interested in helping the Army.

In more recent efforts, the DOD Domestic Preparedness program trained more than 100 cities' firefighters, police, and other emergency responders in preparing for the possibility of CB terrorism. The coordination between Department of Justice (DOJ), FEMA, Department of Energy (DOE), and Department of Health and Human Services (HHS) was executed through the Army's Director of Military Support, a two-star Army general's office. Some have suggested that the Army should continue to play a significant role in the federal response to chemical and biological acts of terrorism, but the Army backed out of the training program when the program transitioned to the DOJ. Congress directed the development of National Guard Weapons of Mass Destruction Civil Support Teams (WMD CSTs), not the Army leadership.

Contrast this to General Charles Krulak's (former Commandant, U.S. Marine Corps) and General James Jones' (current Commandant) strong support for developing and maintaining a Chemical and Biological Incident Response Force, developed from within Marine Corps resources. While the Army has a similar capability (the Technical Escort Unit), its leadership did not support expanding the Technical Escort Unit's capability to support the federal response program. The Army continues to react to congressional interests in this area, rather than seeking to proactively address the issue of responding to CB terrorist incidents.

There are numbers of other issues with similar patterns. The Army develops, executes, and communicates its biological warfare vaccine program and addresses the Gulf War illness issue the same way, as technical topics that require internal deliberation and execution. Congress is seen more as a burden than a potential source of support (and some members of Congress make that perception easy to believe in these two examples). Not only is Congress seen as adversarial, but the general public does not understand the Army's position on these topics, and, more distressingly, nor do the public's own sons and daughters within the military ranks. I can't even convince my own mother that the military is not engaged in some sort of self-serving agenda and conspiring against the public on these issues.

Major General George Friel, commanding SBCCOM in 1993, was personally involved in the initial remediation effort of cleaning up the remnants of a World War I chemical warfare proving grounds in Spring Valley, Maryland (located adjacent to American University in Washington, DC). Today, the Army Corps of Engineers sent majors and lieutenant colonels to discuss their progress and proposed cleanup plan with the public and city council. The Army had a relatively good idea where American University tested and disposed of its chemical agents and disposed of the overwhelming majority of chemical munitions within a year, but the citizens in the community want all properties tested for arsenic traces. "That's not our protocol," the Army's spokesman replied. "We don't care about your protocol," one man shouted. Another resident noted that incidents such as the accidental sinking of a Japanese fishing trawler by a Navy submarine in February 2000 or the loss of a plane flown by John F. Kennedy Jr. in 1998 generated a massive military response. "When John Kennedy [Jr.] was lost, every admiral or general was there," he said. "Where are the generals here?"[16]

The last time a four-star Army general officer addressed Congress on the issue of chemical warfare, he was making the pitch for resuming the binary chemical weapons program in 1985. Army leaders understood the need for retaliatory capabilities short of nuclear response to respond to an adversary using chemical weapons against our forces. In July 1990, President George H. W. Bush and Secretary of State James Baker announced the end of the binary chemical weapons program as a result of a bilateral agreement with the Soviets (just as the 155mm binary artillery shells were starting production at Pine Bluff). Army leadership was not convinced they should give up the goal of developing a modern chemical weapons retaliatory capability, but they were unsuccessful in their attempts to influence the decision through Congress.[17] These are instances of the Army reacting to events rather than anticipating issues and developing a plan that places Congress on your side rather than against your issues.

The Army's execution of the chemical demilitarization program has the same patterns. It is not the Army's attempts to meet congressional intent that makes this a public policy issue; rather, it is how the Army works with Congress and the public to eventually resolve the objective of destroying the chemical stockpiles. The lack of success makes one believe that their approach to executing the congressional mandate must be flawed, or that the leadership is merely incompetent. Having decided that it is not the latter issue, we must examine their policy and direction of the program over the years. The pattern of attempting to deal with an issue internally, without support from the upper Army leadership and by reacting to, rather than working with, Congress, emerges in the following chapters.

This evaluation is not to disparage the Chemical Corps' efforts or to suggest radical changes this far along in the program's execution. The goal is to understand how the Army addresses public policy issues, to identify where its shortcomings are in its execution of public policy issues, and to suggest how the Army can better develop and execute public policy concerns, particularly with sensitive issues related to CB warfare. Army leadership may not like addressing issues of public policy, but the Army is the Defense Department's executive agency addressing CB defense and CB warfare issues, and the public is intimately interested in these issues. The sooner the Army leadership accepts this fact, the sooner it will be able to avoid being the target of congressional committees and front-page headlines.

# 2

# A Legacy of Chemical Weapons

The U.S. military invested a great amount of time and funding over many decades in chemical weapons research, developing several war gases between 1918 and 1990. Most readers will understand the different names and general characteristics of CW agents but may not be aware of the military's abbreviations for them (see Table 2.1). One can describe CW agents by their physical properties or how they affect humans. After World War II, the U.S. military researched and produced several nerve, blister, choking, and psychochemical agents. These were characterized as persistent liquids, meant to contaminate the ground for days or weeks, and non-persistent aerosols, meant to travel downwind as an inhalation hazard and quickly evaporate. Blister agents mustard and lewisite were persistent liquids; the choking agent phosgene was a non-persistent gas. The U.S. stockpile held both persistent (VX) and non-persistent nerve agents (tabun and sarin).

**Table 2.1**
**Chemical Warfare Agents in U.S. Storage Sites, 1968–1990[1]**

| CW Agent | Scientific Nomenclature | Physical State | Military Abbreviation |
|----------|------------------------|----------------|-----------------------|
| Phosgene | carbonyl chloride | Gas | CG |
| Lewisite | dichloro(2-chlorovinyl)arsine | Liquid | L |
| Mustard | bis(2-chloroethyl) sulfide | Liquid | H, HT, HD, HN |
| Tabun | ethyl-N, N-dimethyl phosphoroamidocyanidate | Liquid | GA, TGA |
| Sarin | isopropyl methyl phosphono-fluoridate | Liquid | GB, TGB |
| VX | o-ethyl-S-(2-isopropylaminoethyl) methyl phosphonothiolate | Liquid | VX |
| BZ | 3-quinuclidinyl benzilate | Solid | BZ |

In terms of stockpile storage, mustard, lewisite, and VX, having very low vapor pressures, do not create a very large hazard area as a result of leaks or accidental releases. Under normal conditions, any leaking containers or munitions will not pose a threat past the boundaries of the military base, however the results of coming into contact with VX are severe in very small amounts. GA and GB represent the greater threat as leaking munitions, since these liquids turn to gases about as quickly as water evaporates and could represent a significant off-site hazard if a large number of munitions simultaneously leak or break open. BZ, as a solid, is very stable and unlikely to drift off-post and, as an incapacitant, is relatively nontoxic. Explosions or fires may spread effects from an agent farther from the site, dependent on weather and time of day. With decades of research and past production efforts, there are considerable data and relatively good understanding of CW agent effects on humans.

In 1990, there were a number of different chemical munitions intended for use throughout the battlefield by all branches of the military. Basic artillery shells filled with chemical agents, from mortar rounds to 8-inch artillery projectiles, provided an ability to attack enemy ground forces near the front lines. A short-lived effort led to the development of GB- and VX-loaded 115-mm unguided rockets, similar to the Soviet-style rockets. VX-loaded chemical mines were intended to deny the enemy use of key terrain features. Fixed-wing aircraft could attack enemy personnel with 500-, 600-, and 750-pound bombs loaded with GB agent or deny the enemy use of large areas of terrain using VX-filled spray tanks. There were chemical warheads designed for the Army's guided missiles, intended for deep rear area attacks but never manufactured in large numbers. These missiles were phased out of service and demilitarized long before 1985.

The basic design of a chemical projectile consists of a projectile cavity filled with a chemical warfare agent and a centrally located burster charge. A propelling charge sends the munition on its way to the target. The burster charge is a high explosive charge inside a metal tube. When the projectile strikes the ground, the fuze detonates the burster, rupturing the projectile and releasing the chemical agent into the air. If the chemical weapons planner wanted to disperse the agent from a high altitude onto the ground, a variable time fuze would have been used (same principle; fuze ignites the burster, and boom!). The mortar shells and cartridges are usually stored with fuzes and explosives, while all of the projectiles are stored unfuzed. The Army had prepared a number of the projectiles with bursters to increase their readiness for use in a military contingency.

There are three types of chemical artillery rounds; fixed, semi-fixed, and separate-loaded. Fixed rounds consist of a cartridge case permanently attached to the projectile. The burster, propellant, and fuze are all built into the round. The complete round is loaded into the weapon as a unit, similar to a very large rifle bullet. Semi-fixed projectiles have a cartridge case loosely fitted over the base of the projectile, allowing the loaders to adjust the amount of propelling charge prior to loading the projectile (this allows for greater or lesser ranges). The separate-loading projectile is designed for the projectile, propelling charge, and primer to be loaded into the weapon separately.

The 4.2-inch mortar projectile is the only fixed artillery projectile with a chemical fill, and there are two types in storage, the M2 and M2A1 mortar projectile. Each projectile holds 0.14 pounds of tetryl as its burster. The only difference is that the M2 projectiles are filled with HT, and the M2A1 projectiles are filled with HD. Twenty-four projectiles are loaded on one wooden pallet in the storage igloos. By agent weight, they make up less than 5 percent of the stockpile. Most are stored at Anniston Army Depot, but a number are stored at Pueblo, Tooele, and (formerly) at Johnston Island.[2]

| Munition | Diameter | Length | Weight | Fill Agent | Agent Weight |
|----------|----------|--------|--------|------------|--------------|
| Mortar, M2 | 4.2 in | 21.0 in | 25 lb | HT | 5.8 lb |
| Mortar, M2A1 | 4.2 in | 21.0 in | 25 lb | HD | 6.0 lb |

In the semi-fixed projectile types, there are two types of shells—the 105-mm M60 cartridge, which holds HD, and the 105-mm M360 cartridge, which holds GB. The M60 projectile holds 0.26 pounds of tetrytol for a burster, while the M360 projectile holds 1.1 pounds of tetrylol/composition B burster. About 3 percent of the stockpile is made up of 105-mm cartridges, with 24 cartridges loaded on a wooden pallet. Pueblo Depot Activity holds the majority of the M60 cartridges, with Tooele holding most of the M360 cartridges. Anniston and Johnston Island hold both types of cartridges as well.

| Munition | Diameter | Length | Weight | Fill Agent | Agent Weight |
|----------|----------|--------|--------|------------|--------------|
| Cartridge, M60 | 105 mm | 31.2 in | 42.9 lb | HD | 3.0 lb |
| Cartridge, M360 | 105 mm | 31.2 in | 43.8 lb | GB | 1.6 lb |

In the separate-loaded artillery projectile category, there are one 105-mm projectile (the M360, the same as the cartridge but minus the cartridge case and propelling powders), the 155-mm projectiles, and the 8-inch projectile. The M104 and M110 held 0.41 pounds of tetryol burster, while the M121 and M122 held 2.7 pounds of tetrytol. The 8-in cartridge held 7.0 pounds of composition B burster. In the 1980s, the Army started adding bursters back into projectiles to prepare them for employment, if needed. The 155-mm projectiles make up 12 percent of the stockpile by agent weight, and the 8-inch projectiles only 1.6 percent. Eight 155-mm projectiles and six 8-inch projectiles are stacked on each wooden pallet.

Anniston and Tooele hold the majority of the stockpile's projectiles, with small numbers at Blue Grass, Johnston Island, Pueblo, and Umatilla.

| Munition | Diameter | Length | Weight | Fill Agent | Agent Weight |
|---|---|---|---|---|---|
| Projectile, M360 | 105 mm | 19.7 in | 35.7 lb | GB | 1.6 lb |
| Projectile, M104 | 155 mm | 26.8 in | 95.1 lb | H/HD | 11.7 lb |
| Projectile, M110 | 155 mm | 26.8 in | 94.6 lb | H/HD | 11.7 lb |
| Projectile, M121 | 155 mm | 26.7 in | 97.2 lb | GB | 6.5 lb |
| Projectile, M121A1 | 155 mm | 27.0 in | 98.9 lb | GB/VX | 6.5/6.0 lb |
| Projectile, M122 | 155 mm | 26.7 in | 97.2 in | GB | 6.5 lb |
| Cartridge, M360 | 8 in | 35.1 in | 199 lb | GB/VX | 14.5 lb |

There are three aerial bomb types in the chemical stockpile, a 750-pound MC-1 bomb used by Air Force aircraft and two designed for Navy/Marine Corps aircraft (500-pound Mk 95 and 525-pound Mk-116 "Weteye" bombs). All of them were filled with GB agent, but are not equipped with bursters. The bursters would have been added when arming the munitions prior to a mission. The MC-1 bomb was stored two per wooden pallet. The Navy bombs were stored in individual storage and shipping containers. As these munitions do not have energetics (explosive components such as bursters and fuzes), they are easier to handle and destroy. All the Mk-116 bombs are stored at Tooele, while the other two types are stored at Tooele, Umatilla, and (in the past) Johnston Island. The TMU-28 spray tanks were not filled with chemical agents until immediately prior to their use, so these never posed a demilitarization issue (other than to destroy them as per the CWC protocol).

| Munition | Diameter | Length | Weight | Fill Agent | Agent Weight |
|---|---|---|---|---|---|
| Bomb, MC-1 | 16 in | 50.0 in | 725 lb | GB | 220 lb |
| Bomb, Mark 94 | 10.8 in | 60.0 in | 441 lb | GB | 108 lb |
| Bomb, Mark 116 | 14 in | 86.0 in | 525 lb | GB | 108 lb |
| Spray tank, TMU-28 | 22.5 in | 185 in | 1,935 lb | VX | 1,356 lb |

There were three types of cluster bombs. The M43 cluster bomb contained three stacks of 19 M138 bomblets, each of which held approximately six ounces of agent. Each bomblet had its own fuze and consisted of four M7 canisters filled with a 50/50 BZ/pyrotechnic mix. The M44 generator cluster consisted of three M16 generators, each containing its own parachute and container assembly, and a one time delay fuze. Each generator held 42 M6 canisters arranged in three in-line 14-canister tiers. Each M6 canister contained approximately five ounces of BZ. All of the BZ-filled munitions were stored at Pine Bluff Arsenal (the bulk agent BZ and munitions were destroyed between 1988 and 1989).

Last, the M34 cluster bomb contained 76 M125 bomblets, arranged in four groups of 19 bomblets. Each bomblet held 2.6 pounds of GB, a parachute, opening delay, fuze, and a burster containing 8.8 ounces of tetryl. There were over 21,000 M34 cluster bombs stored at Rocky Mountain Arsenal in 1972. These bomblets were destroyed in September 1976.

| Munition | Diameter | Length | Weight | Fill Agent | Agent Weight |
|----------|----------|--------|--------|------------|--------------|
| Bomb, cluster, M43 | 16 in | 66.0 in | 750 lb | BZ | 86 lb |
| Generator cluster, M44 | 15 in | 60.0 in | 175 lb | BZ | 39 lb |
| Bomb, cluster, M34 | 14 in | 86.0 in | 525 lb | GB | 108 lb |

The traditional use of mines is terrain denial, which meant that chemical land mines were filled with persistent agent. During World War II, the Army filled its chemical mines with mustard agent. With the manufacture of VX, a much more lethal and equally persistent agent, the older mustard-filled mines were replaced. The M23 mine is a circular steel container with a conical burster and side initiator charge. Fuzes were packaged separately within the drums used for storage and shipping (three mines were packed in one drum). The majority of the mines are stored at Anniston, with large quantities at Tooele, Johnston Island, Umatilla, and Pine Bluff, the total sum less than 2 percent of the national stockpile.

The M55 "Bolt" 115-mm rockets are the troublemakers of the stockpile. The rocket consists of an M56 warhead attached to a rocket motor, designed to be launched in salvos either near enemy forces (using non-persistent GB) or to deny key terrain (using persistent VX). The warhead is an aluminum body a bit over three feet in length, at its center a burster cavity with a rear and front burster filled with 3.2 pounds of composition B. The fuze contains a booster made from RDX explosive. All the bursters, fuze, and agent are sealed into the warheads. The rocket motor assembly is a steel tube, pressing 19.3 pounds of propellent grain against an igniter assembly at the base of the rocket's fins. The warhead is assembled to the rocket motor by coating the threads of the two pieces with Pettman cement or a sealing compound and screwing the two components together. In other words, the rockets are not designed to be disassembled or defuzed.[3] Each M55 rocket is stored in a shipping and firing tube made of fiberglass reinforced resin, either epoxy or polyester. They were declared obsolete in 1986.

Most of the rockets are at Umatilla and Pine Bluff, with smaller numbers at Anniston, Blue Grass, Tooele, and Johnston Island; they make up about 7 percent of the stockpile. The rockets make up most leaker incidents, accounting for over half the total number of leakers since 1983, and about 0.5 percent of the total M55 rockets in the stockpile. The danger is not the high incidence of leakers but rather that the agent could react with the propellant and decrease the stability of the propellant. The concern was that, if one rocket "cooked off" due to this lack of stability, it could ignite other rockets in the same igloo. It was difficult to identify the internal leaks, since the rockets could not be disassembled for inspection. While a "cook-off" of an agent-filled rocket has never occurred, the concern that it could happen drove the Army to start disposing of its rockets using concrete "coffins" stored on the Operation CHASE (Cut Holes And Sink Em) Liberty ships that were sunk in deep ocean waters. Elimination of the M55 rockets reduces the risk to local communities in excess of 95 percent.

| Munition | Diameter | Length | Weight | Fill Agent | Agent Weight |
|----------|----------|--------|--------|-----------|--------------|
| Mine, M23 | 13.5 in | 5.0 in | 23 lb | VX | 10.5 lb |
| Rocket, M55 | 115 mm | 78.0 in | 57 lb | GB/VX | 10.7/10.2 lb |
| Warhead, M56 | 115 mm | 34.0 in | --- | GB/VX | 10.7/10.2 lb |

When the Army developed and built ground-to-ground field artillery rockets in the 1950s and 1960s, it experimented with the concept of agent-filled warheads. While the early Soviet FROG and SCUD missile warheads were bulk liquid agent-filled, the Army chose to use submunitions for a more efficient spread and safer handling procedures. There were 106 Honest John warheads stored at Rocky Mountain Arsenal in the early 1970s. Two other warheads (M206 and M212) were designed, tested, and type-classified for the Little John and Sergeant rockets, but production of the warheads was not approved.

The Honest John's M190 warhead held 368 M139 bomblets, each bomblet containing just under 1.3 pounds of GB and 0.16 pounds of Composition B. The bomblet's mechanical fuze was a spin-to-arm type requiring a spinning rate of 1,000–1,200 rotations per minute for arming. This made the bomblets insensitive to normal handling operations. Nearly 60,000 bomblets were manufactured and stored, holding 76,500 pounds of agent. Practically all the M139 bomblets were destroyed between April and November 1976.[4]

| Munition | Diameter | Length | Weight | Fill Agent | Agent Weight |
|----------|----------|--------|--------|-----------|--------------|
| Rocket warhead, M190, Honest John | 762 mm | 100 in | 1,716 lb | GB | 478 lb |
| Rocket warhead, M206, Little John | 318 mm | 57 in | 938 lb | GB | 67.6 lb |
| Missile warhead, M212, Sergeant | 790 mm | 138 in | 2,069 lb | GB | 429 lb |

The one-ton containers make up more than two-thirds of the chemical stockpile, and are referred to as "bulk agent." These steel containers were initially developed and used during World War I for the transport and storage of chlorine (the commercial industry still uses ton containers for storage and transportation of chlorine). The majority of the VX ton containers are stored at Newport, with a few hundred stored at Tooele and Johnston Island. The few GB ton containers reside at Tooele and Blue Grass. The more numerous HT/HD ton containers are among six stockpile sites (all sites except Blue Grass and Newport have them). The containers are among the easiest to demil as they have no energetics or dunnage associated with their storage (meaning no need to incinerate explosives or packing materials, each of which required a dedicated disposal procedure).

| Munition | Diameter | Length | Weight | Fill Agent | Agent Weight |
|----------|----------|--------|--------|-----------|--------------|
| Ton Containers | 31.1 in | 81.5 in | 3,100 lb | H/HD/HT/L | 1,700 lb |
| Ton Containers | 31.1 in | 81.5 in | 2,900 lb | GA/GB | 1,500 lb |
| Ton Containers | 31.1 in | 81.5 in | 3,000 lb | VX | 1,600 lb |

## STORING CHEMICAL WEAPONS

There are eight stockpile sites in the United States and one on Johnston Island, southwest of Hawaii. The exact information on the size and composition of the U.S. stockpile was declassified in 1996 in preparation for declarations under the CWC, which was ratified in 1997 (see Figure 2.1). This chapter is a snapshot of the chemical stockpile sites prior to the initiation of the demilitarization program, except as noted. For instance, all references to what percent of the total national stockpile a particular stockpile site holds is based on the original 31,493 tons when the demilitarization program started in 1985, and does not reflect its current status.

**Figure 2.1**
**Chemical Stockpile Locations in the United States**

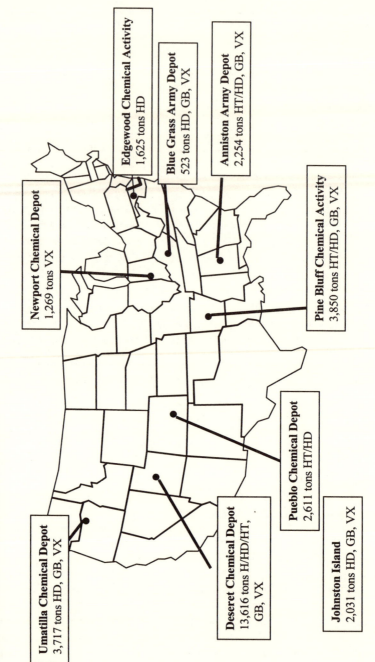

Newport Chemical Depot
1,269 tons VX

Edgewood Chemical Activity
1,625 tons HD

Blue Grass Army Depot
523 tons HD, GB, VX

Anniston Army Depot
2,254 tons HT/HD, GB, VX

Pine Bluff Chemical Activity
3,850 tons HT/HD, GB, VX

Umatilla Chemical Depot
3,717 tons HD, GB, VX

Deseret Chemical Depot
13,616 tons H/HD/HT,
GB, VX

Pueblo Chemical Depot
2,611 tons HT/HD

Johnston Island
2,031 tons HD, GB, VX

Johnston Island is a man-made island of the larger Johnston Atoll, about 825 miles southwest of Hawaii. The Army's chemical stockpile was just one of the many past tenants of the island, which included Air Force, Army, Coast Guard, and civilian contractors. The Navy was the first military manager starting in 1938 (as a Pacific refueling site), with the Air Force assuming control between 1948 and 1973 (as an atomic test site) and Defense Nuclear Agency running the island between 1973 and 1985 (for missile intercept tests). The Army moved its chemical weapons from Okinawa to Johnston Island in 1972, as the island was returned to Japanese governorship. The U.S. Army Chemical Activity, Pacific, came under control of the U.S. Army Western Command. In 1998, the U.S. Pacific Air Force became the official custodians.

After Johnston Island received U.S. chemical munitions retrograded from Germany in November 1990, it held 6.4 percent of the original stockpile (see Table 2.2).[5] The chemical munitions were housed in metal warehouses, given that there were no munitions bunkers built on the island. With hundreds of miles of sea around the man-made island and the military owning the only landing site available, physical security was not initially an overwhelming concern. After 1985, security was increased to ensure the munitions could not be endangered.

**Table 2.2**
**Chemical Munitions Stored at Johnston Island**

| Item | Agent Fill | Item Quantity | Agent Tons |
|------|:----------:|:-------------:|:----------:|
| 4.2-in cartridge, M2A1 | HD | 43,660 | 130.98 |
| 105-mm projectile, M60 | HD | 45,154 | 66.99 |
| 155-mm projectile, M104 | HD | 109 | 0.64 |
| 155-mm projectile, M110 | HD | 5,670 | 33.17 |
| Ton Containers | HD | 68 | 58.15 |
| 105-mm cartridge, M360 | GB | 49,360 | 40.23 |
| 155-mm projectile, M121/A1 | GB | 107,197 | 348.39 |
| 8-in projectile, M426 | GB | 13,020 | 94.40 |
| 500-lb bomb, Mk-94 | GB | 2,490 | 134.46 |
| 750-lb bomb, MC-1 | GB | 3,047 | 335.17 |
| 115-mm rocket, M55 | GB | 58,353 | 312.19 |
| Ton containers | GB | 66 | 50.58 |
| 155-mm projectile, M121/A1 | VX | 42,682 | 128.05 |
| 8-in projectile, M426 | VX | 14,519 | 105.26 |
| Mine, M23 | VX | 13,302 | 69.84 |
| 115-mm rocket, M55 | VX | 13,889 | 70.89 |
| Ton Containers | VX | 66 | 48.68 |
| **TOTAL** | | **412,652** | **2,028.07** |

After awarding the construction contract in 1985, the Army began building the Johnston Atoll Chemical Agent Disposal System (JACADS) in 1987. Raytheon Demilitarization Co., now part of the Washington Group, completed construction of the facility in 1989.[6] Before they could begin operations, the Army initiated a program to operationally test the facility's ability to destroy small lots of different munitions and with each agent class, validating the incineration process on a large scale. The operational verification testing took nearly three years, pushing the official start of full-scale operations to the summer of 1993. On November 30, 2000, the Army announced that it had completed operations, eliminating more than 4 million pounds of chemical agents and over 400,000 munitions without any serious accidents or incidents.

| JACADS | Construction | Setup & Testing | Operations | Closure |
|---|---|---|---|---|
| Original schedule | 1985-1987 | 1988-1989 | 1990-1994 | 1994 |
| 1991 schedule | 1987-1989 | 1989-1990 | 1990-1995 | 1996 |
| 1996 schedule | 1987-1989 | 1989-1990 | 1990-2000 | 2001 |
| Actual schedule | 1987-1989 | 1989-1990 | 1990-2000 | 2001 |

Aberdeen Proving Ground, Maryland, is located on the western side of the Chesapeake Bay, about 12 miles northeast of Baltimore. In addition to being the headquarters for the Army's Program Manager for Chemical Demilitarization (PMCD), Aberdeen Proving Ground is home to the U.S. Army SBCCOM, which researches and develops the majority of the Army's chemical and biological defense equipment (and, formerly, the chemical and biological munitions). The laboratories often use small lots of various chemical agents in their test and evaluation of this equipment. The chemical agent stockpile yard is located on the southern half of former Edgewood Arsenal, behind a high-security fence and ringed with miniature chemical agent monitors (mini-CAMs). At SBCCOM's reorganization in 1996, the chemical agent stockpile yard was renamed the Edgewood Chemical Activity.

The Edgewood Chemical Activity holds 5.2 percent of the original stockpile, all of it bulk mustard agent stored in one-ton steel containers (see Table 2.3). The mustard was produced at Edgewood Arsenal in the 1950s and stored in ton-containers outdoors in the chemical agent storage yard.[7] Most of the ton containers hold 90 percent pure agent by volume. The containers are stored on their sides on steel rails positioned over six to eight inches of crushed rock to minimize contamination or evaporation, if one container were to leak. The filled containers are stacked in groups of 15; 8 containers form the bottom row, with 7 stacked on top, and 6 empty containers on top of those, secured with two thick steel cables. This creates a cushion of sorts if a light plane were to crash into the site.

Because mustard is very persistent, the off-post hazards of a chemical incident at Edgewood is as close to zero as one might ask for, except for the possibility of a plane crash (which is also pretty remote). Before September 11, 2001, this scenario was laughed at. After September 11, the concern to reduce any terrorist targets resulted in all ton containers being moved indoors under Operation Roving Osprey. Physical security measures for all the chemical stockpile sites include controlled and restricted areas, security forces, security fences and barricades, perimeter lighting, and intrusion detection devices.

**Table 2.3**
**Chemical Munitions Stored at Edgewood Chemical Activity**

| Item | Agent Fill | Item Quantity | Agent Tons |
|------|-----------|---------------|------------|
| Ton containers | HD | 1,818 | 1,624.87 |
| **TOTAL** | | **1,818** | **1,624.87** |

The disposal facility, currently under construction, is named the Aberdeen Chemical Agent Disposal Facility (ABCDF). Initially, this was planned as an incineration facility, but due to heavy pressure from citizen groups and the fact that there is only bulk agent here, the Army changed the disposal concept to neutralization. Bechtel National received the contract to build the facility in October 1998, breaking ground in June 1999. The facility will operate for less than two years. The operations schedule may be accelerated if funding is approved, possibly eliminating the agent and decontaminating the ton containers by 2004.

| ABCDF | Construction | Setup & Testing | Operations | Closure |
|-------|-------------|-----------------|------------|---------|
| Original schedule | 1987-1990 | 1990-1991 | 1991-1993 | 1994 |
| 1991 schedule | 1994-1996 | 1996-1997 | 1997-1998 | 1999 |
| 1996 schedule | 1998-2001 | 2001-2002 | 2002-2003 | 2004 |
| Current schedule | 1998-2003 | 2004-2005 | 2005-2006 | 2006 |

Anniston Army Depot, Alabama, is located 10 miles south and west of Anniston, or 110 miles west of Atlanta and 50 miles northeast of Birmingham. Built during World War II, the depot performs maintenance on tanks, missiles, ordnance vehicles, and small arms, including supply and storage of conventional ammunition. The depot holds 1,300 igloos on 18,000 acres, of which 155 hold chemical munitions and bulk agent. It has been holding CW munitions since 1961.

The Anniston Chemical Activity holds 7.2 percent of the original stockpile, which consists of a large assortment of mixed munitions and ton containers (see

Table 2.4). The igloos are 25 feet high and 15 feet wide and vary from 40 to 80 feet long. They are constructed of 10-inch reinforced concrete walls, have steel doors, and are capped by 25 inches of soil. The igloo floors are decontaminable in the event of a leak, and there is a ventilation stack penetrating the earthen cover at the rear of the igloos. In addition to padlocks and intruder alert systems, the igloo door is blocked by a 5,000-pound "King Tut" concrete block. Each igloo is spaced far enough from others to ensure that the blast and shrapnel effects of a detonation of one igloo will not disturb another's contents, and each features lightning protection safeties. The igloos are surrounded with a double-chain link fence topped with barbed wire, automated security systems, and secured by a 24-hour guard force.

**Table 2.4**
**Chemical Munitions Stored at Anniston Chemical Activity**

| Item | Agent Fill | Item Quantity | Agent Tons |
|------|------------|---------------|------------|
| 4.2-in cartridge, M2 | HT | 183,552 | 532.30 |
| 4.2-in cartridge, M2A1 | HD | 75,360 | 226.08 |
| 105-mm cartridge, M60 | HD | 23,064 | 34.25 |
| 155-mm cartridge, M110 | HD | 17,643 | 103.21 |
| Ton containers | HD | 108 | 92.54 |
| 105-mm cartridge, M360 | GB | 74,014 | 60.32 |
| 105-mm projectile, M360 | GB | 26 | 0.02 |
| 155-mm projectile, M121/A1 | GB | 3,600 | 11.7 |
| 155-mm projectile, M122 | GB | 6,000 | 19.5 |
| 8-in projectile, M426 | GB | 16,026 | 116.19 |
| 115-mm rocket, M55 | GB | 42,738 | 228.65 |
| 115-mm rocket warhead, M56 | GB | 24 | 0.13 |
| 155-mm projectile, M121/A1 | VX | 139,581 | 418.74 |
| Mine, M23 | VX | 44,131 | 231.69 |
| 115-mm rocket, M55 | VX | 35,636 | 178.18 |
| 115-mm rocket warhead, M56 | VX | 26 | 0.13 |
| **TOTAL** | | **661,529** | **2,253.63** |

The Anniston Chemical Agent Disposal Facility (ANCDF), an incinerator built after the pattern of the Tooele facility, began testing at the end of 2001 in preparation for the start of operations in 2003. This is the second chemical agent incinerator of the eight disposal sites in the United States to start operations. Westinghouse Electric Corporation initiated building and operating this facility in June 1997, now assumed by the Washington Group (using Bechtel National as a subcontractor). It was initially anticipated that operations will take a little over two years to complete the disposal, but is now projected at five years due to unusually strident "safety" demands by the local politicians.

| ANCDF | Construction | Setup & Testing | Operations | Closure |
|---|---|---|---|---|
| Original schedule | 1987-1990 | 1990-1991 | 1991-1993 | 1994 |
| 1991 schedule | 1992-1994 | 1994-1996 | 1996-1999 | 2000 |
| 1996 schedule | 1997-1999 | 1999-2001 | 2001-2004 | 2005 |
| Current schedule | 1997-2000 | 2000-2002 | 2003-2007 | 2008 |

Blue Grass Army Depot, Kentucky, is actually two separate parcels of land. Lexington Area is 9 miles due east of Lexington and Blue Grass Area, where both the depot headquarters and the chemical munitions are stored, is 27 miles southeast from Lexington. In 1964, Lexington was merged with Blue Grass Army Depot, and the majority of the depot's functions were moved to Blue Grass by 1994. Its primary mission is that of a general supply and ammunition depot activity, to include holding unit sets of chemical defense equipment.

There have been chemical munitions at Blue Grass since 1944. Although the Blue Grass Chemical Activity holds only 1.7 percent of the original stockpile (see Table 2.5), its local citizen group is the most vocal of the eight communities that live near a stockpile site. Located on 250 acres of the depot's 15,000 acres, the 45 igloos (of 914 igloos at the depot) hold a variety of mixed munitions. Similar to Anniston, this site also has security exclusion zones, fences and lights, automated intrusion sensors, and a security force.

**Table 2.5**
**Chemical Munitions Stored at Blue Grass Chemical Activity**

| Item | Agent Fill | Item Quantity | Agent Tons |
|---|---|---|---|
| 155-mm projectile, M110 | HD | 15,492 | 90.63 |
| 8-in projectile, M426 | GB | 3,977 | 28.83 |
| 115-mm rocket, M55 | GB | 51,716 | 276.68 |
| 115-mm rocket warhead, M56 | GB | 24 | 0.13 |
| 155-mm projectile, M121/A1 | VX | 12,816 | 38.45 |
| 115-mm rocket, M55 | VX | 17,733 | 88.67 |
| 115-mm rocket warhead, M56 | VX | 6 | 0.03 |
| **TOTAL** | | **101,764** | **523.41** |

Because of the mix of munition, incineration was initially the recommended disposal technology. Incineration operations would have taken about a year, given the small number of munitions and a single projectile processing line. Planning the design of the Blue Grass Chemical Agent Disposal Facility (BGCDF) came to a halt when Congress directed the Army to investigate alternative technologies for disposing of assembled chemical weapons. The Army cannot dispose of the munitions until it completes a report to Congress identifying all the technologies studied and recommends a final solution. As of November 2002, the decision was made to use "alternative technologies" instead of incineration, probably neutralization or supercritical water oxidation.

| BGCDF | Construction | Setup & Testing | Operations | Closure |
|-------|-------------|-----------------|------------|---------|
| Original schedule | 1987-1990 | 1990-1991 | 1991-1992 | 1993 |
| 1991 schedule | 1994-1996 | 1996-1997 | 1997-1999 | 2000 |
| 1996 schedule | 1998-2000 | 2001-2002 | 2003-2004 | 2005 |
| Current schedule* | 2003-2006 | 2007-2009 | 2010-2012 | 2013 |

*Based on FY99 ACWA report.

Newport Chemical Depot, Indiana, hosted a government-owned, contractor-operated facility that manufactured VX agent between 1960 and 1968. It is located 30 miles north of Terre Haute and 2 miles southwest of Newport, only a few miles east of the Illinois-Indiana state line. In preparation for shipping the final two batches of VX to RMA, the VX agent was transferred from bulk storage to one-ton containers for shipment. In January 1969, reaction to the Dugway Proving Ground incident caused Congress to freeze movements of chemical agents, stopping any shipment options and stranded the VX-filled ton containers at the factory.

The Newport Chemical Depot holds 4.0 percent of the original stockpile, all of it one-ton containers of VX (see Table 2.6). A sample of the containers showed that they hold 90–94 percent pure agent by volume. They are stored in a single warehouse constructed of heavy corrugated sheet metal supported by steel beams. The warehouse lies within a security exclusion zone, security fences and intrusion detection alarms, and is guarded around the clock.

**Table 2.6**
**Chemical Munitions Stored at Newport Chemical Depot**

| Item | Agent Fill | Item Quantity | Agent Tons |
|------|-----------|---------------|------------|
| Ton Containers | VX | 1,690 | 1,269.33 |
| **TOTAL** | | **1,690** | **1,269.33** |

Similar to Aberdeen, the Newport Chemical Agent Disposal Facility (NECDF) was initially charted to use incineration, but, given its unique stockpile of bulk agent, the study to find alternative technologies also identified this facility for potential neutralization technologies. The facility will dispose of its stocks in less than two years, only slightly longer than it would have taken with incineration. Parsons/Honeywell (formerly Parsons/Allied Signal) received the construction and operations contract in February 1999, breaking ground in April 2000. Problems with the alternative technology selected may extend the schedule past 2005.

| NECDF | Construction | Setup & Testing | Operations | Closure |
|-------|-------------|-----------------|------------|---------|
| Original schedule | 1987-1990 | 1990-1991 | 1991-1993 | 1994 |
| 1991 schedule | 1994-1996 | 1996-1997 | 1997-1998 | 1999 |
| 1996 schedule | 2000-2002 | 2002-2003 | 2004 | 2005 |
| Current schedule | 2000-2002 | 2003-2004 | 2004-2005 | 2005 |

Pine Bluff Arsenal, Arkansas, has been an active part of the Army's chemical and biological warfare program since 1941. It is located 8 miles northwest of Pine Bluff and 35 miles southeast of Little Rock and spreads out over nearly 13,500 acres. The arsenal initially produced incendiary clusters, bombs and smoke munitions, and went on to produce and store chemical and biological munitions. It was one of the binary chemical munition production sites, with three separate facilities still awaiting destruction under the CWC protocols. Today, in addition to producing smoke grenades and pots and many calibers of mortar and artillery white phosphorus munitions, the arsenal produces and tests CB defense protective masks, collective protection filters, detection devices and decontamination kits and provides other engineering and technology services for the military.

**Table 2.7**
**Chemical Munitions Stored at Pine Bluff Chemical Activity**

| Item | Agent Fill | Item Quantity | Agent Tons |
|------|-----------|---------------|------------|
| Ton Containers | HT | 3,591 | 3,124.55 |
| Ton Containers | HD | 107 | 94.20 |
| 115-mm rocket, M55 | GB | 90,231 | 482.74 |
| 115-mm rocket warhead, M56 | GB | 178 | 0.95 |
| Mine, M23 | VX | 9,378 | 49.23 |
| 115-mm rocket, M55 | VX | 19,582 | 97.91 |
| 115-mm rocket warhead, M56 | VX | 26 | 0.13 |
| Cluster bomb, M43 | BZ | 519 | 22.32 |
| Cluster generator, M44 | BZ | 973 | 18.97 |
| 16-gallon containers | BZ | 242 | 5.0 |
| **TOTAL*** | | **123,093*** | **3,849.71*** |

* Total numbers reflect original stockpile status not including the BZ agent munitions, which were destroyed separately from the national chemical demilitarization program.

The Pine Bluff Chemical Activity holds 12.2 percent of the original stockpile within a separate chemical storage area on the arsenal (see Table 2.7). The ton containers were kept outdoors, but today all chemical agents and munitions are stored in one of the 100 igloos inside the chemical storage area. It also boasts the standard security fence, intrusion alarms, and guard force to safeguard the munitions.

The Army built a BZ incineration facility at Pine Bluff between 1985 and 1988 and destroyed all the incapacitating agent (bulk and munitions) by 1990. It was decided that a newly designed incinerator was a safer and more efficient option, which lead to a contract competition. The Washington Demilitarization Company completed the construction of Pine Bluff Chemical Agent Disposal Facility (PBCDF) in November 2002, which was originally awarded to Raytheon Demilitarization Co. in July 1997. The remaining chemical stocks will take a little more than three years to destroy.

| PBCDF | Construction | Setup & Testing | Operations | Closure |
|-------|--------------|-----------------|------------|---------|
| Original schedule | 1987-1989 | 1989-1990 | 1990-1994 | 1994 |
| 1991 schedule | 1994-1996 | 1996-1997 | 1997-1998 | 1999 |
| 1996 schedule | 1997-1999 | 2000-2001 | 2001-2004 | 2005 |
| Current schedule | 1999-2002 | 2003-2004 | 2004-2006 | 2007 |

Pueblo Depot, Colorado, lies about 14 miles east of the main city of Pueblo and immediately north of the small town of North Avondale, just north of the Arkansas River. The post was created in 1942 as an ordnance depot. During the late 1950s, this depot was a major Army missile repair and maintenance facility. When the Army maintained the Pershing missile systems, Pueblo had the mission of reconditioning, modifying, and testing the system and its components. Due to a 1988 BRAC decision, the depot moved its conventional small arms, large artillery shells, missiles, propellants, and bombs to other ammunition storage sites between 1989 and 1994. Its buildings and structures are spread out on over 22,650 acres of rolling prairie land. After its chemical demilitarization responsibilities are completed the depot will shut down.

Renamed the Pueblo Chemical Depot, it holds 8.3 percent of the original stockpile, all of it mustard agent-filled munitions (see Table 2.8). The chemical munitions are stored in igloos in a small corner of the depot, surrounded by the usual chain-linked fences, security systems, and guards. Of the 922 igloos at the depot, only 102 are used for chemical munitions storage. They take up a very small part of the 23,000 acres of prairie lands that make up the depot activity. The depot had destroyed mustard munitions by open-pit burning in the 1940s and 1960s, but tests indicate no trace of agent in the ground today.

**Table 2.8**
**Chemical Munitions Stored at Pueblo Chemical Depot**

| Item | Agent Fill | Item Quantity | Agent Tons |
|---|---|---|---|
| 4.2in cartridge, M2 | HT | 20,384 | 59.11 |
| 4.2in cartridge, M2A1 | HD | 76,722 | 230.17 |
| 105-mm cartridge, M60 | HD | 383,418 | 569.38 |
| 155-mm projectile, M104 | HD | 33,062 | 193.41 |
| 155-mm projectile, M110 | HD | 266,492 | 1,558.98 |
| **TOTAL** | | **780,078** | **2,611.05** |

Similar to Blue Grass, the Pueblo Chemical Agent Disposal Facility (PUCDF) was stopped from construction by congressional direction until the Army demonstrated that it had researched alternative technologies other than incineration to destroy chemical munitions. Under Secretary of Defense Pete Aldridge recently (May 2002) announced the disposal site will use neutralization technology. A team composed of Bechtel, Washington Group, and Parsons/Honeywell won the contract in October to build and operate the disposal facility. Originally it was planned that incineration operations would take just over one year to complete.

| PUCDF | Construction | Setup & Testing | Operations | Closure |
|---|---|---|---|---|
| Original schedule | 1987-1990 | 1990-1991 | 1992-1993 | 1994 |
| 1991 schedule | 1994-1996 | 1996-1997 | 1997-1998 | 1999 |
| 1996 schedule | 1997-2000 | 2000-2001 | 2002-2004 | 2005 |
| Current schedule* | 2002-2005 | 2006-2008 | 2009-2011 | 2012 |

*Based on FY99 ACWA report.

Tooele Army Depot, Utah, is a 25,170 acre installation about 12 miles south of Stockton, 20 miles south of Tooele, and 35 miles west of Salt Lake City. Prior to 1993, when the BRAC recommended its closure, Tooele was responsible for a broad degree of ordnance storage, movement, and maintenance, to include administration over several Army ordnance facilities. In 1949, it assumed control of Deseret Chemical Depot, which was consolidated under Tooele Army Depot South Area. The Army moved 888 nerve agent munitions from Rocky Mountain Arsenal to Tooele Army Depot in 1980 to comply with congressional direction.[8]

Deseret Chemical Depot held 43.2 percent of the original stockpile (see Table 2.9) prior to the start of its demilitarization operations in Tooele Army Depot South Area, an area of nearly 20,000 acres. It has held chemical weapons there since 1942. It holds a variety of mixed munitions in three different types of buildings, as well as the mustard agent ton containers once stored outdoors. These buildings include two types of above ground magazines, 68 steel arch igloos nearly 90 feet long, and 140 concrete arch igloos 80 feet long. Security features include a double fence, lighting system, controlled access, and video surveillance in addition to the security guards who patrol the area.

**Table 2.9**
**Chemical Munitions Stored at Deseret Chemical Depot**

| Item | Agent Fill | Item Quantity | Agent Tons |
|------|------------|---------------|------------|
| 4.2in cartridge, M2 | HT | 62,590 | 181.51 |
| 4.2in cartridge, M2A1 | HD | 976 | 2.93 |
| 155-mm projectile, M104 | H | 10,281 | 60.14 |
| 155-mm projectile, M110 | H | 44,382 | 259.63 |
| Ton Containers | HD | 6,398 | 5,691.71 |
| Ton Containers | L | 10 | 12.96 |
| Ton Containers | GA | 2 | 1.41 |
| Ton Containers | TGA | 2 | 0.64 |
| Ton Containers | TGB | 7 | 3.48 |
| 105-mm cartridge, M360 | GB | 119,400 | 97.31 |
| 105-mm projectile, M360 | GB | 679,303 | 553.63 |
| 155-mm projectile, M121/A1 | GB | 67,685 | 219.98 |
| 155-mm projectile, M122 | GB | 21,456 | 69.73 |
| 115-mm rocket, M55 | GB | 28,945 | 154.86 |
| 115-mm rocket warhead, M56 | GB | 1,056 | 5.65 |
| *Weteye Bomb, Mk-116 | GB | 888 | 154.07 |
| 750-lb bomb, MC-1 | GB | 4,463 | 490.93 |
| Ton Containers | GB | 5,709 | 4,299.10 |
| 155-mm projectile, M121/A1 | VX | 53,216 | 159.65 |
| 8-in projectile, M426 | VX | 1 | 0.01 |
| Mine, M23 | VX | 22,690 | 119.12 |
| 115-mm rocket, M55 | VX | 3,966 | 19.83 |
| 115-mm rocket warhead, M56 | VX | 3,560 | 17.80 |
| Spray tank, TMU-28 | VX | 862 | 584.44 |
| Ton Containers | VX | 640 | 455.48 |
| **TOTAL** | | **1,138,488** | **13,616.00** |

* The Weteye bombs arrived from RMA in 1980.

The Tooele Chemical Agent Disposal Facility (TOCDF) is in full operation now, built and operated by EG&G Defense. This facility was particularly important as it is the first dedicated chemical agent incinerator on continental U.S. territory (if one does not include Pine Bluff's BZ disposal facility or the previous disposal operations conducted at RMA). It included a number of improvements over the pilot plant and was initially planned for operations lasting more than three years to destroy nearly half the U.S. military's chemical stockpile.

| TOCDF | Construction | Setup & Testing | Operations | Closure |
|---|---|---|---|---|
| Original schedule | 1987-1990 | 1990-1991 | 1991-1994 | 1994 |
| 1991 schedule | 1989-1992 | 1992-1994 | 1994-1999 | 1999 |
| 1996 schedule | 1989-1994 | 1994-1996 | 1996-2003 | 2004 |
| Current schedule | 1989-1994 | 1994-1996 | 1996-2004 | 2005 |

Umatilla Chemical Depot, Oregon, is approximately 7 miles west of Hermiston, 33 miles northwest of Pendleton, and just a few miles south of the Columbia River and the state of Washington. It has been holding chemical munitions since 1962. The depot's original mission was to receive, maintain, ship, and dispose of conventional ammunition, until the 1988 BRAC recommended it be shut down. The depot's grounds cover nearly 19,700 acres. Because of a nearby American Indian reservation, the government must coordinate chemical demilitarization issues with the Confederated Tribes of the Umatilla Indian Reservation.

The Umatilla Chemical Depot holds 11.8 percent of the original stockpile (see Table 2.10). Of the 1,001 igloos at the depot, 89 store the chemical munitions. These igloos are slightly smaller but wider than Anniston's, approximately 12 feet high and 26 feet wide with lengths of 40 to 80 feet. They are constructed of steel-reinforced concrete and are capped with approximately 2 feet of soil and 4 inches of gravel. The ton containers and spray tanks are kept in metal warehouses. The requisite fences, security systems, and guard forces protect the stockpile.

**Table 2.10**
**Chemical Munitions Stored at Umatilla Chemical Depot**

| Item | Agent Fill | Item Quantity | Agent Tons |
|---|---|---|---|
| Ton Containers | HD | 2,635 | 2,339.52 |
| 155-mm projectiles, M121/A1 | GB | 47,406 | 154.07 |
| 8-in projectile, M426 | GB | 14,246 | 103.28 |
| 115-mm rocket, M55 | GB | 91,375 | 488.86 |
| 115-mm rocket warhead, M56 | GB | 67 | 0.36 |
| 500-lb bomb, Mk-94 | GB | 27 | 1.46 |
| 750-lb bomb, MC-1 | GB | 2,418 | 265.98 |
| 155-mm projectile, M121/A1 | VX | 32,313 | 96.94 |
| 8-in projectile, M426 | VX | 3,752 | 27.20 |
| Mine, M23 | VX | 11,685 | 61.35 |
| 115-mm rocket, M55 | VX | 14,513 | 72.57 |
| 115-mm rocket warhead, M56 | VX | 6 | 0.03 |
| Spray tank, TMU-28B | VX | 156 | 105.77 |
| **TOTAL** | | **220,599** | **3,717.38** |

The Washington Group has finished construction of the Umatilla Chemical Agent Disposal Facility (UMCDF), which was awarded to Raytheon Demilitarization Co. in June 1997. It will be the third chemical agent incinerator to start operations in the United States, anticipated to begin in the fall of 2003. It was initially projected to run its operations over two and a half years before ceasing operations prior to the 2007 CWC deadline.

| UMCDF | Construction | Setup & Testing | Operations | Closure |
|---|---|---|---|---|
| Original schedule | 1987-1990 | 1990-1991 | 1991-1993 | 1994 |
| 1991 schedule | 1993-1995 | 1995-1996 | 1996-1999 | 2000 |
| 1996 schedule | 1997-1999 | 1999-2001 | 2001-2004 | 2005 |
| Current schedule | 1997-2000 | 2000-2002 | 2003-2005 | 2006 |

One can see how complex the challenge is from this array of issues. There are eight stockpile sites in the United States (the ninth being in the Pacific) with differing mixtures of munitions and agents at each site. Some munitions have explosives in them, others do not, and much of the agent in bulk ton containers. On top of reporting to the House and Senate Armed Services Committees and Appropriation Committees, there are eleven sets of state and congressional delegations, one Tribal nation, assorted activist citizens groups, a number of companies interested in the multibillion-dollar construction and operations efforts, and, of course, the ever-vigilant local and national media watching every move. Who wouldn't relish running this operation?

# 3

## Death and Birth of a Program

In 1969, the year following the alleged sheep kill near Dugway Proving Grounds,[1] the United States government had to deal with public concerns with dumping chemical weapons at sea (Operation CHASE), was told by the United Nations that all nations should stop developing chemical and biological weapons, and had publicly acknowledged ownership of chemical stockpiles in Okinawa and West Germany for the first time. In response to these events, the Army was told to comply with congressional restrictions on the use, transportation, and storage of chemical agents. Because of the controversy surrounding the CHASE operation, the DOD Director of Defense Research and Engineering (DDR&E) requested that the National Academy of Sciences (NAS) assess the hazards of disposing of chemical warfare materiel by various means. The NAS convened an ad hoc National Research Council (NRC) review committee, chaired by Dr. G. B. Kistiakowsky, a professor of chemistry at Harvard University. In June 1969, the NRC review committee delivered its report, which recommended that DOD:

- Adopt basically the same approach to chemical agents and munitions that the Atomic Energy Commission had adopted toward radioactive waste products from nuclear reactions.
- Assume that all chemical agents and munitions will require eventual disposal.
- Avoid ocean placement.
- Undertake a study of optimal disposal methods at appropriate military installations that involve *no hazards* to the general population and *no pollution* of the environment [emphasis added].
- Require large-scale disposal facilities as a counterpart to existing stocks and planned manufacturing operations.
- Construct facilities for gradual demilitarization and detoxification of the remaining M55 rockets as a first step in this direction.[2]

This was not a remarkable report except for the observation that the panel had made its recommendations more as measures of what it saw as common sense rather than as ones based on scientific evaluations. It had decided that ocean placement should be a last resort largely based on parallel studies supporting a ban on ocean placement of radioactive waste.[3] After all, the U.S. government did not want a radioactively spawned Godzilla to rise up against New York City. The "CHASE" Liberty ships scuttled in 1967 and 1968 had contained 1,706 concrete "coffins," each weighing more than six tons and containing 30 M55 rockets, sunk to a depth of 7,200 feet. Even if the coffins had cracked open and the agent had leaked out, the chemical would have been diluted by many millions (billions?) of gallons of seawater. There was no evidence then, and there has been no evidence since, of any impact to sea life or any threat to humans swimming off beaches nearly 250 miles away.[4]

A subsequent NRC report[5] noted that the language in its 1969 report, referring to no hazard and no pollution, was unfortunate, since the very existence of the chemical stockpile represented a potential public hazard in and of itself. Both storage operations and disposal operations entail a certain degree of risk (as all activities do); it would require the elimination of the chemical agents to end the hazard completely. It became incumbent on the Army leadership to develop a storage plan that *minimized* risks while effectively and efficiently *eliminating* leaking and obsolete munitions. The Army had some experience incinerating approximately 3,000 tons of mustard agent in a special furnace located at Rocky Mountain Arsenal, but at that time, had explored neutralization technologies only for GB munitions. Because GB munitions were still relatively young in the inventory, the Army simply had not demilitarized GB munitions in similar quantities as it had mustard. There was no way to gain experience upon which to make decisions. The NAS committee recommended that the Army should consider both technologies for continued disposal operations.

In November 1969, President Richard Nixon announced that he would stop production of chemical weapons until binary weapons were available, and renounced the U.S. offensive biological weapons program. This announcement effectively killed the offensive CB warfare program and unintentionally decreased funding of CB defense programs.[6] His administration had also recommended the Defense Department destroy its mustard agent stocks, remove the chemical munitions from Okinawa to the United States, and brief the West German government on the U.S. chemical munitions in its country and volunteer to remove those munitions.[7] Congress was intent on "helping" the Army's decision process and passed no less than four public laws over four years to restrict the military's movement of chemical weapons. Public Law 91-121, passed in November 1969, restricted the transportation and open-air testing within the United States, short of issues involving national security, and restricted movement of chemical weapons overseas without informing the host nation. The law also directed the Secretary of Health, Education, and Welfare (HEW, later HHS), to direct the Surgeon General to review the public and worker health and safety issues involved with transportation and testing.

The following year, Congress amended that law by adding restrictions on nonemergency disposal operations and ocean placement in international waters.

In 1970, Congress denied funds to transport chemical munitions from Okinawa to the United States, in response to the governors of Oregon and Alaska seeking to stop the Army from moving these stocks to defense facilities in their states. The Army resorted to moving those stocks from Okinawa to Johnston Island between January and September 1971 under Operation Red Hat. This major movement of more than 10,000 tons of chemical munitions took place without incident. Finally, in October 1972, Congress passed the Maritime Protection, Research, and Sanctuaries Act, which prohibited any ocean placement of radiological waste, biological warfare agents, or chemical warfare agents, to include herbicides intended to be used for military applications during wartime.[8]

## EARLY ARMY DISPOSAL OPERATIONS

The Chemical Corps had lost much of its past power and prestige by the early 1970s. Edgewood Arsenal was merged into neighboring Aberdeen Proving Ground in July 1971, causing the Chemical Corps to lose autonomy over its main laboratory. In 1972, Army leadership directed the transfer of Edgewood Arsenal's intelligence division to the Army Intelligence Agency, Fort Detrick; control over biological defense research to the Army Surgeon General and transfer of Pine Bluff Arsenal and Rocky Mountain Arsenal to the Munitions Command. In a time of downsizing and consolidation within the Army, Edgewood Arsenal was a prime target, given its loss of the offensive chemical weapons program.

In early 1972, Headquarters, Army Materiel Command (AMC) established a senior advisory panel, including eight experts from industrial, educational, and research institutions, to review the Army's chemical demilitarization program. They concluded that the NRC recommendation to consider both methods of demilitarization was still valid based on existing research data but desired a single disposal process that might be applicable to all chemical agents and stockpiles. The panel recommended that the Army continue to conduct laboratory and pilot incineration tests with chemical agents. To oversee and execute this responsibility, a new program office was created, deliberately separate from the traditional agencies that had designed, tested, and produced the munitions.

On October 11, 1972, HQ AMC approved the charter of the first Program Manager for Demilitarization of Chemical Materiel. The office, headed by Colonel Sampson Bass (a Chemical Corps officer), was moved from Dover, New Jersey, to Edgewood Arsenal for "planning, direction, and control of the chemical demilitarization program to include design, development, and acquisition of special equipment and facilities, site decontamination as authorized, and the execution of operational aspects of the program."[9] He reported through Munitions Command to the Commanding General of AMC. The Program Manager's responsibilities ran from technical decisions to budgeting and development of the facilities and coordinated with DOD offices, the EPA, and HEW. The office addressed the disposal projects at 12 installations as its first priorities (see Table 3.1).

**Table 3.1**
**Initial Chemical Disposal Projects, 1972**

| Installation | Demilitarization Responsibilities |
|---|---|
| Johnston Island | Leaking munitions[10] |
| Dugway Proving Ground, UT | M55 rocket residue, bomblets, leaking munitions, Carr Facility demilitarization |
| Umatilla Army Depot, OR | Bulk agent, leaking munitions |
| Tooele Army Depot, UT | Bulk agent, leaking munitions |
| Pueblo Army Depot, CO | Leaking munitions |
| Anniston Army Depot, AL | Leaking munitions |
| Blue Grass Army Depot, KY | Bulk agent, leaking munitions |
| Newport Army Ammunition Plant, IN | Bulk agent |
| Edgewood Arsenal, MD | Bulk agent, concrete drums |
| Rocky Mountain Arsenal, CO | Bulk mustard, M34 cluster bombs, GB war reserve stocks, bulk phosgene,[11] and arsenal cleanup |
| Pine Bluff Arsenal, AR | Bulk agent, leaking munitions |
| Fort Detrick, MD | Inactivated anti-crop agents |

The first issue to be addressed was aging stocks of mustard agent left over from World War II stocks. The Army had planned to move over 2,214 tons of levinstein mustard and 857 tons of distilled mustard, produced in the 1940s, stored in ton containers, and considered excess stocks, on the next CHASE ship, along with over 20,000 M34 cluster bombs holding over 2,000 tons of GB. When that operation was canceled in 1969, the Army began planning Project Eagle–Phase I to drain the ton containers and incinerate the mustard agent. The mustard agent could be incinerated at RMA's furnace, as had been done several times in the past (albeit in smaller quantities). Of anecdotal interest, the Environmental Impact Statement (EIS) for this operation was the Army's first ever EIS delivered to the newly created EPA. Given the emerging environmental restraints as a result of the recently enacted public laws, as well as emerging political and public scrutiny, this effort set the stage and put in place many of the principles for the follow-on programs.

Project Eagle–Phase I required about two years to develop and set up a process that would drain the ton containers, incinerate the agent, and clean up the facility after operations were complete. Mustard agent decomposes rapidly at 425 degrees centigrade to produce three gases—sulfur dioxide, carbon dioxide, and hydrogen chloride. These products were removed from the exhaust stream and converted to harmless salts. Between August 1972 and September 1973, over 3,070 tons of mustard were incinerated, using a basic concept of preheating and draining the ton containers, incinerating the agent and thermally decontaminating the containers, controlling furnace emissions, and treating and disposing of the 7,000 tons of brine salt. This equated to about 2.3 pounds of waste per pound of mustard agent treated. While the waste products were not deemed hazardous under the Resource Conservation and Recovery Act (RCRA), the Army wanted them transported to a hazardous waste site to be safe-sided, given potential public concerns that the waste products had originated from a chemical warfare agent.[12]

The Army had investigated neutralizing mustard agent, using mono-enthanolamine (MEA) as the catalyst. Other chemicals had either not completely neutralized the agent or took very long times to complete reactions. The problem with using MEA was that the reaction produced a hazardous organic chemical waste that had to be incinerated itself. If the waste products had to be incinerated, why not just start with that process up front? In addition, there were three other reasons not to use MEA: first, MEA had a high flash point, which meant that it was prone to exploding. Second, the neutralization process had to be temperature-controlled or the reaction could run away with itself, leading to an explosion. Third, the process did not completely eliminate the mustard agent, leaving about 0.25 milligrams per liter of waste product behind. These factors, developed by years of field and pilot plant experience, led the Army (and later the NAS) to support incineration as the ideal technical approach for mustard disposal.[13]

In July 1973, a Pentagon safety board stopped Denver city officials from extending a runway of Stapleton International Airport onto 600 acres of land formerly owned by RMA. The fact that chemical weapons were still present at the arsenal (888 Weteye aerial bombs) caused considerable concern at city, state, and federal levels of government. Discussions between the Secretary of the Army and the Deputy Secretary of Defense in October of that year led to an agreement to rid the arsenal of all chemical munitions and agents. The GB production facilities, however, would remain standing in the event that they were required for mobilization production. Because the Army had not budgeted for such a large demilitarization effort for fiscal year (FY) 1974, it would require some time to develop the cost data that would support building the facilities required to dispose of the agents and submit to OSD for execution in the FY 1975 budget.[14]

The Deputy Secretary of Defense's memorandum authorizing this action did permit the Army to begin detailed planning to expand Project Eagle and to award the design/construction contracts in 1974. It also set two precedents as a result of the public concerns: first, DOD appointed the Army as its executive agent for the disposal of all chemical agents and munitions stored at RMA. The executive agent role meant that the Army had to coordinate with the other Services for the disposition of their munitions in addition to its own. Second, the Army appointed the Assistant Secretary of the Army for Installations and Logistics (ASA[I&L]) to oversee the execution of the Army's chemical demilitarization program.

Project Eagle–Phase II would address the neutralization of GB agent in RMA's underground storage tanks holding 189 agent tons, the M34 cluster bombs holding more than 2,000 agent tons and 441 tons of explosives, 2,422 ton containers amounting to 1,802 agent tons, and 38.5 tons of agent in the M139 bomblets.[15] A special facility would have to be constructed for handling and draining the bomblets. Originally, the project was also scheduled to dispose of the Navy's 888 Weteye bombs, but the Navy requested that these bombs be retained in the active inventory until the binary chemical munitions could replace them.

The neutralization process consisted of three elements: storage and delivery of a caustic solution of 18 percent sodium hydroxide (stored in three 10,000-gallon tanks), storage and delivery of the GB agent (similarly stored in a 10,000-gallon tank), and reactor filling, neutralization, and emptying. For one complete cycle, 1,500 gallons of GB was sent to a 3,500-gallon mixing tank, where the caustic was added. The mixture was agitated at a high temperature until the reaction was completed, using water jackets to control the exothermic reaction. After sampling the mixture to verify that the GB had been neutralized, it was sent to the spray dryer in a different building and reduced to brine salts. After removal of the dried salts, the heated air and water vapor were scrubbed to remove particulates before releasing the gases. The explosive components were incinerated. As with the mustard incineration process, the salts were packaged and sealed in 55-gallon drums for transportation to a landfill.

In total, Phase II was to dispose of nearly 4,100 tons of sarin between October 1973 and November 1976. The munitions and ton containers were disassembled and drained in different facilities, while the nerve agent was neutralized in the same building in all cases. The entire process generated 43,000 drums of brine salts, or about 2.6 pounds of salt for every pound of agent neutralized. While the salt's heavy metal levels were below the RCRA maximum concentration limits for hazardous waste, the Army managed the salts under hazardous waste policy. This was for two reasons; first, the salts had a high corrosive nature due to high sodium fluoride levels, and second, Army scientists believed that minute amounts of nerve agent, not neutralized completely, remained in the salts despite high temperatures in the spray dryer.

## THE DEMILITARIZATION PROGRAM MATURES

On August 22, 1975, Colonel Bass' job position expanded to become the Program Manager for Chemical Demilitarization and Installation Restoration (PM CDIR). This new charter included the responsibility for installation restoration technology for all DOD sites. The PM CDIR would develop technologies and procedures to clean up all DOD installations that had chemical, biological, or radiological contamination. This agency, staffed by about 100 personnel, would conduct hazard assessments and development of safety and toxicity standards, and submit these assessments to applicable federal regulatory agencies for approval. Less than a year later, Colonel Bass was promoted to Brigadier General and left the position, with Colonel Frank Jones assuming command. Colonel Jones' deputy project manager was Charles Baronian, who would later be involved in the 1985 PMCD organization.

These duties and the potential scope of the disposal operations that lay ahead eventually led the Army to propose that a formal agency be created to plan and execute building facilities, developing disposal technologies, coordinating with interagency government offices, and running the operations that would dispose of the agents and munitions. The U.S. Army Toxic and Hazardous Materials Agency (USATHAMA) began operations in September 1978, allowing the PM CDIR charter to be withdrawn. Colonel Jones became USATHAMA's first commander and continued the Army's demilitarization and installation restoration research.

One of USATHAMA's first major efforts was building the Chemical Agent Materiel Disposal System (CAMDS) at Tooele Army Depot as a test facility to develop proven industrial and military processes and equipment and demonstrate their applicability to large-scale demilitarization facilities. Tooele was chosen because it had the most diverse collection of chemical munitions (29 different types, to be exact). In addition, the facility would dispose of Tooele Army Depot's obsolete and/or leaking munitions.[16] The facility was not put into operation prior to the development and testing of demilitarization protective ensembles, which required approval by the Army Surgeon General. CAMDS would become the primary tool used to develop processes to conduct disposal operations on a larger scale, evaluating various technologies and procedures to destroy chemical munitions and agents between September 1979 and August 1986.

The Army had originally intended to design a mobile disposal plant that could be transported to the various chemical stockpile sites, a much simpler operation than building separate disposal facilities at each site or transporting all the munitions to a central site. This concept was designated the Transportable Disposal System. The one problem with this concept was that it would be very challenging to move the plant to Johnston Island to dispose of the leaking and obsolete munitions there. Congressional direction had stopped any actions on transporting the munitions to the States, which meant that there had to be a disposal plant built on Johnston Atoll to eliminate leakers and obsolete munitions.

The transportable disposal concept lived on as the Drill and Transfer System (DATS), a transportable facility mounted on a series of trailers, designed to drain chemical agents from leaking munitions at the installations where they were currently stored. It did not destroy the agent but transferred the agent to a second storage container. The drained munition would be chemically decontaminated and then fractured by detonation in a fragment-containing chamber. The decontamination solutions were stored for drying, and the munition residue were stored for final thermal treatment. The DATS could process only three to six rounds per day, but it represented a capability to minimize the hazard caused by leakers. By 1988, DATS had processed 900 munitions, averaging 150 munitions per year.[17]

The Army built a number of separate facilities at Tooele to develop test data on various functions of the demilitarization process, including an agent destruction system for the agent neutralization process and a liquid incinerator for the agent incineration process. All explosive components were sent through a deactivation furnace system to ensure that any residual agent was destroyed with the explosives. This included all M55 rocket parts, as the explosives could not be separated from the munition. All metal parts of the munitions were sent through a metal parts furnace (appropriately named) to remove all chemical agents from their surfaces. Once the scrap metal was thermally decontaminated, the Army could sell the scrap metal to recycling firms (as is done with conventional munition demilitarization). Finally, a toxic dunnage incinerator would destroy any packing material or pallets that might have become contaminated. All of these systems, save the agent destruction system, used high-temperature (1,000–2,000 degrees Fahrenheit) incineration technologies.

CAMDS started operations in September 1979 using neutralization technologies in two major chemical agent disposal operations. The first one, initiated in September 1979 and completed by April 1981, processed 13,951 M55 rockets. Since the explosive components of the rockets could not be removed, the rockets were cut into seven sections by a rocket demilitarization machine, drained of GB agent, and decontaminated with a caustic solution. All metal parts, propellants, and explosives went through the deactivation furnace system. Similar to the RMA process, the nerve agent was mixed in the agent destruction system with sodium hydroxide in large reactors and sampled after a time to ensure that the concentration of agent was less than 2 nanograms per milliliter (this level was required to meet drinking water standards). The brine was drum-dried through two parallel, steam-heated, twin-drum dryers with circulating pumps, the resulting salts packed into plastic-lined fiberboard storage drums and sent to a RCRA-approved landfill. The M55 disposal project disposed of nearly 64 tons of GB agent.

The second neutralization operation addressed the disposal of 4,731 105-mm projectiles and 7,942 155-mm projectiles, all filled with GB agent. None of these projectiles had bursters in the shells. CAMDS destroyed the 155-mm projectiles first, between July 1981 and February 1982, with the 105-mm projectiles following in March 1982 through July 1982. A "projectile pull and drain" machine opened the projectile bodies by removing the burster wells and draining the agent into tanks. The metal parts went to the metal parts furnace, and the agent went to the agent destruction system, undergoing the same process as described earlier. This disposal project was much safer given the lack of explosive components in these artillery projectiles. In total, the second project destroyed approximately 27 tons of GB nerve agent.

Between the two neutralization projects, CAMDS generated more than 1 million pounds of waste salts, or about 6.0 pounds of waste salts for every pound of GB agent. This was more than twice what had been seen at RMA and over three times what had been demonstrated in a laboratory setting. In addition, while sodium hydroxide neutralizes GB very quickly in the lab, in the bulk process it was taking as long as 13 days. Scientific theory said that it should have taken no more than four or five hours. The engineers could not pin down the inefficiencies of the bulk agent process. This exacerbated the disposal schedules. Adding more sodium hydroxide sped up the reaction, but this in turn created more waste salts. Including the scrubber salts, the total amount of waste could rise as high as 27 times the amount of agent neutralized.

There had been attempts to examine how one might neutralize VX agent in laboratories and pilot-scale levels, but they did not seem potentially successful. The neutralization of VX agent by acid chlorinolysis had a possible risk of explosion and created a very corrosive mixture. An accident occurring in the CAMDS agent destruction system could cause a significant health risk. Second, there was no reliable, low-level detection capability for VX during the neutralization process at that time. Poor extraction recovery, detection interferences with other chemical agents, and a required sensitivity standard of 600 micrograms per liter of brine contributed to the problem. It was thought that HHS would never permit approval of the neutralization process based on these issues.

One of USATHAMA's initial incineration projects was the disposal of Chemical Agent Identification Sets (CAIS). The Army had used CAIS to train its soldiers in detection and identification of chemical warfare agents between 1928 and 1969. Each CAIS had two dozen or more glass ampules, each ampule holding about 100 milliliters of agent, and each set held between one and five different CW agents. These included sarin, sulfur mustard (diluted and distilled), nitrogen mustard (types 1 and 3), lewisite, phosgene, cyanogen chloride, and chloropicrin. There were three major varieties (of 18 different set configurations): a toxic gas set, containing bottles of sulfur mustard for decontamination exercises; war gas identification sets containing ampules of agents and simulants for outdoor training; and "sniff sets" for use in indoor classroom training.[18]

These CAIS were declared obsolete in 1971 and were recalled from Army installations in two movement operations, Operation Set Consolidation (SETCON) I in 1978, and SETCON II in 1980. Over 21,400 CAIS were sent to Rocky Mountain Arsenal for incineration, using the same buildings that were used for disposing of the Honest John warheads and bomblets. As an example of what the CAIS held, one can examine the K951/2 variant, which made up about a third of the recalled CAIS. One CAIS of this variant held 0.07 pounds of mustard agent, 0.10 pounds of lewisite, 0.87 pounds of chloropicrin, 1.46 pounds of phosgene, and 3.81 pounds of chloroform. Only 1,335 sets had the nerve agent sarin, totaling 46 pounds in the entire collection.

The Army conducted an operational test of the disposal equipment between October and December 1979, destroying 1,761 sets.[19] By the completion of the disposal, 36,694 pounds of chemical warfare agents had been destroyed, three-quarters of which had been phosgene and chloropicrin (see Table 3.2). This operation was unique in the sense that, as the chemical ampules were not easily sorted and separated prior to incineration, multiple chemical agents were incinerated simultaneously.[20] In general, all the incineration efforts had been, and today continue to be, pure agent disposal operations.

**Table 3.2**
**Chemical Agent Identification Set Disposal Schedule**

| Phase | Number of CAIS destroyed |
|---|---|
| Oct. – Dec. 1979 | 1,761 |
| May 5, 1981 – Jan. 28, 1982 | 4,634 |
| Feb. 2, 1982 – Apr. 19, 1982 | 2,968 |
| Apr. 22, 1982 – Dec. 22, 1982 | 12,095 |
| **TOTAL** | 21,458 |

CAMDS incineration operations for GB agent and munitions ran from September 1979 through August 1986, starting with the destruction of the M55 rockets from the neutralization process. All of the trials included operations with GB agent, save one that employed VX-filled ton containers. The intent of these trials was to test the furnace/incinerator start-up operations in support of a test, testing and evaluating the furnace/incinerator and its pollution abatement system or, in the one case, incinerating the drained M55 rockets from the neutralization tests without formally evaluating the incineration process. For reasons explained later, the Army had given up on neutralization around 1982, resulting in a larger scope of furnace/incineration tests, ironically referred to by the Army as the "alternative technology." As Table 3.3 illustrates, nearly 42 tons of chemical agents were disposed of in these tests.

The deactivation furnace system underwent four specific evaluations: incineration of drained M55 rockets, incineration of undrained M55 rockets, incineration of polychlorinated biphenyls (PCBs), and evaluation of the furnace pollution abatement system. Results of the tests showed an efficiency of 99.999999 percent removal of GB from the rockets and 99.9999 percent removal of all PCBs from the rocket shipping containers. In engineering terms, this was called achieving "eight 9s" and "six 9s," respectively. The pollution abatement system was tested to evaluate how it might remove agent from the furnace exhaust if the furnace shut off suddenly. It tested out at 99.9998 percent removal of GB agent from exhaust.

**Table 3.3**
**CAMDS Incineration Operations**[21]

| Munition/ Source | Number | Agent/ Quantity | Furnace | Dates of Disposal |
|---|---|---|---|---|
| Drained M55 Rockets | 13,951 | GB - 0.0 tons | Deactivation Furnace | 9/79 - 6/81 |
| Ton Container* | | GB - 0.5 tons | Metal Parts Furnace | 4/81 - 11/81 |
| Drained 155-mm projectiles | 9,157 | GB - 2.7 tons | Metal Parts Furnace | 7/81 - 2/82; 6/82 |
| Drained 105-mm projectiles | 7,771 | GB - 0.6 tons | Metal Parts Furnace | 3/82 - 6/82 |
| Ton Container* | | GB - 5.1 tons | Metal Parts Furnace | 3/82 - 1/84 |
| Undrained 155-mm projectiles | 2,703 | GB - 8.8 tons | Metal Parts Furnace | 10/82 - 11/83 |
| Ton Container* | | VX - 3.9 tons | Metal Parts Furnace | 6/84 - 8/84 |
| Drained M55 Rockets | 4,357 | GB - 1.2 tons | Deactivation Furnace | 11/85 - 5/86; 11/86 |
| Ton Container/ Drained M55 Rockets | | GB - 19 tons | Liquid Incinerator | 8/85 - 8/86 |

* Contents of the ton containers were spray-injected into the furnace; the ton containers were not destroyed.

The metal parts furnace also underwent four specific evaluations: incineration of agent sprayed into the furnace, thermal decontamination of drained projectiles, incineration of undrained munitions, and evaluation of its pollution abatement system. The engineers sprayed agent directly into the furnace to test its ability to handle bulk agent; while the results were promising, the Army decided to send the bulk agent into a separate and dedicated incinerator for control purposes. Its results showed a greater than 99.99999 percent elimination of GB for bulk agent, greater than 99.999999 percent for elimination of GB in undrained munitions, and greater than 99.9999998 percent for VX. The furnace thermally decontaminated the 105-mm projectiles to a level that tested free of any traces of agent. The pollution abatement system performed similarly to the deactivation furnace's system.

The liquid incinerator was tested to burn organic matter in waste liquids and spent decontamination solutions as well as chemical agents. It used two incinerators, a primary incinerator that reached levels of 2,500 degrees Fahrenheit, and a second afterburner maintained at 2,000 degrees Fahrenheit. This design is different from that of commercial incinerators, which have only one furnace. After 17 test burns disposing of 19 tons of GB, there was zero agent detected. Even the other two furnaces had some minute traces of agent detected (albeit below 0.00001 percent), but this liquid incinerator destroyed it all. The particular concern became one of tracking the metal leachates in the waste and particulate emissions, to ensure that the Army could develop future disposal systems that would meet RCRA and clean air standards for heavy metals.

As with mustard agent, neutralization of nerve agent was not seen as an optimal technology, especially after comparison to the incineration results. The neutralization process had to be carefully monitored at all stages, as there were numerous parameters to the chemical reactions that would either slow down the process or result in hydrolysis reversal reforming minuscule amounts of nerve agents. One had to monitor the temperature, pH, and concentrations continuously, resulting in additions of cooling systems and controlled injections of the caustic solutions. Incineration was relatively straightforward—inject agent in this end, remove the slag at the other end, and monitor the exhaust gases. Incineration took milliseconds to destroy the agent, while neutralization could take between 5 and 16 days. Some of the older munitions had jelled agent, which did not react well or mix with the caustic solutions. Most important in process evaluation, the neutralization products had to be certified to be less than two nanograms per milliliter of brine, or the batch went back through the process. These many parameters all played a role in the delays to certify the neutralization process, which the incineration process did not have.

While neutralization was generating waste at a ratio of 2.6 to 6 times the agent treated, incineration resulted in a fairly constant waste generation ration of 1.5 times the agent treated (again, not counting the scrubber salts, which made the total neutralization waste products even higher). In laboratory exercises, both processes should have been about the same. Another point against neutralization was that it was possible to regenerate GB agent from the waste products, while that was impossible with incineration. A final point on the waste issue was that neutralization resulted in organic waste, while incineration resulted in inorganic waste. While this means little to the layman, hazardous waste treatment often calls for additional treatment and higher standards for organic waste, meaning that neutralization is only one step (not the final step) in the disposal process.

In an examination of the costs of the two technologies, incineration won out over neutralization, primarily because of reduced or eliminated consumption of chemical feedstocks (the caustic solutions), reduced production of waste salts, and reduced maintenance requirements. In a study examining a theoretical employment of both systems at Johnston Island, the result was that employing incineration would result in a net savings of $16.9 million in capital costs and $2.7 million in operating costs. This was based on the number of chemical munitions at Johnston Island in 1982, prior to the arrival of the U.S. chemical weapons from Germany.

The final point in favor of incineration was that it was required even if neutralization was chosen as the main technology for disposing of the chemical agents. The explosive and propellent components had to be destroyed, and the munition cavities and metal parts had to be thermally decontaminated to permit their release to recycling plants. Operating two technologies to dispose of parts of the chemical munitions would make operations more complicated than running one that could do both. As a result, March 9, 1982, the Army officially adopted the "reverse assembly" approach of component disassembly of munitions, followed by incineration and treatment of the off-gases by a pollution abatement system to be used at JACADS and at the proposed BZ disposal facility at Pine Bluff Arsenal.[22]

USATHAMA had no orders to dispose of the entire stockpile, but it had been directed to focus on developing an approach to dispose of the obsolete and leaking munitions. At least 40 percent of Johnston Island's stockpile, by one estimate, was assessed as in that category, much of it being the M55 rockets.[23] In March 1981, USATHAMA began designing a disposal facility that would destroy the rockets, with an eye to possibly adapt the facility to destroy the M23 mines (as obsolete, not leaking, munitions). USATHAMA began preparing its Environmental Impact Statement for constructing a disposal plant on Johnston Island and would use the CAMDS-proven technologies to develop it. The decision to construct a facility at Johnston Island would be made in 1984 (no military construction funds had yet been authorized).[24]

In August 1981, USATHAMA oversaw the movement of the 888 GB-filled Weteye bombs from RMA to Tooele Army Depot. Public Law 96-418 required that the Army remove or destroy all chemical munitions at RMA by October 10, 1981. All other chemical munitions had been moved, save for these bombs, based on the Navy's request to retain the munitions on active inventory status. After HHS approved the required environmental documentation, the Army completed the transport over 17 days, costing nearly $3.5 million.

## ENVIRONMENTAL STANDARDS

Throughout all these disposal operations at RMA and Tooele Army Depot, the Army had to ensure that its operations met the HHS-approved safety guidelines. The National Environmental Policy Act (PL 91-190), which created the EPA in 1969, called for the preparation of an Environmental Impact Statement for major federal actions significantly impacting the environment. In 1974, the Safe Drinking Water Act (PL 95-523) established national drinking water regulations in all states, standardizing the many differing policies and measures across the nation. The RCRA was passed in 1976 to establish solid waste management information and guidelines for hazardous waste management. That same year, the Toxic Substances Control Act (TSCA) was passed to authorize the federal government to require testing and regulation of potentially hazardous chemicals at production and disposal sites. In 1977, the Clean Air Act (PL 95-95) and Clean Water Act (PL 95-

217) established air and water quality standards to protect the public health and welfare.[25]

The Army had to ensure that Project Eagle and CAMDS met all these federal regulations and coordinated with EPA to ensure that their disposal operations were within acceptable parameters. This was not the difficult issue. The controversy was determining what level of chemical agent exposure was safe for stockpile and disposal workers as well as the general public. The final EIS for CAMDS had to elaborate in great detail all the destruction problems that they might encounter and how the Army would minimize these risks. Project Eagle had created much of the groundwork required to prepare these assurances.

The Army developed safety guidelines, identifying that all personnel involved in agent operations would be given intensive training in handling chemical agents, in addition to operation and maintenance of the demilitarization equipment. There had to be first aid kits at numerous points in the buildings and a medical facility with decontamination showers and standby emergency medical personnel. The Army noted that there was a chance that extremely small quantities of agent might be released into the atmosphere during demilitarization operations but that these emissions would not be allowed to exceed limits established by the Army Surgeon General as safe for operations.[26]

One might think instinctively that the desired safe emission level would be as near to zero as possible, but that is an emotional and not a scientific response. The logical response is to identify, based on known toxicological data and technical ability to measure low agent quantities, what exposure levels would provide adequate protection to civilians working in and living near the stockpiles (Congress intervened when there was disagreement as to "adequate protection" versus "maximum protection"). The Army Surgeon General developed process emission standards for each agent, which were approved by HHS prior to any disposal operations. Detectors throughout and outside the plant monitored the air for trace emissions, with action limits that caused immediate shutdown of operations. As seen in Table 3.4, the limits for alarms were extremely safe-sided.

Three types of monitoring were conducted to ensure compliance with these standards: in the disposal facility, in the pollution abatement system stacks, and around the perimeters. In the plants, the Army used M8 automatic chemical agent alarms and Demilitarization Chemical Agent Concentrators, the latter using bubbler technology to track long-term, low-level agent concentrations. The M8 alarm sensitivity was 0.2 mg/m3 in less than a minute; the bubblers could detect down to 0.0001 $mg/m^3$ over a two-hour period or 0.0000003 $mg/m^3$ over 13 hours. Personnel had to mask if a bubbler sampler showed anything greater than 0.001 $mg/m^3$ for one hour or longer. One can see from Table 3.4 that an agent leak of 0.001 to 0.2 $mg/m^3$ is not immediately lethal or even incapacitating, but there was the desire to ensure that there was minimal, if any, extended exposure to low levels of chemical agents. More sensitive meant greater time to safely evacuate the potential danger area.

Table 3.4
Chemical Agent Exposure Occupational Health Standards[27]

| Definitions | GA | GB | VX | H/HD/HT | L |
|---|---|---|---|---|---|
| Lethal Concentration Dose for 50 percent of population ($LCt_{50}$) - inhalation | 200-400 mg-min/m$^3$ | 70-100 mg-min/m$^3$ | 30-100 mg-min/m$^3$ | 1,500 mg-min/m$^3$ | 1,400 mg-min/m$^3$ |
| Effective Concentration Dose for 50 percent ($ECt_{50}$) | 2-3 mg-min/m$^3$ | 3 mg-min/m$^3$ | less than 1 mg-min/m$^3$ | 10 mg-min/m$^3$ | 30 mg-min/m$^3$ |
| Source Emission Limit (automatic shut-down) | 0.0003 mg/m$^3$ | 0.0003 mg/m$^3$ | 0.0003 mg/m$^3$ | 0.03 mg/m$^3$ | 0.03 mg/m$^3$ |
| 8-hour Time Weighted Average (unmasked agent worker limits) | 0.0001 mg/m$^3$ | 0.0001 mg/m$^3$ | 0.00001 mg/m$^3$ | 0.003 mg/m$^3$ | 0.003 mg/m$^3$ |
| General Population Limit (non-agent workers) for 72 hours | 0.000003 mg/m$^3$ | 0.000003 mg/m$^3$ | 0.000003 mg/m$^3$ | 0.0001 mg/m$^3$ | 0.003 mg/m$^3$ |
| Visible Opacity | Air contaminants (particulates, smoke, vapor, gases) being emitted from stack must not reduce an observer's vision more than 20 percent or less of normal ambient air (not counting water vapor or steam condensate). | | | | |

The exhaust stacks were also monitored with the same equipment, but with more drastic actions required. If a bubbler noted a concentration of 0.0003 mg/m3 for one hour or more, the operations were shut down. At RMA, there were nine fixed-site sampling stations around the perimeter. Each station held a Technicon air monitor for continuous sampling of nitrogen dioxide, a high-volume sampler for suspended particulates, mast ozone meters for measuring total oxidants, GB bubblers, and an anemometer and wind direction transponder/recorder. Engineers took samples every 12 hours every day to monitor for any releases.

This is not to say that it was a perfect process. Particular attention focused on the pollution abatement systems; the stacks rising out of the facility gave the most concern to citizens and regulators as a source of airborne hazards. Tests of the liquid incinerator and metal parts furnace stacks showed that the particulate concentration in the stack gases had exceeded the RCRA limits, but it was a correctable problem with some minor engineering and closer control. The system removed 97 percent of the particles prior to releasing the gases to the stack. There were no products of incomplete combustion (PICs) detected in the liquid incinerator stacks. In tests of the deactivation furnace, there were no RCRA-specified PICs, but other organic compounds were identified.

In all cases, the brine and waste products were testing out as below RCRA standards for nonhazardous waste. In particular, tests for heavy metals such as silver, barium, cadmium, chromium, lead, mercury, selenium, and arsenic showed traces far below RCRA criteria. The engineers had tracked the brine products for over 30 different chemicals in their tests, across all agents and all incineration furnaces. Reams of data available from this period show that the incineration process had proven out as executable, efficient, and safe to operate.

Throughout the early years of CAMDS operations (1979–86), there had been no any indications of agent migrating off-post, either through the air or through the groundwater. These seven years of operations resulted in a high level of technical expertise within the Army, not only in the area of chemical demilitarization but in areas of risk assessment and compliance with EPA regulations. When it became time to take the next step, planning to dispose of the entire U.S. chemical stockpile, the PMCD's office thought that it understood the issues and had the right people to execute a safe and cost-efficient plan. It had not, however, considered the full impact of the Army leadership's interest, the citizens groups' fears, and, perhaps most importantly, what federal, state, and local politicians expected out of the program.

# 4

## Public and Congressional Interests

It is important to identify all the major players of the chemical demilitarization program and their roles prior to beginning discussions on the public policy aspects. In the realm of policy processes, Charles Jones identifies four types of participants that may be involved: rationalists, technicians, incrementalists, and reformists.[1] Depending on the time period examined, each participant has larger or smaller roles in the execution of policy.

The rationalists are those policy analysts who examine the problem, develop goals, identify and evaluate all the alternatives, and choose the best course of action. This very methodical and careful examination of the issues seems the most comprehensive approach. The challenge facing rational goal-making is that numerous institutional and political goals and objectives counter the realization of completing policy objectives. Rationalists are often accused of not understanding the human nature side of the issues, often as a result of being geographically distant from the challenges and dealing with many other competing issues. In our case, the rationalists are the Army and OSD leaders dealing with incineration policy, in particular the Under Secretary of the Army, the ASA(I&L), later the Assistant to the Secretary of the Army for Research, Development and Acquisition (ASA[RDA]),[2] and the Assistant to the Secretary of Defense for Nuclear and Chemical and Biological Programs (ATSD[NCB], reporting to the Under Secretary of Defense for Acquisition, Technology and Logistics (USD[AT&L]). To clarify, the rationalists include those Army general officers in Headquarters, Department of the Army but not the general officers in the Chemical Corps or those running the chemical demilitarization program.

The technicians are specialized rationalists in a sense, using their particular subject-matter expertise toward a particular assignment within a policy area. What makes them different (in addition to their expertise) is that they often have their goals set by others (the defense program oversight office). These technicians include the scientists, engineers, and statisticians involved with the program's execution. While technicians are very confident of their analyses in their particular area of expertise, they are not comfortable making more extensive decisions.

Technicians can be overly narrow in their focus on the problem, choosing not to address areas outside their interests. In the demilitarization program, these technicians would include the office of the Program Manager for Chemical Demilitarization, their supporting contractors, and managers of the stockpile sites.

In public policy reviews, incrementalists are often identified as the politicians, concerned with constantly adjusting the process to fit near-term desired outcomes. Because incrementalists do not expect to have all the information that they need to make perfect policy based on truly rational or technical observations, it may be said that they build upon the existing program and tinker at the margins. Incrementalists constantly compromise competing demands based on the most recent context, rather than taking bold, strong actions. Status quo is often seen as better (or at least safer) than change, and incrementalists do not have to consider the long-term effect of their decisions. State and local politicians and Congress play major roles as incrementalists in the chemical demilitarization program. Consider that every sitting Congress since 1969 has passed a regulatory (as well as budgetary) law on some aspect of the chemical demilitarization program, constantly tweaking the program to fit its immediate concerns.

Reformists are very similar to incrementalists in that they do not expect to have all the information desired in a particular area, but believe that this lack of information means that government must take every precaution in making its decisions. Impatient with incremental changes, reformists expect to see government address their concerns immediately and can be very confrontational. Not surprisingly, reformists are seen as the activists in any policy process, often voicing the concern that the government is not making the right decisions. Their demands are often unrealistic and uncompromising in nature. In our case, these include the small, but vocal, citizen groups living near the chemical stockpiles and some national citizen groups, concerned about the presence of the chemical munitions as well as the method of their disposal. Many consider science and facts as mere minutiae that can be twisted as required to fit their specific agenda.

To complicate the situation, the chemical demilitarization program was being dragged into two closely related policy areas with very different agendas. The Army leadership had always been interested in retaining some kind of retaliatory capability in the form of chemical weapons. Even when General Creighton Abrams moved to disestablish the Chemical Corps in 1972, his intent was to merge these chemical specialists into the Ordnance Corps as special weapons handlers, not to do away with chemical weapons altogether.[3] There was a concern that, lacking a retaliatory capability in kind, the only U.S. military option available to counter Soviet use of chemical weapons would be to respond with tactical nuclear weapons. The current inventory of chemical weapons had been aging for years, and there was a desire to modernize the capability and to make handling chemical weapons more safe. The Army and OSD leadership began its overtures to Congress in May 1974 to fund procurement of binary chemical weapons.[4]

At the same time frame, the arms control program shifted its initiatives to include chemical weapons, beginning with a Moscow summit meeting in June 1974 between President Nixon and General Secretary Leonid Brezhnev. The two leaders had agreed to try to formulate a joint initiative on chemical weapons for presentation to the 31-nation Conference of the Committee on Disarmament, later the 40-nation Committee on Disarmament. This agreement was later reaffirmed between President Gerald Ford and Brezhnev in November of that year. In August 1976, the two nations initiated bilateral talks in Geneva on chemical weapons. Two and a half years later, the Joint Chiefs of Staff reported that talks had not been substantive. There were significant challenges in trying to retain a retaliatory capability for deterrent purposes, on one hand, as another branch of government, on the other hand, was attempting to negotiate their complete destruction.[5]

The interesting point of this defense policy review is the observation that both the arms control community and the binary weapons proponents saw the chemical stockpiles and associated chemical demilitarization program as an integral part of their agenda. The Army's chemical demilitarization efforts had been going on for several years on a smaller scale to eliminate the leakers and obsolete weapons at the stockpile sites. If it made political and common sense to align the national chemical demilitarization and the binary weapons modernization programs together, the Army leadership was going to link the two efforts.

## DOD WANTS BINARY CHEMICAL WEAPONS

The exact nuance of the U.S. national policy on offensive use of chemical weapons has changed several times over the decades, but from 1917 through 1990, military commanders were tasked to prepare contingency plans for the employment of chemical weapons in their areas of responsibility. While the United States was a signatory of the Geneva Protocol of 1925, the Senate chose not to ratify that treaty until 1975. Technically, this gave the U.S. government a legal loophole up to 1975 to order the first use of chemical weapons in a conflict, although the government had always been careful to note that it had always lived by the intent of the treaty. Even if the Senate had ratified the treaty, it would not have prevented the U.S. military's option to respond to an adversary's chemical weapons use with its own chemical weapons. President Franklin D. Roosevelt set the first national policy on June 5, 1942, stating:

Use of such weapons has been outlawed by the general opinion of civilized mankind. This country has not used them, and I hope we never will be compelled to use them. I state categorically that we shall under no circumstances resort to the use of such weapons unless they are first used by our enemies. . . . Any use of gas by any Axis power . . . will immediately be followed by the fullest possible retaliation upon munition centers, seaports, and other military objectives.[6]

While most portray Roosevelt as an opponent of chemical warfare in general and of the U.S. Chemical Warfare Service's plans to develop and employ chemical weapons in particular, he did recognize the need to develop and retain a retaliatory capability to deter possible German and Japanese employment of chemical weapons. At the beginning of World War II, that retaliatory capability was practically nonexistent; by the end of the war, the U.S. military had thousands of tons of agent weaponized and stockpiled overseas in a ready status.

Through World War II, the Korean War, and most of the Cold War, the Army continued to develop and move stockpiles of chemical weapons to ensure that an adequate and responsive retaliatory capability existed. In the late 1950s, this included transporting and storing chemical munitions at Army depots in Germany and Okinawa to ensure a retaliatory option existed. President Truman had made clear that the Korean conflict was to be a "limited" military operation, meaning one limited by the lack of nuclear, biological, or chemical weapons as well as one limited geographically to the Korean peninsula. The possibility that the Soviet Union might arm either China or North Korea with chemical or biological weapons haunted military commanders, however, leading to the development of stocks in Okinawa and a reinvigorated offensive CB warfare program at Pine Bluff Arsenal and Rocky Mountain Arsenal.

After the war, the DOD revisited its policies in response to concerns that the military should be prepared to engage in a military operation, including the use of CB munitions. In 1956, the military policy changed to the effect that the United States would be prepared to use CB weapons in a general war to enhance military effectiveness. The president would have the decision to employ these weapons. This was a step beyond just a retaliatory capability. In part, this was to answer increasing Soviet aggressiveness, and, in part, the military was recognizing a need to develop a response to an adversary's employment of CB weapons with something other than a tactical nuclear weapon (which might cause escalation to strategic exchanges).[7]

All four branches of the military began investing in production, testing, and stockpiling of modern unitary chemical munitions in the 1960s. In November 1969, that ended with President Nixon's announcement stating the U.S. CB warfare policy as no first use of lethal chemical weapons (to include incapacitating chemical agents such as BZ). The alleged Dugway sheep kill was still being investigated in Congress more than a year after the incident, and Congress took this announcement as reason to severely decrease funding for the military's chemical and biological warfare and defense program. This was, unfortunately, just the time frame that the Army had been considering a start of production for its binary chemical weapons program.

Edgewood Arsenal had been researching the potential feasibility of manufacturing binary munitions since 1958, initially because the Navy was seeking a way to safely store chemical weapons on aircraft carriers. Thinking about the potential catastrophe as a result of a leaking chemical munition on a ship, the Navy suggested that Edgewood Arsenal investigate binaries as a way to ensure a safe storage capability. By 1969, it had conducted significant research into a 155-mm binary artillery projectile and a "Bigeye" BLU-80/B binary bomb. Plans to continue tests and development of these munitions and to develop production facilities were shelved after the Nixon announcement and resulting congressional cutbacks in the program. The result was a sudden stop to all plans to produce chemical munitions, but this was not in line with the DOD leadership's desires. It still wanted a modern retaliatory capability, and that meant retaining the capability to produce and store chemical munitions.

What caused this desire was the very casual observation—that the Soviet armored vehicles captured from the Egyptian military during the Arab–Israeli 1973 conflict had collective protection systems for its crew and inhabitants. The Egyptian soldiers had Soviet protective masks, skin decontamination kits, and manual chemical detection kits. This information, combined with the knowledge that the Egyptian air force (trained by Soviet military advisors) had dropped mustard and nerve agent munitions on Yemeni royalists during the Yemeni civil war, meant that the U.S. military had to acknowledge that the Soviet military was intent on developing a capability to operate under chemical warfare conditions. While some noted that the Soviets might be taking these precautions against possible U.S. military use of chemical weapons, DOD had to examine the potential that its European forces could be potential chemical targets. If that was true, U.S. forces were dangerously vulnerable, given the overall lack of defensive training and equipment and the recent disestablishment of their primary specialists—the Army Chemical Corps—in 1972.

Intelligence analysts were identifying the Soviet Union as the best-prepared nation, offensively and defensively, in the world in the area of chemical warfare. Their doctrine suggested that chemical warfare was a tactical capability, not a strategic weapon equivalent to nuclear weapons. The Soviets had a very active research and development program in the 1960s and 1970s and had weaponized missiles, bombs, rockets, and artillery projectiles with chemical fills. Their military exercises included practice in simulated and actual toxic environments. In the face of this threat, the U.S. military had to consider the need for a retaliatory capability. Even given defensive equipment and time to train, U.S. forces would be at a serious tactical disadvantage if they were forced into protective postures while only the Soviet forces were free to choose the time and place of chemical contamination of the battlefield. There were only two clear options available: develop a policy to respond to Soviet initiation of chemical warfare by escalation to tactical nuclear weapons or lower the nuclear threshold by retaliating in kind.[8]

The U.S. military had to demonstrate it had a prompt and effective capability to retaliate in kind, thus leveling the playing field. It was hoped that the Soviets, seeing that their forces would be similarly degraded by the effects of chemical weapons, would not resort to first use. This policy necessitated development of an adequate stockpile ready for employment, with operational plans developed for specific areas of command. The Joint Chiefs of Staff had determined that the current stockpile, with much of its stocks predating 1960 and packaged in bulk ton containers, was not adequate for the task. This led to the Army's investigations of what would be required to modernize its chemical stockpile with binary chemical munitions. The proposal was first put to Congress in 1974 by the acting Assistant Secretary of Defense for International Security Affairs, Amos Jordan.

The military was convinced that there were significant operational and safety advantages over unitary chemical weapons by turning to binary munitions. The binary munitions made the same nerve agents that unitary weapons held, used the same delivery means and provided the same target effectiveness. Because they could be transported in two different configurations (not assembled as nerve agent munitions), they were safer to store in peacetime, safer to transport across the battlefield, and safer to demilitarize after they were obsolete. The bottom line was that the use of binary weapons would be no different from the use of unitary weapons, since both employed the same nerve agents to produce the same battlefield effect. This was merely a modernization effort that would provide a deterrent against Soviet employment of chemical warfare against U.S. forces.

Of course, the problem was that, in the midst of bilateral U.S.–U.S.S.R. arms control talks on chemical and biological disarmament, the U.S. military was going to manufacture chemical munitions of its own. In a post-Vietnam, post-Dugway-sheep-incident, firmly Democratic Congress, the idea that the military would rearm itself with these weapons was seen as not well thought out. Then-Representative Pat Schroeder (D-CO) hinted that the Army Materiel Command merely wanted to manufacture chemical munitions in an attempt to build up its business and maintain a large infrastructure and that development of these binary weapons, either as a retaliatory option or as a deterrent, would not serve national security objectives.[9] Some in Congress were concerned that the initiation of a binary program would result in an arms race with other nations, increasing the threat to U.S. military forces facing hostile nations overseas rather than acting as a deterrent. Others noted that, if arms controls in Geneva were successful and the Soviets signed a chemical weapons disarmament treaty, the U.S. military could even stop research and development of defensive equipment, saving taxpayer money. As the years went by, additional studies and the rhetoric surrounding the feasibility of binary chemical munitions only increased.

The debate raged throughout the military and political community, with various think-tanks and varied "experts" composing discussion papers and making speeches on the pros and cons of chemical warfare deterrence through a retaliatory capability. Critics decried chemical weapons as immoral weapons of mass destruction but also voiced doubts that the binary weapons would be effective at all or that conventional weapons would surpass chemical weapons in lethality and thus render the need for chemical weapons moot. Many thought that a chemical arms race would result and that, unless the European allies would accept having binary chemical weapons on their soil, a stockpile based in the United States was of little value. The odd part was that, before any binary munitions were even manufactured or tested, these self-designated technical experts were already debunking their utility and effectiveness. Because the Chemical Corps was on the ropes in the 1970s, critics interpreted the binary munitions program to be a lifeline for the weakened Chemical Corps and thought that its leaders were "selling" the program under false pretenses.[10]

While these critics lacked any political, military, or diplomatic credentials in the area of chemical weapons programs or military policy, they were very articulate in stating their opinions on what the Soviets could do with their chemical weapons stockpile, on the value of a U.S. chemical weapons stockpile, and on whether the U.S. military needed a binary weapons capability. Very often their testimonies were a blend of assumptions, selective facts, and academic theory, leading to statements that had no basis in logic but were elaborated upon with great confidence.

It may have been merely opportunism on the part of some individuals, stating what certain Congressional leaders wanted to hear in times of nuclear arms control and disarmament, use of riot control agents in Vietnam, and environmental awareness. Public opinion certainly seemed to support a complete prohibition of chemical weapons. Most government arms control experts were dealing with nuclear disarmament issues and did not spare serious thoughts or time to the issue of CW policy options, which was the military's realm. The number of true CW doctrine and policy experts outside the Army was very limited, and this allowed an opening for other articulate academic graybeards to theorize in this area.

Because issues related to chemical warfare often appear very technical and distant from traditional military topics, it became easy for some in Congress to rely on these experts. They were stating what the majority party wanted to hear: that chemical weapons were not really useful, that this issue was an attempt by the Chemical Corps to remain relevant at whatever cost to international security, that binary weapons (although untested) were sure to fail. Consider these two passages from J. Perry Robinson, a British arms control expert, in 1975:

One such [alternative] policy is that of participation in international chemical disarmament—a policy of counter-threat, which for several reasons could prove ineffectual, it offers the possibility of removing the threat altogether. It also offers the possibility of checking nerve-gas proliferation, an eventuality which would create far more serious security dangers than exist at present in Europe, and which a counter-threat policy is likely to promote, particularly if binary technology is used to support it.

As it happens, the United States possesses enormous quantities of nerve gas in bulk storage. These stocks, which apparently are to be destroyed, could be used in existing munition filling facilities to provide an increase in the quantity of immediately useable weapons. Moreover, for technical reasons, binary weapons are militarily inferior to those weapons they are intended to replace. These two considerations, taken together, hardly suggest cost-effectiveness.[11]

These statements seem foolish and without merit today, but in 1975, this was the general tone of arms control proponents intent on stopping the U.S. binary munitions program. Despite the lack of knowledge of chemical weapons employment doctrine and without any actual operational test data on the binary munition's capabilities, these critics were already dooming the binary program as ineffective, overly costly, and worsening the security of Europe.

On the other side, binary proponents noted that the Soviet Union obviously did not consider chemical weapons immoral but rather a part of tactical military operations, that the binary munitions would be as effective as the unitary munitions that they replaced, that arms control talks had led nowhere for years, and that the Europeans might more readily accept safer binary munitions rather than potentially leaking unitary munitions. There were obvious technical challenges, such as how the Army would test munitions when it was severely limited by restraints to open-air agent testing (answer: they would use chemical agent simulants),[12] but the bottom line was that the Army leadership at the top levels believed that this modernization effort was necessary to deter possible Soviet use.

The Ford administration largely held the same views on CW policies as the Nixon administration, with President Gerald Ford pushing both the Geneva Protocol of 1925 and Biological Weapons Convention through the Senate as ratified treaties in 1975. Requests for construction funds for a binary munitions production plant, initially identified to be built at Pine Bluff Arsenal, were rebuffed both by legislative and the executive branches through 1976. In particular, Congress directed that the president would have to certify to the House and Senate leadership that the production of these binary munitions was essential to national interest prior to the release of any production funds.[13]

In May 1977, President Jimmy Carter directed a full review of the DOD CW policy and military posture. The National Security Council review examined the U.S. and Soviet CW capabilities and recommended both modernizing the U.S. chemical stockpile and leveraging progress in arms control negotiations. Focusing on arms control issues and stopping major weapons programs such as the B1 bomber and neutron bomb, the Carter administration hoped to bring the Soviets to the negotiating table. Not only were negotiations fruitless, but the Soviets were seen as continuing to improve their CW capabilities while the U.S. military had no offensive research and development program.

The Army leadership had hoped at least to construct a binary munitions facility, while not producing any munitions, to minimize the lead time required to develop a retaliatory capability if authorized. The Carter administration eventually agreed with the push for binaries and included funds for the facility in the president's final budget, but the president pulled it out at the last moment. His decision was that no immediate policy changes would be made and that the chemical stockpile would be maintained without improvement. The Reagan administration was left to make that decision. The military continued to state its official position as seeing the binary program and eventual chemical disarmament as complementary, rather than competing, objectives. Congress viewed this position as a bid to develop a full offensive capability, which ran counter to the tone of the arms control talks. The funds were not authorized for the facility, let alone authorization to produce binary munitions.[14]

The Reagan administration changed the tempo, picking up the initiative and advancing it considerably. Events such as the Soviet Union's invasion of Afghanistan, reports of chemical warfare in Laos, and the Sverdlovsk anthrax release in 1979, combined with a Republican majority in the Senate, supported Army requests for funding the production of a binary munitions facility. In 1980 and 1981, it was obvious that Soviet chemical warfare efforts had not diminished, leading to a National Security Council recommendation to modify the U.S. chemical warfare policy. This was a two-pronged initiative: to eliminate the chemical warfare threat by achieving a complete and verifiable chemical weapons treaty and to deter the use of chemical weapons against the United States and its allies by revitalizing the U.S. military's CW capabilities until such a treaty was ratified.[15]

Construction of the binary munitions facility at Pine Bluff Arsenal was finally authorized in September 1980 with starting funds of $3.15 million in planning funds and in 1981 an addition of $20 million, but Democrats in Congress still drew the line at authorizing actual production of binary weapons. Meanwhile, Edgewood Arsenal had reinstated some research and development, designing an 8-inch binary artillery projectile and beginning investigations into a Multiple Launch Rocket System (MLRS) binary chemical warhead.[16]

All the discussions on the need for a chemical retaliatory capability brought attention back to Rocky Mountain Arsenal and its store of Weteye bombs filled with nerve agents. Public concern, stirred by the media, focused on the fact that traffic at the Stapleton airport had grown considerably over the past 10 years and on what might happen if an airplane crashed into one of the depot's ammunition igloos. Congress added a section to the DOD Military Construction Act for 1981 specifically to direct the Army to move the chemical weapons out of the Arsenal.

While the lack of success in arms control talks had not been enough to persuade Congress, the downing of Korean Air Line 007 by Soviet fighters in 1983 pushed the moderates over to support the binary program. This passenger plane had strayed into Soviet air space while flying from South Korea to Anchorage, Alaska. The death of 269 civilians on board enraged the public, pushing Congressional legislators into a "get tough" attitude. Public Law 98-94, passed in September 1983, tied the binary program to the chemical stockpile by withholding production funds until the president certified to Congress that, for every binary projectile or bomb produced, the Army would destroy a serviceable unitary artillery projectile from the existing stockpile. Because the start of the binary program appeared to be still distant, the Army began rearming its chemical bombs with bursters and renovating 155-mm and 8-inch artillery projectiles in their U.S. and overseas stockpiles, as interim measures to rebuild its retaliatory capability.

In the following year, Congress directed the formation of a Chemical Warfare Review Commission (CWRC), which would review the U.S. military's chemical warfare posture and recommend whether the United States should produce binary chemical weapons. This commission began its work in January 1985 and in April released its report to Congress. The commission noted that only 10–18 percent of the unitary stockpile was useful or available for limited use, and 11 percent was either unrepairable or obsolete munitions. Over 61 percent of the stockpile was not usable in any form (mostly the ton containers, which, lacking a filling facility and empty munitions, were not deemed to be useful in a future military contingency). The report concluded that (1) modernization of the chemical stockpile would more likely encourage negotiations for a multilateral, verifiable ban on chemical weapons; (2) only a small fraction of the current stockpile had any deterrent value, while the bulk was militarily useless and should be destroyed; (3) the proposed binary program would provide an adequate capability to meet the present armed forces' needs and was necessary; and (4) any expectation that protective measures alone could offset the advantages gained from a Soviet chemical attack was not realistic.[17]

In June 1985, Defense Secretary Casper Weinberg sent a letter to Representative Les Aspin (D-WI), the chair of the House Armed Services Committee, telling him that "the production of binary chemical munitions is essential to the national interest." That same month, the House voted to authorize resumption of chemical weapons production, contingent on the DOD's certifying that technical difficulties surrounding the Bigeye bomb were solved, that the DOD would store the separate parts of the binary chemical munitions in different states, and that the European allies would formally agree to forward deployment of binary weapons on their soil. On November 26, 1986, the Office of the Project Manager for Binary Munitions was provisionally chartered at Aberdeen Proving Grounds-Edgewood Area, Maryland.

The Army leadership finally made its case, and was successful because they had gotten the Army and OSD leadership (the rationalists) to agree on the retaliatory policy that called for the development and employment of binary chemical munitions (a research and development program developed by the technicians) to the politicians in the executive and legislative branches (the incrementalists). Within this military policy program, the reformists (largely members of nongovernmental arms control groups) had not energized public reaction to the Army's initiation of its binary program enough to create any obstacles to the binary program's initiation. That is not to say that arms control groups had not tried their best.

## THE STATE DEPARTMENT DOES NOT WANT CHEMICAL WEAPONS

The international arms control community was very busy in the 1960s and 1970s, with successes, for example, in completing the Partial Test Ban Treaty in

1963, the Outer Space Treaty in 1967, and Seabed Treaty in 1971. The Strategic Arms Limitation Talks (SALT) were ongoing through the late 1960s and into 1970, and international attention now turned to chemical and biological warfare. Arms control experts had been discussing how the international community might continue to disarm the military of chemical and biological weapons in the mid-1960s, but progress was slow. One of the obstacles seen was that, while biological weapons were largely limited to the two major superpowers, several smaller nations had developed chemical weapon stockpiles. Warring nations had used chemical weapons in past conflicts, while they had not used biological weapons. It was far easier to develop agreements among the nations for a weapon system that many did not possess. This led to Britain's negotiators presenting a draft arms control protocol in 1968 intended to curb biological warfare, negotiated separately from the chemical warfare discussions, although the Soviets continued to insist on the need to treat both chemical and biological warfare issues together.

In 1972, President Nixon had submitted the Biological Warfare and Toxins Convention (BWC), the Geneva Protocol of 1925, Anti-Ballistic Missile treaty, and SALT I Agreement to Congress for ratification. It was a busy decade for the Senate and arms control experts, as the debates began over the pros and cons of ratification. The Senate would debate the Geneva Protocol for two years on and off, questioning (among other things) the potential restrictions on the use of riot control agents and herbicides imposed by the treaty and whether this protocol would restrict the U.S. government from modernizing the chemical weapons stockpile. President Ford's executive order renouncing first use of riot control agents and herbicides in April 1975 made it possible for the Senate to agree to ratification of the Geneva Protocol, with the provision that military use of riot control agents or herbicides was addressed outside the protocol.[18] Interlaced in this debate were discussions on the U.S. military's defensive capabilities (which, lacking a Chemical Corps, had been significantly reduced), the growth of the Soviet chemical warfare capability, and the realistic expectations of deterrence through retaliation in kind.

Differing views of the United States and Soviet Union continued to keep discussions on a chemical weapons convention unproductive for several years. The binary program was seen as a major obstacle that, fairly or unfairly, was perceived as making the United States less willing to negotiate a treaty banning all chemical weapons. With Britain, Japan, the Soviet Union, and other countries submitting drafts for consideration, the U.S. negotiators were seen to fence over technical details on verification issues. Critics began to remark that if the United States embarked on a binary weapons procurement program, there would be no confidence in the U.S. position or its good intentions to eventually disarm. Despite the U.S. military's protestations that the binary munitions program was necessary as a deterrent until the treaty was ratified, arms control pundits continued to voice that the best policy to prevent chemical warfare was international chemical disarmament. If the United States had to unilaterally disarm its chemical weapons prior to the Soviet Union to show its sincerity, so be it.

Idyllic views of deterrence through disarmament, without any supporting facts or experience, were routinely developed and quoted to diminish the U.S. military's chemical weapons program goals and to keep the emotional fever for chemical disarmament high. This is not to say that this attitude was unique to chemical weapons; this was typical of much of the arms control program of this time. The U.S. government's preoccupation with arms control in the 1970s had spun up a life of its own, creating a moral or almost religious mandate to continue arms control processes at all costs, even if this practice ran counter to military and political strategic objectives or made the United States look weaker than it really was. The result of these efforts would embolden the Soviet Union's negotiators to continue to fence with the U.S. negotiators with no real interest in concluding an arms control treaty for chemical warfare.[19]

At the Moscow summit meeting in June 1974, President Nixon and General Secretary Brezhnev agreed to work toward a bilateral chemical weapons agreement for presentation to the 31-nation Conference of the Committee on Disarmament. The Geneva talks would proceed much more smoothly, it was felt, if the two major countries with chemical weapons arsenals had agreed on a few points in general. This agreement was reaffirmed by President Ford and Brezhnev in November 1974, and the two countries began formal bilateral meetings in Geneva on chemical weapons disarmament in August 1976. While the spotlight was on nuclear arms discussions (SALT II), there seemed to be measurable progress in the chemical arms control talks.[20]

The U.S. delegation presented a number of options. One option might be to reduce existing chemical weapons stocks to a certain agreed level and to restrict production that would increase the stockpiles, similar to the nuclear arms control process. A second option was to ban all future production or transfer of current chemical stocks to other countries, and to require a phased destruction of stocks over a period of time. A third option was the complete ban of all chemical weapons production and destruction of a specified amount of munitions over a period of time. What the negotiators really wanted was to completely disarm all nations of all chemical weapons and their production facilities.[21]

The work began under the Carter administration, with Paul Warnke as the director for the U.S. Arms Control and Disarmament Agency. Warnke was not a fan of military force and held the view that the Soviet Union would follow the United States' example of unilateral disarmament in arms control. During his Senate confirmation as the lead negotiator on SALT II, a senator noted that Warnke had recommended against the B-1 bomber, the Trident submarine and missile, submarine-launched cruise missiles, the AWACS program, mobile ICBMs, MIRV deployments, improvements to the current ICBM, and development of the XM-1 tank and for reductions of U.S. tactical weapons in Europe, withdrawal of forces from the North Atlantic Treaty Organization (NATO), holding the Army to 13 divisions vice 16 divisions, and continued cuts in the defense budget.[22] This was the man who was going to set the pace for chemical arms control talks, as the administration indicated new interest in continuing negotiations with the Soviets.

They began talks on what a draft convention might include. Certainly, as a first step of confidence, the nations would have to declare their total stockpile prior to opening their file cabinets for inspections. Assuming that the declaring nation was not concealing any parts of the stockpile, the inspectors would move in to verify these accounts. An exchange of data between participating countries was seen as necessary to build trust, but it was a daunting task. The number of records supporting the production, transportation, storage, testing, import/export of precursors, consumption, and testing alone would be immense for the major powers. Verification depended on a number of both technical and political variables, many of which depended on the openness of the country declaring its stockpile. The technical details of how to verify then get more difficult, as the arms control negotiators had to agree on:

- What is to be declared as far as what constitutes a chemical warfare agent? Do riot control agents, herbicides, incendiaries, and smoke munitions count, since they all disperse chemicals that cause a physical or physiological action? What about toxins, which the Soviets considered as chemicals derived from biological organisms and the United States considered as biological warfare agents?
- What chemical precursors should be included for verification that they are not being used for chemical warfare production? What about dual-use chemicals? Will inspectors have to visit commercial industries not declared as CW production sites? Will these measures be so restrictive as to impair the commercial industry's ability to operate?
- Could facilities that had produced CW agents be converted to make commercial products? How do the inspectors ensure that the facilities are not switched back, if these plants are converted? Do all facilities have to be destroyed?
- Who conducts the inspections, and who chooses the inspectors and observers? How does a country know that the inspectors are not political or industrial espionage agents? What equipment will they carry, and how will the equipment be certified? How will the inspectors test and validate the samples taken at sites?
- How much time does a nation have to prepare for inspections? Do the inspectors have the right to challenge a nation on undeclared sites? Do the inspectors get to observe the destruction processes, or do they merely verify the absence of CW agents and precursors?
- How much of the defensive program is open for inspection? Are the countries permitted to develop chemical warfare agents to test their defensive equipment? Is it likely that a country developing a defensive program is planning to use chemical weapons in an offensive posture?
- Can the chemical warfare agents be converted into a useful commercial product rather than being destroyed? How does one ensure that the commercial products are not reassembled into CW agents? What are the limits to complete and irreversible destruction of agent? 99.99 percent? More or less?
- Is the treaty broad enough and are destruction measures affordable enough to permit all nations to participate? What happens if one country starts a destruction effort and finds out that its neighbor is not complying with the treaty? What is the deterrent then?

There were many more technical issues, all of which had to be addressed and agreed upon by the two major powers and their allies, let alone the nonaligned countries, before they could draft a common treaty. While many participating nations did not have chemical warfare stocks, they were interested in shaping the debate and ensuring that the treaty was enforceable for all nations without being overly intrusive or costly to implement. There was optimism that, as long as the two major powers were talking, there was hope of coming to a middle ground.

By 1980, these hopes had faded somewhat. There had been at least three draft chemical weapons treaties and numerous working proposals reviewed by the Conference of the Committee on Disarmament in the 1970s, without any agreement of a final product. The Reagan administration was more willing to play hardball with the Soviets, to the point that some in the Soviet Union believed that President Ronald Reagan was prepared to initiate nuclear war against them. Certainly, Reagan's gaffe on the radio in 1984, when he jokingly announced that he had outlawed the Soviet Union and would begin bombing in five minutes, did nothing to contradict that view.[23] In 1983, the Reagan administration returned to Geneva to press for an aggressive arms control initiative, both in nuclear and in chemical arms control. Vice President George Bush presented a draft chemical disarmament treaty before the Conference on Disarmament in April 1984, again calling for a strict verification process.

The Soviets continued to press for a verification process similar to that of the BWC, that is, no verification other than voluntary and chaperoned visits permitted at a time and location agreed to by the host nation. The U.S. government pushed for more strict measures, to include challenge inspections and on-site verification of destruction of chemical munitions and facilities. Waiting in the shadows was the production of binary chemical weapons as a bargaining chip to force the Soviets to the table, which eventually worked.

The general U.S. arms control position in the early 1980s could be stated as an iron-clad commitment to effective and complete chemical weapons disarmament, calling for the total destruction of an entire class of existing weapons. As an example of this commitment, the U.S. government announced that it had deliberately refrained itself from manufacturing binary chemical weapons or otherwise modernizing its offensive capability. On the other hand, there was a measurable imbalance in offensive chemical warfare capability between the Soviet Union and United States, which was aggravated by the lack of any progress in bilateral discussions since 1976. When the decision was made to initiate the binary production program, there was considerable angst in the arms control community. Many saw the binary weapons production and the U.S. government's calling for continued chemical arms disarmament talks as contradictory. Yet, when Congress approved the construction of a binary chemical weapons facility in 1985, the Soviets denounced the effort but suddenly became more willing to discuss the verification issue at Geneva.

In this review of policy, the participants' roles and accomplishments are a bit less clear. The Department of State and associated DOD arms control agencies had not been successful in their attempts to shape and develop an international treaty banning all chemical weapons. They had not gotten the OSD and military leadership (the rationalists) to fully back their agenda of chemical weapons disarmament, especially in the light of any lack of Soviet willingness to disarm and the U.S. military's resulting perceived disadvantage. The policy initiatives debated in Geneva (developed by the arms control technicians) had the support of the executive and legislative branches (the incrementalists), as long as the initiatives could be sold to the public as leading the world to become a better and safer place. The reformists (again, largely non-governmental arms control individuals and groups) were more than willing to assist the U.S. government, supplying the participants with any number of studies using selective facts, making poor assumptions about military issues that they did not understand, and endorsing the disarmament of all chemical weapons.

## WHICH WAY DOES THE CHEMICAL DEMIL PROGRAM GO?

Up to 1983, the Army's chemical demilitarization agency had a limited agenda, focusing on its original charter to dispose of leakers and obsolete munitions and to test and develop safe and efficient means to conduct that disposal. Without a ratified chemical weapons treaty, there was no definable guidance or timetables for disposing of chemical weapons while the arms control talks continued. With the passage of PL 98-94 (DOD Authorization Act for 1984) in September 1983, the Army received the first formal directive that it had to plan for the disposal of all the unitary chemical weapons, and that this directive was to make room for the binary chemical weapons. While there was not a clearly identified timeline for this process, there certainly was top-level military interest in starting the binary program. The Army would need to execute both the demilitarization and the binary program to be successful, since eventually it would have to replace all the unitary chemical weapons that were destroyed.[24]

The Army thought that it understood what it needed to do to complete a chemical disposal program, having developed a tentative schedule and cost based on the CAMDS experiments. Its end-goal was the timely destruction of the chemical stockpiles while ensuring protection for the general public, for personnel involved in destruction activities, and for the environment. To execute this, it would develop effective and safe facilities designed solely for the destruction of lethal chemical agents and munitions. It had decades of experience in this area and knew that it could execute the program once given adequate funding and the go-ahead to begin. It had Congress supporting the need for quick and safe disposal of the existing stockpile. The Army leadership slow to recognize a need for close public involvement in what they felt was clearly a technical process to be executed under military management.

The OSD and Army leadership, with the CB defense research and development community, had successfully set the agenda for the chemical demilitarization program. They had identified the objective of disposing of the aging, unitary chemical munitions through incineration technology and making room for the binary chemical munitions. This agenda was formed without input from citizens living near the stockpile sites who had just realized that the Army was ready to start building rather large incinerators next door. While they may not have liked living next to chemical weapons stockpiles, they were less pleased about living next to a toxic chemical agent incinerator. National environmental groups and other critics did not care about arms control or binary program issues and were willing to take a position against the Army's plans. The public policy challenges were only just starting.

# 5

## Developing a Disposal Program

In 1983, USATHAMA's chemical disposal agenda was very straightforward; it was to: (1) support the Army depots in the safe storage of chemical munitions and agents, using DATS to handle and contain leakers; (2) develop facilities to destroy the bulk BZ and BZ-filled munitions, all the M55 rockets in the stockpile, and the obsolete and leaking stocks on Johnston Island; and (3) conduct experiments and analyze alternative methods for disposal of the remaining chemical munitions and agents through CAMDS. This was an executable program agenda, bounded by available funding and supported by the Army leadership.

Public Law 98-94 required the Army leadership to expand its program to examine what chemical munitions would be demilitarized and how the Army might destroy the entire unitary chemical munition stockpile. An oversight group, including Brigadier General Bobby Robinson and Colonel Bob Orton on the Army staff, worked with Under Secretary of the Army James Ambrose and Amie Hoeber, Deputy Under Secretary of the Army for research and technology, to develop a strategy to approach Congress. This strategy was to pitch both the binary chemical munitions program and the chemical demilitarization program on the Hill as a concurrent effort to eliminate aging stocks and modernize a key military capability. The OSD and Army leadership recognized the need for both programs to be successful, and eventually they would need to replace all the unitary munitions. USATHAMA decided to evaluate three disposal options: disposal facilities at each site, a single national site at Tooele Army Depot, and two regional sites (Tooele and Anniston).

Some early critics accused the Chemical Corps of conspiring with the chemical industry and lobbying Congress to make billions of dollars in profits, but the evidence just does not exist to support that accusation.[1] The Corps had suffered a decade of neglect after General Creighton Abrams' attempt to disestablish it in 1972 and had lost its general officer position on the Army's Office of the Deputy Chief of Staff for Operations and Plans. There was no Chemical Corps leadership in Washington, DC, to influence Congress or industry leaders. In the early 1980s, the U.S. defense industry in general and the chemical industry in particular were wary about getting back into the offense or defense sides of the chemical warfare program. Industry had seen no reason to jump into what could be a very risky and short-term investment, should the Army leadership decide to pull out of the chemical warfare program again. The U.S. chemical industry saw a strong public stigma associated with the binary chemical munitions program, and there did not appear to be billions of dollars in the chemical demilitarization program or remediation efforts, at least not in the early 1980s.[2]

As an example, the RMA remediation effort was not moving forward as swiftly as one might expect. The Army had to negotiate with its tenants (Shell's lease ran out in 1987) and the state government on the responsibilities and costs of cleaning up the post, while continuing interim measures to minimize the potential impact to public health. In December 1982, the EPA, the ASA(I&L), Shell Oil Company, and the Colorado Department of Health had announced a jointly developed remediation plan for RMA. The group had examined more than 40 technologies to dispose of the waste and was set to begin work. The Army had already begun removing underground sewer lines that ran to Basin F and built a dike around the pool to prevent further runoff. They had also installed an enhanced evaporation system to reduce the existing volume of liquid. Unfortunately, the agreement fell apart in determining who would foot the remediation bills, and the Army had to initiate legal actions against Shell a year later to sue for cleanup costs. The state of Colorado followed by suing both the Army and Shell Oil to recover its respective cleanup costs.

The destruction of BZ agent and munitions at Pine Bluff Arsenal had been under study since 1977, including evaluations of munition sensitivity and transportability, development of interim exposure standards, and examination of potential incineration processes. USATHAMA continued its preparations to destroy the BZ munitions and bulk agent stored at Pine Bluff Arsenal, with development of a construction and operation plan published in August 1983, complete with a full environmental assessment. The BZ facility was to be designed with the flexibility to be modified later to dispose of the M55 rockets and M23 mines stored at Pine Bluff. The maximum credible event had been developed a year prior, using the scenario of an M43 cluster munition accidentally going off. Because the BZ fill was a powder with a very low vapor pressure, USATHAMA estimated that the 1 percent incapacitating-level plume would travel only 688 yards in the summer and 847 yards in the winter. The nearest residential group was 3,828 yards from the facility. These distances would not even permit the agent to leave the post, let alone imperil the residents on-post or local citizens.[3] Dick Roux, a very competent USATHAMA engineer, was the manager of the BZ disposal process. He was particularly focused on the safety of the operation and created a basis for the safety and security plans for all future disposal sites.

There were a number of proposed alternatives, starting with the comparison of neutralization (sodium hydroxide-based chemical hydrolysis) and incineration. Based on bench- and large-scale test experiments, incineration was shown as a much more thorough and predictable process. Chemical treatments were abandoned due to the nature of the explosive mix in the munition, having a historical nature to deteriorate in storage with the result that the munitions became unstable and were likely to detonate during handling. Alternatives included modifying an existing facility at PBA for disposal operations, building a new disposal facility on PBA, transporting and disposing of the munitions and agents at RMA, or transporting and disposing of the munitions at the CAMDS facility at Tooele. Perhaps not surprisingly, USATHAMA saw the building of a new disposal facility at PBA as the least risky and the best engineering solution to successfully disposing of the entire BZ stockpile.

The disposal facility would include a munitions holding area (a temporary holding site), a munitions demilitarization building (to unpack and inert the munitions and drums), a liquid incinerator, afterburner system (to incinerate the exhaust gases), pollution control system, and site control center. The Army planned to begin construction in 1984 with facility operations starting in October 1986, continuing for at least 18 months. When in operation, it was planned to process 12 M43 or 20 M44 munitions a day, or 16 drums of bulk BZ or solid and liquid residues (stored as a result of the BZ production). With good planning in the design of the equipment and buildings, this facility might be turned around to continue the disposal of the chemical munitions and agent stored at PBA.

Dick Roux was able to complete the entire project ahead of schedule and only $300,000 over budget. The Army, however, never took advantage of the public relations value of this project. To this day, there is still little mention of this very safe and successful program in the PMCD's literature or information sites.

As the CAMDS operations continued, USATHAMA's commander, Colonel Pete Hidalgo, organized the next phase of the demilitarization program: ridding the Army of its obsolete M55 rockets. These munitions had been intended for disposal back in the late 1960s and were the top priority given their unstable nature (relative to the other chemical munitions). USATHAMA began developing the JACADS facility design in 1981, focusing on equipment that would dispose of the chemical-filled M55 rockets using incineration technology. This facility would permit the Army to eliminate what it considered the most unstable and unsafe munition in its inventory. With minor modifications to the processing machines, it was thought that the same equipment could be used to disarm and dispose of the M23 mines, the second identified, obsolete class of chemical munitions. The incinerator would be capable of destroying all the CW agents and energetics at the site, but processing equipment specifically designed for the M55 rockets would be built at first.

The JACADS EIS was completed in 1983, which opened the door to the Army's decision to request military construction funds to build the facility. The fact that the disposal facility was located over 800 miles from Hawaii probably made this decision easier. Before making this request, the Army had formally asked the NAS to independently review existing disposal plans and to evaluate the safety of continuing to store the munitions rather than destroy them. This review was just getting under way in 1983, leading the Army to plan for initiating construction for JACADS in 1984 or 1985. Under Secretary Ambrose had endorsed the plan to construct the facility, hoping that if the tests and operations were successful, the PM's office could bring the technology to the planned CONUS disposal sites. In fact, he directed that the U.S.-based disposal sites be designed as closely to JACADS as possible. Creating cookie-cutter images would increase public confidence in the sites, he felt, assuming that JACADS worked as anticipated. It would also save money as a result of duplicating the facility design and procuring common equipment.

USATHAMA had planned to announce its intent to prepare an EIS in the Federal Register on the proposed construction, operation, and decontamination of three new chemical agent disposal facilities: Anniston Army Depot, Blue Grass Depot Activity, and Umatilla Army Depot Activity. The focus of the disposal operations was on destroying only the chemical-filled M55 rockets. The Army began holding public "scoping" meetings, as per NEPA requirements, to allow the public to participate in identifying significant environmental impacts or issues related to the planned disposal process.[4]

After these first meetings, USATHAMA recognized that the Army required a more comprehensive plan that would address the disposal of all M55 rockets, including those at Tooele Army Depot and Pine Bluff Arsenal. This led to the planned development of a draft EIS that would examine at least three alternatives: continued storage of the rockets at the five storage sites, disposal of the rockets on-site at each of the storage sites, and transportation and disposal of the rockets at one or more regional disposal sites. USATHAMA initiated a study of these alternatives, an effort that would take nearly two years. USATHAMA formally published the EIS in the Federal Register on January 31, 1984, and released the completed EIS in April 1985.

## THE NATIONAL RESEARCH COUNCIL'S REPORT

In late 1982, Under Secretary Ambrose requested the NRC's Board on Army Science and Technology to recommend the most effective, economical, and safe means for disposing of the Army's obsolete chemical agents and munitions. The board established a Committee on Demilitarizing Chemical Munitions and Agents (also known as the Stockpile Committee) in August 1983 and kicked off its first meeting in October. Of the chairman and the 10 panel members, only one had military experience (a retired major general); 9 were members of academe (professors of toxicology, material science, chemical engineering, law, public health, infectious diseases); and one was from industry. They would visit the CONUS facilities and meet with Army and industry experts to gather information on the state of the chemical agents and munitions, the stockpile sites, USATHAMA's plans for disposal, and alternative technologies. Included in this assessment were a hazard assessment and identification of the urgency of disposing of the chemical agent and munitions.

Six months later, the committee completed its assessment and drafted its report. The 1984 NRC report became a very influential document in evaluating and critiquing the Army's agenda. It is significant to review the NRC's findings, if merely to identify what findings arose from the NRC report rather than from the Army leadership's desires.[5] Later, citizen reformers would accuse the Army of contemplating actions that had existed only as recommendations of the NRC's report and had never been actually considered by the Army.

First of all, the NRC noted that the Army had competently managed the task of preserving the chemical stockpile's agents and munitions. Given the age of the munitions and agents (between 16 and 40 years at the time of the report) and the potential risk to off-site citizens and depot workers, the committee recommended their destruction as soon as possible. The most appropriate strategy seemed to be disposing of the obsolete and unserviceable munitions that pose the greatest risk to the workers and nearby residents and developing new technologies that would enable the safe disposal of the remaining stocks at the lowest feasible cost. The committee did not rule out transportation of some of the stocks to other facilities as an option. It did, however, call for on-site disposal of the M55 rockets, as soon as possible, as the Army's top priority. The committee saw no evidence that waiting for the development of more advanced technology for disposing of the M55 rockets would reduce either costs or risk.

As to alternative technologies for disposal, the committee reviewed a number of options. Noting that ocean placement had been outlawed, it examined chemical processes (various neutralization techniques), thermal processes (incineration, molten metal, steam pyrolysis, etc.), and the use of nuclear explosions for disposal of the agents and munitions. The last option, while unconventional, offered a simplicity of design, in that the Army would not have to unpack or disassemble the munitions. The political aspects and transportation requirements of that option (transporting all the munitions to an underground site, exploding a nuclear device, and verifying total destruction of all agents) gave it little chance for acceptance. Interestingly, many years later, Russian scientists proposed this same approach using elaborate financial models showing the attractiveness of disposing of chemical weapons through nuclear detonation.

In reviewing the Army's past decade of experience in disposal technologies, the committee agreed with the Army's decision to abandon chemical neutralization processes in favor of incineration. It did recommend that the Army continue to research cryofracture processes as a means of replacing the need for munitions disassembly. In this handling process, the entire munition would be submerged in a liquid nitrogen bath, causing the chemical-filled munition to become brittle. A hydraulic press would fracture the munition, and the metal parts would be sent to a rotary kiln, while the agent would be sent to an incinerator. This process would reduce the probability of burster detonation and increase the ability to safely handle the munitions in the dismantling process. While this reduced the hazard of handling toxic agents, the engineers were not sure about the idea of sending the explosive components of the munition into the same incinerator as pounds of chemical agents. Any explosion might force a cloud of hot vapors out of the towers, if they were not designed for that sudden pressure. Cryofracture was an untested concept, as far as disposing of chemical-filled munitions at the rate that the traditional incineration process was expected to achieve.

There were a few programmatic issues as well; obviously, this process would not be required for the bulk agent within the ton containers. The M55 rockets could not be frozen; the aluminum skin of the rockets would not become brittle at low temperatures as the steel aerial bombs and artillery projectiles would. An incinerator was required to eliminate agent contamination and dispose of the explosive components. Certainly, the Army had not developed the necessary engineering tests and evaluation to determine the parameters of how well a disposal facility, using cryofracture, would work, as it had with neutralization and incineration. While cryofracture was of interest to reduce the risk of an agent's escaping during the disassembly of chemical munitions, adding a second technology to the disposal process was seen as potentially increasing the overall costs and technical risks to the program.

The PMCD had been against cryofracture from the beginning, not because of the technology itself but rather because its immaturity would not allow the program to be completed by 1994. There was no information on what cryofracture did to fuzes, whether it could safely destroy the energetics, and if it disposed of irregular shapes without incident. Brigadier General Dave Nydam, who would be the first PMCD under public law 99-145, testified to Congress that it would take 8 years of research, testing, and operational verification prior to use. Despite these concerns, there were friends of industry in Congress that would push funding specifically for cryofracture through the program.

The NRC committee noted that the Army's research was aimed at substantially reducing the estimated costs and time of disposal and that the correct first step in this effort was the need for a careful assessment of the cost and time required using currently available and tested technology. The emphasis on "currently available and tested" focused on the Army's desire to proceed immediately with disposal operations at Johnston Island. Since it was a strong likelihood that the Army would use the disassembly and incineration technology proven out during CAMDS operations, this would become the "baseline technology" by which to measure all other options. If the current processes would cost $4 billion and nine years to develop and produce the disposal facilities, operate the facilities to dispose of the munitions, and close out the program, one could evaluate what new technologies, processes, or equipment would add or detract from the overall program in terms of cost-effectiveness and time. The term "baseline technology" would soon become a well-used phrase in future public discussions.

Assuming on-site disposal using incineration technology, the NRC committee estimated that, according to the Army's estimates (using CAMDS as a measure), the total cost for destruction of all chemical weapons and agents in the continental United States and Johnston Atoll would be about $1.4 billion, assuming no movement between the depots (then the costs would go up). That figure included construction, support facilities, security, training, startups, changeover of equipment between munition types, shutdown, cleanup, and so on.[6] Naively, the NRC did not foresee additional costs due to environmental and public health concerns, the costs of additional start-up testing at Johnston Island, or the scope of emergency response preparedness capabilities in the surrounding communities. Nor could they predict the financial impact of the involvement of a well-funded and politically-active "anti-incineration" movement.

The committee recommended that the Army explore the potential for using the chemical disposal facilities for disposal of DOD wastes, to include wastes and hazardous materials from other agencies. This was seen as a way to substantially reduce the life-cycle costs of the program, especially if the plants could be designed to generate power as a result of their disposal operations. While this was an entirely valid observation, it would later be immediately rejected by Congress (in PL 99-145). In future years, citizen groups would believe that the Army was seriously considering this issue, not based on any evidence but rather on the mere supposition that DOD and Congress would not let these very expensive facilities be destroyed after their primary purpose was filled.

The committee was to examine the issue of transportation of the chemical munitions from one depot to another but did not establish a special panel to do this due to extenuating circumstances. It lacked the expertise and information to quantitatively analyze the safety, cost, legalities, and politics of transporting chemical munitions. Significantly, the members did not recommend transportation, especially any transportation of the M55 rockets. They did recommend that the Army initiate a technical study of transferring chemical munitions as a risk-mitigation method. In general, the committee thought that the disposal at on-site facilities would cost less than disposal at regional disposal centers or a national disposal center. Their final observation was to issue a concern that any "delay in disposing of the stockpile in the face of opposing public pressures" could only result in decreases in cost efficiencies and public safety. They were certainly correct about the escalating costs.

USATHAMA had continued testing its incineration process at CAMDS during the summer of 1984, as it finalized its disposal plant design. Between June and August, the liquid agent incinerator had destroyed approximately eight tons of VX agent, with a removal efficiency of 99.9999998 percent. This test data gave the Army the confidence to begin construction of JACADS. In addition to its primary role of disposing of the chemical weapons stockpile at Johnston Island, it would demonstrate that incineration technology could be safely and effectively utilized to destroy different CW agents and munitions, while meeting all the required national environmental regulations.

USATHAMA initiated its M55 Rocket Disposal Program in 1985, which would allow an independent evaluation of the M55 rocket inventory to provide an assessment of its continued storage, movement, or disposal. The Army needed more quantitative data to determine exactly how much of the inventory was stable and how rapid the rate of deterioration was and to identify rockets that were developing leaks in storage. The disposal program would use these data to determine the ability to continue storing the rockets, support decisions on disposal activities, and create the basis for continued monitoring of the stockpile.

The program sampled several lots of rockets, taking several components of the rockets for further analysis at several laboratories. The assessments revealed that most of rockets were in good condition, including the propellant stabilizer, which was the main source of concern. Given the continued concern over potential rocket incidents and the major effects that an ignited rocket could cause in a bunker, HQ AMC ordered an M55 rocket surveillance program following the assessment, to be implemented by the owning depots and arsenals. This surveillance program would allow the continued monitoring of potential leakers and increase the safety of the workers and nearby civilians. These were dangerous weapons, but not seen as potential hazardous chemical incidents on the same scale as large industrial spills; or so the Army thought.

The state of Kentucky thought otherwise, citing Blue Grass Army Depot as being not in compliance with RCRA, and stating that the storage of M55 rockets should be treated as hazardous waste prior to their demilitarization. Many critics thought that all chemical munitions and bulk agent should be declared "hazardous materials" by their nature as chemical warfare agents, which would be contrary to the EPA's definition. Army representatives traveled to Lexington to review the state's concerns and while there, publicly acknowledged that, because of the presence of PCBs, the M55 rockets and their packing cases met certain hazardous waste criteria. There was, however, no health hazard resulting from handling the rockets in storage.

This statement sent shock waves through HQ AMC and created a year long fight between AMC and the EPA. The EPA claimed that RCRA regulations took effect once it was announced that a particular class of ammunition was to be demilitarized, and all subsequent storage and transportation issues should immediately be handled as hazardous material measures. The Army leadership disagreed, stating that chemical ammunition should not be subject to RCRA until the demilitarization actually began. Had the EPA view held, the Army would have had to negotiate the storage and on-site transportation of the chemical munitions with every state involved on a site-by-site, case-by-case basis. Declaring an entire class of serviceable (but obsolete) military chemical munitions as "hazardous materials" had grave implications for the Army's storage and demilitarization of conventional military munitions as well. It would have imposed unreasonable and unwarranted regulations on the Army's wartime munitions capability.

## U.S. CHEMICAL WEAPONS GAIN ATTENTION

In February 1985, General John Wickham, Chief of Staff of the Army, told the House Armed Services Committee that the Army "must modernize our deterrent stockpile with binary munitions and rid ourselves of the obsolete and potentially hazardous chemical munitions we currently store."[7] The Army leadership recognized that the U.S. chemical weapons in Germany were rapidly becoming outdated and would have to go. In April, production tests of the Phase I (155-mm binary) munition factory at Pine Bluff Arsenal had taken place. Production of binary artillery projectiles could begin by September 1987, but not before the president certified to Congress that the production of these munitions was essential to the national interest.

The other binary chemical munitions had been in testing for several years and were moving toward the date where the decision had to be made whether to continue into production. The Bigeye bomb had been redesigned in 1983, correcting several technical design deficiencies and allowing the munition to be operated at lower altitudes. There were continued questions as to the effectiveness of the device, but it would be ready for limited production as early as 1985. Congressional approval for military construction of a production facility had not yet been made, and building a full-scale facility could take up to 26 months. The MLRS warhead was the newest binary chemical munition, initiated after the Army made the decision to retire its 8-inch artillery systems. Development had begun in 1981 and, with successful testing, binaries could be ready for production by 1990. The MLRS warhead would use the same chemical precursors as the 155-mm projectile but would require a dedicated production facility as well.

At the DOD level, the DDR&E took the opportunity to update DOD Directive 5160.5, titled "Responsibilities for Research, Development, and Acquisition of Chemical Weapons and Chemical and Biological Defense." The directive was released in May 1985. Its predecessor, published in March 1976, focused on research, development, test and evaluation. This updated directive called on the Army to coordinate the joint procurement of chemical weapons and CB defense equipment, not merely the research and development of same. In addition to updating the CB defense program execution to the new DOD acquisition regulations, it tasked the Army with the development of the Annual Report to Congress, as required by Public Laws 91-121, 93-608, 95-79, and 97-375. While one might see the release of this directive as a mere affirmation of the Army's existing leadership role in the DOD CB program, its timing clearly emphasized the Army's commitment to developing modern chemical weapons.

The CWRC report, as mentioned in the last chapter, was released in June 1985, which would provide the president with the necessary recommendations to proceed with the binary munitions program. Shortly thereafter, President Reagan and General Secretary Gorbachev agreed to intensify bilateral discussions on all aspects of a chemical weapons ban and to initiate a dialogue on preventing chemical warfare proliferation. The only obstacle in the Army's path in developing a retaliatory chemical weapons capability and advancing its arms control agenda was the demilitarization of the existing chemical stockpile.

Johnston Island would receive much more attention and not just because it was the first planned disposal facility. In 1984, the island was evacuated due to an approaching hurricane (not the first or last time that this would happen). When the military contingent returned, it noticed Soviet spy trawlers gathered nearby to snoop on the island's activities. The Army's Vice Chief of Staff, General Max Thurman, traveled to the atoll to examine the Johnston Island Chemical Activity in November 1984 and was not pleased with the security situation. He directed the formation of a task force to make recommendations that would upgrade the island's security. Part of the problem was that the man-made island was maintained by the Air Force, and "owned" by the Defense Nuclear Agency through its Albuquerque, New Mexico, office.

The result of the Johnston Island Assessment Task Force was to increase the grade of the Army commander overseeing the CW stockpile from a major to a colonel and to add 176 personnel to be stationed on the island. This included 76 military police and 31 civilians joining the chemical ammunition company, all of whom would fall under U.S. Army Western Command instead of the Air Force or Defense Nuclear Agency. There was even serious consideration to stationing armored personnel carriers and anti-aircraft missiles on the island.

Once indications became clear that the disposal program would not be relegated to merely the M55 rockets, the Army began to develop details on the potential costs of establishing and operating a disposal program for the entire stockpile.  Judging from the technologies evaluated by CAMDS, the Army estimated total program costs for the first option (on-site disposal) to run about $1.7 billion, plus or minus 30 percent.[8] Studies for the two other options would continue into 1986, with data required on transportation options, accident risks, special shipping containers, movement scenarios, security, and environmental impact before finalizing their costs. The option 1 costs (seen in Table 5.1), while optimistic, were based on life-cycle cost estimates, including inventory site equipment, production costs, labor requirements, and general program support.

Design costs for Blue Grass, Anniston, and Umatilla included $4.5 million for an M55 rocket-processing plant (one-third of the planned cost of the prototype design) and $0.4 million for site-specific modifications to that design. The lower design and construction costs for Pine Bluff were due to the assumption that the BZ disposal facility would be modified for the chemical disposal mission. In other costs, the $76 million included $50 million for transportation of the U.S. stockpile in Europe to Johnston Island and $26 million for program management costs for planning and development of JACADS. Another $31 million would cover the additional disposal costs of the chemical munitions moved to Johnston Island. The disposal facility at Johnston Island would be the most expensive disposal facility (compared to the CONUS facilities) largely due to its remote location, the need to build up the plant's infrastructure, and the unforeseen challenges that it would cause as the first CW disposal facility.

**Table 5.1**
**Estimated On-Site Chemical Stockpile Disposal Costs (in millions, 1985)**[9]

| Stockpile Sites (as they were called in 1985) | Design and Construction | Equipment and Operations | Closure | Total |
|---|---|---|---|---|
| Aberdeen Proving Ground | $13.1 | $60.1 | $4.8 | $74.2 |
| Anniston Army Depot | $30.2 | $153.0 | $5.8 | $189.0 |
| Blue Grass Depot Activity | $30.2 | $112.8 | $5.8 | $148.8 |
| Newport Army Ammunition Plant | $13.1 | $56.3 | $4.8 | $74.2 |
| Pine Bluff Arsenal | $5.1 | $80.1 | $5.0 | $90.2 |
| Pueblo Army Depot | $20.6 | $117.4 | $5.8 | $143.8 |
| Tooele Army Depot | $25.7 | $256.9 | $6.0 | $288.6 |
| Umatilla Depot Activity | $30.2 | $164.6 | $5.8 | $200.6 |
| Johnston Island | $78.0 | $261.0 | $6.0 | $345.0 |
| Other costs at Johnston Island | $0.0 | $31.0 | $76.0 | $107.0 |
| **Total** | **$246.2** | **$1293.2** | **$125.8** | **$1665.2** |

The initial cost estimate of $1.7 billion has been a constant source of reference for critics and the media to attack the program's inability to restrain cost growth, so some mention of the assumptions should be stated here. The Army leadership believed that, based on the CAMDS tests and engineering results conducted to that point, it could get the job completed by 1994 if they executed disposal operations at all nine sites simultaneously, if all environmental documentation was completed promptly, and assuming that Congress would not impose any measures to block disposal operations (such as the JACADS operational trial tests as a predecessor to the construction of CONUS disposal facilities). The estimate did not include the continued costs of operating CAMDS, transporting chemical munitions, developing and executing emergency response plans, or addressing non-stockpile chemical materials. This estimate was what engineers refer to as a parametric estimate, meaning that it was based on similar equipment and results (in this case, CAMDS), and not based on experience derived from running a full-scale disposal facility.

The BZ disposal facility at Pine Bluff Arsenal was over half completed, with scheduled completion of construction in the fall of 1986. The plant equipment was nearly all procured and would be installed by the end of the year. DATS continued its mission of disposing of leakers in Umatilla and was moving to Pueblo to start operations in 1986. CAMDS was testing new process equipment, procedures, monitoring systems, and other demilitarization components to evaluate their impact on personnel safety, environmental acceptance, and overall efficiencies. All these chemical demilitarization efforts would be grandfathered into the disposal program upon its formal initiation.

For comparison, costs to continue to store the chemical munitions would run about $64 million a year (1985 dollars), with about 60 percent of that going to security costs. Estimates for the binary chemical program, which included research, development, and production of the BLU-80 Bigeye bomb, M687 155-mm artillery projectile, and M135 MLRS warhead, ran at about $2.8 billion (1985 dollars) over the period 1985–1992.[10] All in all, the $1.7 billion costs were seen as reasonable and executable. The unexpected challenges from developing and operating JACADS would provide data that showed that this estimate was not realistic at all, and would change after the new PMCD office was established a year later.

## PUBLIC LAW 99-145

In November 1985, Congress released its formal guidance on how the national program was to be executed. In what would become the legislative foundation for the chemical demilitarization program, Congress passed language under PL 99-145 (DOD Authorization Act for 1986, November 8, 1985) that outlined specific guidance on production of binary chemical weapons and the destruction of the unitary chemical weapons. The language called for the president to certify that the military had a viable contingency plan for employing binary chemical weapons as a measure to deter the use of chemical weapons against NATO and its allies, that the production of the binaries was in the national security interest, that the binaries would be safe to handle and store, and that the Defense Secretary had a disposal plan for the unitary munitions ready for implementation.

The bill called for the destruction of all unitary chemical weapons by September 30, 1994, noting that the demilitarization program would provide for "maximum protection for the environment, the general public, and the personnel" involved and "adequate and safe facilities designed solely for the destruction of lethal chemical agents and munitions," and an evaluation of alternative destruction concepts.[11] The legislation also called for a new Army management organization headed by a general officer to be established not later than May 1986, with funds set forth as a separate account not to be included in any other military account (to track and control the money) and submission of annual reports on the chemical stockpile, proposed demilitarization activities by site, and related funding actions.

The creation of a program office requiring an Army general officer was not a surprise to the Chemical Corps leadership. Colonel Hidalgo, now at HQ AMC (he had been transferred in February 1985), recognized that the new responsibilities would dwarf USATHAMA's installation restoration tasks, and that a new office was required to effectively manage the demilitarization program and the binary weapons production. He had suggested the new program office to General Richard Thompson, Commander of AMC, and Under Secretary Ambrose; both supported the concept of linking the two efforts. Colonel Bob Orton, as the chief of chemical and nuclear division in the office of the Army Deputy Chief of Staff for Operations and Plans (DCSOPS), worked with the Army leadership and congressional staffers to develop legislative language that would outline what authority and responsibilities were required to successfully execute the program.

Colonel Orton had been working closely with the Arkansas congressional delegation on the binary weapons language as well, since Pine Bluff Arsenal was to be the site of the binary weapons production facility. Following his DCSOPS position, he would report to Johnston Island as the commander of the stockpile site in June 1985. USATHAMA had completed facility and process designs for JACADS, initiated equipment procurement actions, and awarded construction contracts in September 1985 to build, equip, and test the facility. The creation of this office was both timely and necessary to execute this national disposal program and start the binary production effort.

Before the reformists yell "Gotcha," it should be explained that this was (and remains) a pretty routine process between military legislative liaison offices and congressional staffers. Congressional staffers often discuss specific military issues with the armed forces, not pretending that they always know all the right answers on all topics. These politicians preferred executable legislation, if for no other purpose than to be able to tell their constituents that they were doing something positive to address their respective stockpiles as well as support the binary program. The development of PL 99-145 was one instance in which the Army leadership coordinated with congressional representatives to ensure that the PMCD would receive reasonable guidance that would permit the successful initiation of the chemical disposal program. In this case, the Army had three champions supporting this legislation, Representative Glen Browder (D-AL), Representative Burle Anthony (D-AK), and Representative Helen Bentley (R-MD). This is not lobbying; it is listening to relevant subject-matter experts, and it is the way that many successful programs are started.

The Army would address the public's concern through the development of the environmental impact statement. USATHAMA published a notice of intent to prepare an EIS addressing the disposal of the entire CONUS stockpile of chemical agents and munitions on January 28, 1986. The agency contracted with Oak Ridge National Laboratory to draft the EIS, based on Oak Ridge's support to USATHAMA in studies evaluating how to destroy the M55 rockets. In April, representatives from HQ DA, USATHAMA, Oak Ridge National Laboratory, and the President's Council on Environmental Quality met to discuss the merits of developing a programmatic (addressing all eight sites) versus a site-specific EIS for the chemical stockpile program. The group agreed that a programmatic approach made more sense, given the national and regional impact of transporting chemical munitions and agents from site to site under some of the alternatives, and that similar actions would be executed at the several disposal sites. The general counsel for the President's Council approved this approach.[12]

The new office for a Program Manager for Chemical Munitions (Demilitarization and Binary) was formally established at Aberdeen Proving Ground-Edgewood Area on May 1, 1986, initially headed by Brigadier General David A. Nydam, who had just completed a tour as the commander of Dugway Proving Ground. He and his deputy, Charles Baronian, would oversee two project managers who would head the binary munitions program and the chemical demilitarization program. Colonel Bob Orton, returning from Johnston Island, would be the Project Manager for Binary Munitions, and Colonel Jan Van Prooyen would be the Program Manager for Chemical Demilitarization. Brigadier General Pete Hidalgo had moved from HQ AMC to return to Edgewood and became the Commanding General of CRDEC.

The challenge facing any new office is obtaining the necessary manpower and resources to start the program. It had the funding, but HQ AMC was not providing the 250 bodies that one manpower study suggested that it needed. The office had to transfer or matrix its core personnel from USATHAMA and neighboring U.S. Army Chemical Research, Development and Engineering Center (CRDEC), ending up with about 100 people.[13] USATHAMA would continue its installation restoration work under the leadership of the AMC Deputy Chief of Staff for Engineer (they had formerly reported to the AMC Deputy Chief of Staff for Chemical and Nuclear Matters).

The binary office had only three people and needed more support. Brigadier General Nydam was not sure he wanted both programs run under one office. He felt that the binary program would have a strong momentum once initiated, and that might sap the chemical demilitarization program's efforts. He interpreted the public law's intent as focused on the demilitarization program, not the binary program. In 1987, the binary munitions program moved under Dr. Billy Richardson, who had just transferred from Technical Director of CRDEC to become the new Program Executive Officer (PEO) for Chemical and Nuclear Matters (until that PEO position was disestablished in 1989).[14] Brigadier General Nydam became the Program Manager for Chemical Demilitarization (PMCD) in October 1988, and Colonel Van Prooyen moved to become the first Product Manager for NBC Defense Systems (PM NBC) under the new PEO.

The PMCD office would report directly to the ASA(I&L), but Under Secretary Ambrose's close and personal involvement would continue to heavily influence the program's direction. A new DOD agency required a new funding line; this program line, "Chemical Agents and Munitions Destruction, Defense," was established in February 1986 to cover research and development, procurement, and operations and maintenance (O&M) costs, but not military construction. The Army was charged to fund military construction at its sites but to identify it separately from other military construction efforts. The Army Corps of Engineers would execute any construction efforts for the program.

The draft Programmatic EIS (PEIS) was issued on July 1, 1986, to federal agencies, the states that either held stockpiles or might have to deal with the transportation of munitions moving across their boundaries, and the public in general. The Army announced the initiation of the demilitarization program through full-page, one-day adds in 31 newspapers over 20 different states. Letters were sent to governors of all 50 states. The report announced the Army's intent to pursue a site-specific disposal strategy as its preferred alternative, citing the ease of emergency planning and preparedness and avoidance of off-site transport of any munitions or agent. The draft PEIS had many comments from a large number of readers, all of which had to be answered in the final PEIS. The main point of interest was its review of the risks involved in storage and disposal operations. Much rode on the success of this document, and it would be a difficult job to win over the public on the Army's plan to dispose of its chemical weapons.

# 6

## Risk Management

How the government communicates the general risk to the public of storing and destroying chemical munitions and materiels is perhaps the major factor of the chemical stockpile disposal program. There are several elements of risk: the risk of continued storage of chemical weapons and materiels as a result of accidents or incidents; the risk of releasing chemical warfare agents or dangerous incineration by-products during disposal operations; and the risk of accidents or incidents while transporting chemical munitions on- or off-site. The NRC has noted that the risks associated with this program are low in comparison with other measured public risks (driving on public highways, living near nuclear plants, lightning strikes, etc.). Discussions about risk are often overcome by emotional responses focusing on the issue that the program deals with toxic chemical warfare agents far more potent than industrial chemicals, significantly raising concerns higher than those associated with the safety of commercial or private incineration plants. Critics often use advocacy science to distort the Army's successful safety record and to justify their claims that the program is inherently unsafe. In the NRC's view, risk management is more important in this program than in other defense efforts because:

- Risk *is* the major source of public concern. Although there are widely varying opinions on the significance of the different sources of risk, risk is virtually the only common ground among interested parties.
- Anxiety and uncertainty tend to be the response to low-probability, high-consequence, involuntary risk [author's translation: even if the odds are 10 million to one, people don't like long odds of dying as a result of someone's managing a dangerous program].
- The risk of stockpile storage, while not high, is nevertheless gradually increasing due to such phenomena as destabilizing propellants and deteriorating containment. Uncertainties in both the stockpile condition and disposal schedule leave open the possibility of a significant increased hazard if disposal is significantly delayed.[1]

As the NRC noted, there is a need for better understanding of not only the levels of risk involved but also the contributing factors to that overall risk. There are well-established methodologies for conducting risk assessments, and there is no end of data for determining risk in the demilitarization program. Far more complex is discerning how people react to potential exposure to hazards and associated risks and communicating the risk assessments to Congress and the public in a way that facilitates overall agreement on the program's goals and approach. Federal regulations require that the managers actively try to reduce the risk of any program that could impact on the public's safety or the environment. Risk management is done by evaluating the hazard, identifying risk reduction alternatives, and implementing decisions that will reduce the overall risk to an acceptable level.

To fully understand risk assessments and risk management, one might require a moderate education in statistical analysis and mathematics. My intent is to permit the reader to understand the language and process by which the analysts develop these assessments, without attempting to make the reader a risk assessment expert. We can begin with basic definitions, the following developed by the NRC[2]:

- A *hazard* is a possible source of danger.
- *Receptors* are people, components of the environment, or physical property exposed to a hazard.
- *Exposure* is an opportunity for a hazard and a receptor to interact, creating an at-risk situation for the receptor.
- *Risk* is the possibility or probability that an undesirable outcome might result during or as a consequence of an activity or event that involves a hazard (the measure of how the receptor might come out of an exposure).
- *Risk assessment* is the process by which one assembles and integrates relevant data to provide a quantitative estimate of the probability of a particular outcome(s).
- *Risk management* is a decision-making process by which one can balance alternative strategies and consequences associated with risk reduction and implement those decisions.
- *Risk perception* is the personal, although usually informal, assessment of risk that includes the values, concerns, and beliefs of people in communities impacted by a hazardous technology.

As a risk assessment example, assume that you are a homeowner with a sidewalk bordering your front lawn, and the sidewalk has a large crack and raised edge as a result of a tree root's growth. The crack presents a hazard (source of danger) to people (receptors) walking on your sidewalk (exposed to the hazard). There is a probability that people could trip on the crack and fall, perhaps injuring themselves or even dying as a result of those injuries. Perhaps inadvertently, you have allowed a hazard to exist to those using the sidewalk. Those walkers who see the crack in the sidewalk and stride onward are voluntary risk-takers, while those traveling at night who do not see the crack are involuntary risk-takers. If you decide to repair the crack, put up a sign warning walkers, or otherwise reduce the risk of people's tripping on the crack, you are taking risk management steps. The final measure of what you, the homeowner, do to mitigate this risk, depends on a risk assessment, by which you measure the probability of whether people will injure themselves seriously against the costs of taking steps to minimize the hazard. This might be a qualitative assessment as just described, based on a discussion of the process rather than hard figures on probabilities of events' occurring.

If you wanted to take the extra step of developing a quantitative risk assessment, then you need a more detailed methodology and a calculator. There are four major components of a quantitative risk assessment: hazard identification, consequence (or dose-response) assessment, exposure assessment, and risk characterization. In a hazard identification one determines the hazard or hazards associated with a particular condition. In the sidewalk example, there is a need to identify what outcomes would result as a condition of people's hitting the crack in the sidewalk. They might trip and recover without incident. They might trip and bruise their foot or twist an ankle. They might trip and break an arm or leg or hit their head, suffer a traumatic injury, and die. This simple assessment does not consider other scenarios, for example, bicyclists, baby strollers, or skateboarders using your walk. One could develop a fault tree that identified each scenario with differing results and outcomes, all leading back to the crack.

Upon determining the various hazards, one would need to identify probabilities for the consequences of each exposure. That is, what percentage of walkers would trip as a result of their impacting the crack in the sidewalk? What percentage would fall after tripping on the crack as opposed to stumbling? How many would hit their head as opposed to another part of their anatomy? These data might be available from similar situations elsewhere or as estimates from subject-matter experts or just might be assumed as a certain value. Maybe 1 in 50 walkers hits the crack and stumbles, and 1 of 2 who stumbles actually falls. Of those who fall, 1 in 10 hits his or her head after tripping on a sidewalk crack, and, of those, 1 in 1,000 actually dies as a result.

The exposure assessment identifies how many potential exposures could take place in a given time period, what particular critical path of decisions leads to the hazard exposure, and the size and nature of the exposed population. Maybe your sidewalk is particularly busy and receives 10,000 walkers at one time or another, with an average of 1,000 walkers per day. One might go so far as to identify the age, sex, height, weight, and physical condition of the walkers to better categorize and understand the consequences of particular walkers' tripping on the sidewalk crack.

All of these data are gathered for the quantitative risk characterization, which leads to a conclusion about the nature and magnitude of the risk. The probability that a walker will trip on your crack, fall, and die as a result can be determined by multiplying the associated probabilities: chance of tripping (1 in 50) times chance of falling (1 in 2) times the chance of hitting his or her head (1 in 10) and dying as a result (1 in 1,000), which gives 1 in a million odds of such an incident. To put a time frame on this probability, 1 death per 1 million times 1,000 users per day yields 1 death every 1,000 days, 0.37 deaths per year, or 0.001 deaths per day.

Given all these statistics, you, the sidewalk custodian, must now make the decision on what steps could reduce the risk of someone's dying on your front lawn and whether those steps are beneficial considering the cost of implementing the decision. Do you (1) rip out the sidewalk and lay down fresh concrete, (2) lay a carpet over the crack to minimize the impact, (3) put up warning signs and detour walkers around the crack, or (4) do nothing? That's it; you're now a risk manager!

It is important to note that the measure of risk is the probability of an event's happening multiplied by the consequences of the event. Risk assessments get much more complicated as the number of factors increase, and developing an assessment for a disposal facility that destroys a number of toxic chemical warfare agents has many variables. Given the long history of chemical manufacturing in the United States, some particular examples illustrate how managers assess the risk associated with toxic chemical disposal operations. As one identifies the hazards of a certain chemical, remember that any chemical can have adverse effects on people if the dose is high enough (even water can cause fatal reactions if ingested in large enough quantities over a long period of time).

What requires particular attention are those chemicals that could be harmful in small quantities. Some chemicals are automatically tested as potential hazards, such as pesticides (which are designed to kill) and food additives (since they are intended for ingestion). Other chemicals are tested after discovering that there are adverse effects in the population as a result of uncontrolled exposure outside the production plant. In the early twentieth century, industry participated in identifying toxic substances and harmful doses in part because it had a self-interest in keeping its workers healthy and later, to understand health and legal consequences arising from its disposal methods.[3] The process of assessing these risks is illustrated at Figure 6.1.

The need to identify tolerable exposure levels led to the involvement of industrial hygienists and waste managers in the consequence assessments, which in the chemical hazards field is referred to as dose-response assessments. Once it is decided that a particular chemical merits a risk assessment, scientists can run animal test models to determine equivalent exposure concentrations for humans. The standard methodology is to expose a healthy group of rats, mice, or guinea pigs with a low dose of a chemical over a period of weeks, months, or even years. A second group of similar animals is not exposed to the test chemical and is monitored over the same time period as the experimental group. A third group gets a larger dose, and a fourth group a larger dose than the third. The highest dose that does not cause an adverse reaction is the no observed adverse effect level (NOAEL).[4]

The second step is to translate the animal data to human exposure levels (assuming all you have is animal data). The animal NOAEL is divided by an uncertainty factor, which typically assumes that humans are 10 times more sensitive to the chemical than the test animals. On the outside peripheries of the

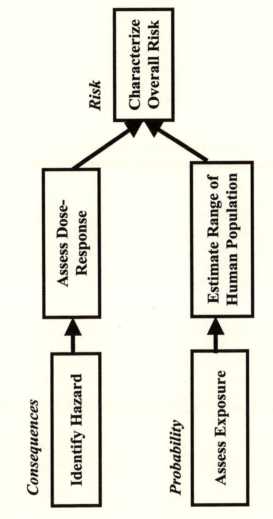

**Figure 6.1**
**Example of a Risk Assessment Model**

Consequences

Identify Hazard → Assess Dose-Response

Risk

Characterize Overall Risk

Probability

Assess Exposure → Estimate Range of Human Population

Risk = Probability x Consequences

human population, some people might be ten times more sensitive than the norm. This yields an uncertainty factor of 100 (10 times 10). If the animal data resulting in the NOAEL are questionable, another multiple of 10 is introduced, leading to an uncertainty factor of 1,000. Dividing the animal NOAEL by the uncertainty factor gives one the human exposure dose, often called the reference dose or acceptable daily intake.

In the last step of risk assessment, researchers have to identify how humans become exposed to the chemical in question. This includes the route of exposure (is it in the water you drink? the air you breathe? the food you eat?) and in what concentrations the chemical exists in these forms. The locations may be specific to a particular chemical; for instance, the chemicals in car exhaust are perhaps a greater threat to city dwellers than to rural farmworkers, so the study focuses on exposure limits for those living in the city. Contaminants in well water might be evaluated as to their effects in the country as opposed to an urban population's using chlorinated water. As described in the sidewalk example, these factors can all be quantitatively stated as statistical probabilities.

Once these data are collected and analyzed, a risk assessment can be developed, and appropriate information can be passed on to the decision makers. The only caution in this process is the tendency towards making every assessment a worst-case scenario, especially if there is a lack of historical data to validate the assessment results. Consider the following case to illustrate this example. In 1982, the Food and Drug Administration (FDA) had recommended banning red dye number 3 from foods based on animal tests where rats were fed fruit cocktail (including red cherries). This dye had been in use for 12 years. When the fruit cocktail made up 4 percent of the rats' diet, a large number of the rats contracted thyroid cancer. For a human to ingest an equivalent amount, one would have to consume nearly 14,000 servings of fruit cocktail over a 70-year lifetime of exposure. Despite this very obvious worst-case scenario, the red dye was banned until recently, causing many baby boomers to wait out their formative years without red M&Ms.[5] Anecdotal stories such as these are more the exception than the rule, but people react to the perception that hazard exists, rather than under-standing the very long odds of a hazardous exposure leading to a fatality.

In most cases dealing with hazardous chemicals such as ammonia, arsine, carbon tetrachloride, phosgene, and toluene, industrial hygiene experts determined the recommended maximum allowable concentrations the hard way—through human exposure studies resulting from toxicity cases on the job. Most of these situations occurred prior to 1950, when complying with concentration limits was still voluntary. As industry developed these data to deal with increasing local and federal regulatory concerns, it had hard data with which managers could make defendable risk management decisions.

Recognizing the hazards and determining the frequency of human contact with toxic chemicals permitted managers to identify means to limit their liabilities stemming from exposure (both worker and the general public). There was also the more humanitarian role of protecting their workforce to ensure that the company did not lose valuable talent or (less humanitarian) suffer heavy lawsuits. These means included use of protective suits and masks for the workers under certain exposure conditions and, in the case of waste treatment, either diluting the waste stream in the environment, geographically isolating the waste from the public, containing the waste, or, as a last (most expensive) measure, treating the waste.[6]

## ASSESSING THE DEMIL PROGRAM'S RISKS

First and foremost, understand that there are several different risk assessments and for each one, a considerable number of factors and variables to be considered. There is the initial risk assessment as to the disposal strategy (on-site versus regional sites), downwind hazard risk calculation, and disposal site quantitative risk assessment for the EIS, health risk assessment for RCRA permits, and hazard evaluations. This book does not intend to justify the chemical demilitarization program's approach (even if risk is the number one issue). It is more important to identify and understand the process by which the Army developed, communicated, and executed its risk management program. Not surprisingly, the Army used the same methodology that most industrial hygienists use, that is, hazard identification, consequence assessment, and exposure assessment. The Chemical Corps, in particular, has had a long history of working with the chemical industry on toxic industrial chemical handling issues and, in many cases, has led the industry in development of these issues.

The Chemical Warfare Service (CWS), as it was formally designated in 1920, was established as a result of America's involvement in World War I to develop offensive war gases and defensive equipment. Its headquarters at Edgewood Arsenal, Maryland, initiated most of the research on hazardous chemicals to include construction of a plant to manufacture mustard gas. After the war, the American Chemical Society supported the Chemical Warfare Service's continued existence before Congress, stressing the danger posed by hostile nations that could develop war gases based on their strong commercial chemical industries. Thus began a close relationship between the civilian chemists and Army chemists in developing safety concerns related to toxic chemicals. In peacetime, when the CWS was limited in its wartime preparations (due to a decrease in all military efforts between the wars), the Army chemists worked with industry to investigate chemical-related fatalities and develop protective suits and masks.[7]

When World War II broke out, the Army had a very small stockpile of mustard, lewisite, and phosgene munitions. To build a credible retaliatory capability, the Army built three additional arsenals (Huntsville, Pine Bluff, and Rocky Mountain) to support construction of chemical agent and incendiary weapons. The precursors to develop these weapons came from hundreds of commercial plants across the country. The CWS developed specific guidance for safe waste disposal and inspected not only its own arsenals and depots but commercial industries supporting military efforts as well. This level of oversight and involvement called for the CWS to research and publish chemical hazard information and handling.[8]

The primary chemical agents manufactured for filling munitions in World War II were mustard agent, lewisite, and phosgene. During the interwar period, scientists and medics had ample opportunity to examine these agents, as well as examine the effects on World War I veterans (over 70,000 Americans were injured as a result of chemical warfare agent exposure, over half by mustard agent). The toxicology data were well known, if not the long-term effects. In fact, it was an element of chemical warfare training to place a drop of mustard agent on a soldier's arm so he could observe the blistering effect (to better acquaint the soldier with early signs and symptoms). This practice was discontinued in the 1970s when it was later discovered that this practice actually increased an individual's sensitivity to mustard agent.

After World War II, the involvement of civilian and military chemists continued at Rocky Mountain Arsenal. As the Army investigated the new nerve agents, sarin and soman in particular, former German scientists worked with the Army to develop and design new munitions. Again, there was a large volume of human test data from German work conducted during the war, both as a result of involuntary worker exposure and deliberate experimental exposure to test subjects. While some might see use of data where such experiments took place as unethical, during the Cold War using these data were seen as the only sane thing to do in the race with the Soviets to develop nerve agent munition stockpiles. Animal tests continued for decades at Edgewood Arsenal and Fort Detrick in developing both offensive munitions and defensive equipment. During this time, occasionally scientists got "bit" by nerve or blister agents due to accidents or incidental exposure; while there were no deaths from accidental chemical warfare agent exposures in the United States, these events provided more data on hazard identification.

After 1969, the Army instituted formal risk management principles to identify the possible consequences of an accident at one of their stockpile sites. In addition to physically inspecting samples of each munitions lot, surveillance teams performed vapor tests on munitions to determine if there were trace leaks. The Army sampled a number of chemical munitions to test the deterioration of the agent and explosive components with a mobile analytical laboratory. It would have been easier to conduct test firings to evaluate the condition of the munitions, but that was severely restricted by congressional law. There had been metallurgical analysis of the artillery projectiles and bombs to determine their shelf life, but no such tests had been carried out on the M55 rockets.

When the PMCD initiated its program in 1985, it developed a maximum credible event (MCE) for each stockpile site. In the course of normal handling and storage operations, there was the remote chance that a given quantity of agent would be released as a result of an accident or incident, caused by human interaction or otherwise. Given a certain MCE, the Army calculated the downwind hazard plumes for what would cause more than 1 percent fatalities, for no deaths, and for no effects to an unprotected population. The length of the plume would vary based on the CW agent, the munition or container, the amount of agent released, the local weather conditions, and the time of day. Terrain was not a factor in these calculations, only because the models were not sophisticated enough to account for terrain and microclimate weather effects.[9]

For the bombs and projectiles, tests had shown that it was not credible that more than one munition would explode at any given time (i.e., no sympathetic detonations while in storage). For two other munitions, that was not necessarily true. The explosion of one M23 mine, stored three in one container, might cause the other two to detonate, but not another container of mines. Stacks of M55 rockets, however, could be detonated if one M55 rocket were to self-ignite and explode inside an igloo. Tests at Black Hills Army Depot, South Dakota, and at Dugway Proving Ground had shown this could happen. While 97 percent of the agent would be consumed in the high temperatures created in the igloo, there could be an open-air release of up to 570 pounds of GB or 37 pounds of VX. Since five of the eight CONUS stockpile sites held rockets, this became their MCE.

The exact length of the agent plume then depended on the MCE, the particular agent, and the meteorological conditions at the time of the incident. In the cases of three CONUS stockpile sites that do not hold rockets, the MCE does not extend past the military boundaries. The MCE for the other five stockpile sites that have M55 rockets filled with GB agent, however, does extend far past the boundaries in worst-case conditions. This was the basis for PMCD to decide it should institute additional measures to ensure the protection of the populace living outside these sites and to dispose of the rockets as quickly as possible.

This approach lacked some specificity; notably, it relied on a Gaussian dispersion model that was not reliable more than a mile from where the release took place, given the possible terrain features and meteorological conditions that would be sure to affect the agent release. It also did not consider scenarios including earthquakes, lightning strikes, airplanes falling onto the depots, forest fires, or terrorist incidents. Last, it did not assess the probability of the events; while the M55 rocket explosion seems extreme, what were the odds that a rocket would cause such a chain reaction? No one really had worked out that scenario. The Army accepted these estimated values despite these limitations since it was seen as better to err on the side of conservatism. More sophisticated models have since replaced these older models, allowing for more sensitive analyses, and the results of these analyses are shared with the local emergency responders.

What it did show is that, at least for three sites, the expected vapor hazard from an incident would not cross the post boundaries and harm the public. Once the M55 rockets were destroyed at that site, the overall risk to the local populace plummeted nearly to zero. The information reinforced to the Army the need to dispose of the rockets and mines first to reduce the overall risk of continued storage and later disposal of the other munitions. This is what drove the 1981 decision to build an on-site disposal facility for M55 rockets first, using CAMDS lessons learned, and then to modify the equipment to dispose of other obsolete munitions.

We examined RMA's struggle with risk management and attempting to mitigate the chemical hazards in the 1950's through 1970's in Chapter 1, and we examined the steps taken to ensure that CAMDS met environmental regulations in Chapter 3. There is little question that the Army had significant experience both in understanding the health hazards of chemical warfare agents and in the production and disposal of these agents. As of 1985, we could identify almost 30–40 years of experience with nerve agents and more than 60 years of experience with mustard and lewisite. By 1985, the Army had neutralized about 8.4 million pounds and incinerated 6.3 million pounds of chemical warfare agents. The Army felt that what was required now was a more holistic examination on how to identify the best option for disposing of the remaining stockpile. Would it be better to continue to store the chemical agents and munitions at their stockpile sites for decades, dispose of the agents and munitions on-site at each stockpile site, or transport all the agents to one or more regional (or a national) sites for eventual disposal? This programmatic review would form the basis of the PEIS report and the PMCD's recommendations for action.

## ANALYSIS OF ALTERNATIVES

The first risk assessment was the evaluation of three different disposal alternatives: on-site disposal sites for each stockpile, regional disposal sites (West Coast and East Coast centers), and a national disposal site. The National Environmental Protection Act also required consideration of a "no action" alternative, that is, continued storage of the chemical weapons. This risk assessment did not consider the hazards of incineration against alternative technologies. In the development of each option, PMCD used planning constraints that would ensure maximum protection for the environment, general public, and workers; provide adequate and safe facilities designed solely for destruction of chemical agents and munitions; meet all applicable laws and regulations; and allow them to meet a deadline of September 30, 1994.

In the risk assessment, the Army evaluated a very large number of events, including what might happen during short-term storage during disposal operations (one to four years), handling and transportation to the disposal facility, temporary storage at the disposal facility, plant operations, and, in the case of the regional and national alternatives, off-site transportation from one site to another site. The accident scenarios covered weather and seismic effects, aircraft crashes into an igloo, equipment failures, and human error. Accidents that created an agent plume less than half a kilometer were excluded, as those plumes would not leave the stockpile site, let alone stray beyond the boundaries of the military post.

To compare the public risk of the disposal alternatives, the Army identified four measures to calculate the human health impact: probability of one or more fatalities, maximum number of fatalities, expected fatalities, and person-years at risk. The probability of one or more fatalities was the sum of the probabilities of all accidents at the sites that could cause one or more fatalities. The number would always be less than 1, since only a small fraction of the hundreds of possible accidents was expected to actually cause a fatality. The maximum number of fatalities was the number of fatalities in a worst-case scenario for all the accidents at a site, where an agent release would be carried the farthest by weather conditions over the most dense populations surrounding the site, without allowances for any sort of protection or emergency services. The expected fatalities was the sum of the risk contribution of all accidents at a site, where each risk is the potential fatality count (if an accident were to cause fatalities) multiplied by the probability of such an accident's taking place. In these three measures, keep in mind that the Army's calculations covered several hundred potential events. The person-years at risk was the number of years equal to the population density living within a distance of the plume's downwind hazard area for 1 percent lethalities, multiplied by the time period that chemical agents or munitions would be resident at the stockpile and disposal operations. This number included anyone who might suffer ill effects but is not a fatality count.

Those disposal concepts that were significantly superior to others in the area of human health impacts would be selected for further consideration. Those concepts surviving the first cut would then be examined against ecosystem and environmental impacts, by measuring their expected plume area. If that did not narrow down the list to one concept, the concept with the best potential effectiveness in emergency planning and preparedness would be chosen. *Cost of operations was not a determining factor in this selection*, a fact that should be kept in mind. In this methodology, the Army demonstrated that it intended to make a recommendation based on Congress' concern expressed in its legislation.

The national disposal center alternative would establish Tooele Army Depot as the main receiving facility from the other seven CONUS stockpile sites, given that over 40 percent of the stockpile was already located there. Additionally, the personnel at Tooele were trained on CAMDS, and there were relatively few communities nearby. The preferred mode of transportation would be railcars, as airplane or trucks were seen as less preferable in terms of overall safety, security, feasibility, and cost considerations. A little over half the U.S. stockpile would be moved. The national disposal center would require five facilities, three for processing munitions and two for processing the bulk agent, to meet the 1994 deadline. This alternative would minimize the number of personnel exposed but might increase the chance of accidents and the resulting impact on the citizens surrounding Tooele Army Depot's South Area.

The regional disposal center alternative would establish Tooele as the West Coast site, receiving just over 21 percent of the total stockpile from Pueblo and

Umatilla. Anniston, as the East Coast site, would receive over 22 percent of the U.S. stockpile from Aberdeen, Lexington, Newport, and Pine Bluff. Again, the movement would be by rail. Tooele would require three facilities to process its 63.8 percent of the stockpile, while Anniston would have two facilities to process its 29.6 percent of the stockpile. This alternative significantly reduced the number of personnel exposed, as did the national alternative, but again, it increased the potential impact on the surrounding area.

In both the regional and national disposal center options, the transportation plans initially called for the Army to route the trains through cities with fewer than 100,000 citizens. This was an effort to reduce the potential number of persons who might be exposed by any accident. In discussions with the railroad industry, the PMCD was told that this logic was actually faulty, in that they should route the trains on the best-maintained rails, and these were not the ones going through small cities. If the Army wanted a smooth and safe ride, it would have to travel through larger metropolitan areas with well-maintained rail systems, rails that were used for transportation of hazardous chemicals on a constant basis.

The on-site disposal center alternative is not too hard to figure out. Each site would receive its own disposal facility, designed to its unique munitions mix. There would be no off-site transportation, limiting the need for incident response to a much smaller area. A greater number of people (around the eight disposal sites as opposed to one or two) would potentially be affected, but for a shorter duration than for those living near a regional or national disposal center.

A twist on the three disposal alternatives was a partial relocation of munitions, specifically moving the stockpiles at Aberdeen and Lexington to Tooele by air transport, with the remaining sites employing on-site disposal.[10] Because Aberdeen and Lexington had the highest surrounding population, it was felt that moving these stocks would reduce the overall risk to the nation's populace. Ocean transport was not one of the ways that these stocks would be moved. Because of the complexity of attempting to develop an environmental assessment of the many waterways and coastlines that a water transport might pass through and by, the Army leadership felt that the required environmental analysis would take too long and unnecessarily delay the program, given that there were other transportation options available to a partial relocation plan. Since the two sites had a relatively small number of munitions and to avoid rail transport through the more heavily populated communities, the Army chose to evaluate the option of using air transport to move the munitions to Tooele.

Continued storage of the munitions would mean that the potential hazards and risks associated with storing the CW agents and munitions would remain and perhaps increase. This option would assume that security features and monitoring equipment would be constantly updated and maintained. For calculation purposes, the Army chose to examine the potential risks that could result over a 25-year period of continued storage, from 1985 through 2010.

**Table 6.1**
**Risk with Mitigation: Comparison of Programmatic Alternatives for All Locations (with normalized values)**

| Alternatives | Probability of One or More Fatalities | Maximum Fatalities | Expected Fatalities | Person-years at Risk | Expected Plume Area (km$^2$) |
|---|---|---|---|---|---|
| Continued Storage | $2.4 \times 10^{-3}$ (7.5) | $8.9 \times 10^{4}$ (17) | $4.5 \times 10^{-1}$ (480) | $1.4 \times 10^{8}$ (61) | $4.4 \times 10^{-2}$ (96) |
| On-site Disposal | $3.2 \times 10^{-4}$ (1.0) | $5.4 \times 10^{3}$ (1.0) | $9.4 \times 10^{-4}$ (1.0) | $2.3 \times 10^{6}$ (1.0) | $4.6 \times 10^{-4}$ (1.0) |
| Regional Disposal | $1.8 \times 10^{-3}$ (5.6) | $4.2 \times 10^{4}$ (7.8) | $9.5 \times 10^{-3}$ (10.0) | $5.5 \times 10^{6}$ (2.4) | $2.0 \times 10^{-3}$ (4.3) |
| National Disposal | $3.4 \times 10^{-3}$ (11) | $4.2 \times 10^{4}$ (7.8) | $3.0 \times 10^{-2}$ (32) | $5.4 \times 10^{6}$ (2.3) | $3.8 \times 10^{-3}$ (8.3) |
| Partial Relocation | $3.7 \times 10^{-3}$ (12) | $2.3 \times 10^{4}$ (4.3) | $2.5 \times 10^{-2}$ (27) | $3.1 \times 10^{6}$ (1.3) | $6.6 \times 10^{-3}$ (14) |

Source: U.S. Army, Final Programmatic Environmental Impact Statement, 1988.

When the calculations were run on all the potential accidents that could happen given their respective probabilities of occurring, the following results emerged (see Table 6.1). The exact numbers and assumptions used in developing these figures would be a book in and of itself and of questionable interest to anyone other than a statistician. What is important is how the Army interpreted these numbers and how they influenced the Army's decisions.

The Department of Energy defines "reasonable assuredness" of protection as 1 in 10,000,000, as they develop their nuclear reactor safety measures. In the continued storage scenario, the odds of an earthquake or small aircraft's crashing into the stockpile in any given year was seen as 1 in 10,000. A large plume of agent could result in high casualties. Executing on-site disposal would reduce the chances of an agent release during a 25-year period to 1 in 100,000,000. The PMCD thought that, if the risk management decision resulted in a selection of an option that was an order of magnitude better than Department of Energy standards, surely that met the intent of Congress to develop a program that ensured "maximum protection" to the people and environment.

The most probable scenario was an accident's occurring as a result of routine storage activities, someone's dropping a munition while in the process of maintenance and surveillance of the stockpile. While these odds were only as high as 1 in 100, the resulting agent release would be minimal and in most likelihood would not escape the post boundaries. These activities, accumulated over a 25-year period, account for a range of possible casualties from one a year to a catastrophic event causing 90,000 casualties and the largest number of person-years at risk (61 times that of on-site disposal). The fact that there had been no public deaths as a result of continued storage between 1968 and 1988 was not because of errors in analysis but rather the factor of very long odds of any catastrophic event's happening within any given year.

On-site disposal has the lowest potential fatalities (maximum or expected) primarily because of smaller stockpiles (smaller targets for aircraft accidents and smaller plume releases), shorter length of time for disposal operations, and no off-site transportation risks. Most accidents would be caused by chemical disposal plant operations. As in the continued storage option, the handling accidents would result in a minimal downwind hazard that probably would not leave the post boundaries. The maximum potential fatality event (resulting from a VX spill that was carried aloft by burning fumes) would cause 54 casualties. Over the entire duration of disposal operations (three to five years, less than three years at any one site), the maximum theoretical casualties from an absolutely worst-case scenario was around 5,000.

Regional disposal had a high risk factor due to the transportation of M55 rockets by rail. While the overall person years at risk for transportation was low (due to the very small amount of time that any population would be exposed to a potential train wreck, minutes to hours), one rail accident could cause up to 1,400 casualties. The actual odds of this happening was 1 in 1,000. Other than the expected risks of disposal plant operations and on-site transportation, storing munitions arriving from the other sites at a short-term holding facilities was seen as a potential additional source of risk. Again, the rockets were seen as the greatest risk, but the probability of their igniting was seen as less than 1 in 10 million. The larger numbers of munitions at the regional sites accounts for the larger plume projections, which might occur if a catastrophic event took place.

In examining the criteria for selection, a probability of one or more fatalities had not ruled out any option, with no significant difference in scores for any alternative. Likewise, the maximum fatalities measure had not clearly shown any alternative as better, at least to any statistically meaningful degree. Looking at expected fatalities, continued storage was seen as significantly worse than the other options, and the national disposal center and partial relocation alternative were ranked somewhat worse than on-site disposal. The last human effects measure, person-years at risk, shows continued storage as only slightly worse than the other options. This left on-site disposal and regional disposal alternatives as the two clear possibilities.

Comparing the possible ecosystem and environmental impacts of the two alternatives, on-site disposal has a slight edge based on the expected plume area, but not enough to clearly identify it as better. The final measure, emergency planning and preparedness, put on-site disposal over the top, largely because it would be difficult to mitigate the risk of transporting the munitions and agents by rail to the two centers, as opposed to controlling the risk at any one site. Just to be certain, the Army evaluated the options from the perspective of each site and the overall program. For Aberdeen, Pueblo, and Umatilla, the risk assessments clearly suggested that on-site disposal was the optimal solution. From an overall program perspective, on-site disposal was best for each site because it had the least amount of overall risk in each site's analysis, no matter how insignificant the difference.

## PUBLIC PERCEPTION OF THE RISKS

To say that this risk assessment was controversial would be an understatement. State and local officials were relieved that they would not have to deal with chemical munitions moving through their territories. The public, however, thought that the Army was stating that "we might kill people if we store chemical munitions, we might kill people if we burn chemical munitions, and we might kill people if we move chemical munitions." There was risk in every option, and that was not explained well, nor was it well received. The residents around Blue Grass Army Depot were particularly upset over the on-site disposal decision, preferring the partial relocation, or regional or national disposal center alternatives, anything but disposal at their site.

What was driving the public fear was deeper than merely the mysteries of chemical warfare; it was a basic misunderstanding of the element of risk itself. Emotion has driven the U.S. public citizens, in particular, to become a society in which the government makes decisions based on the overused expression, that "any risk is unacceptable." Yet the risks that citizens face daily are often more deadly than industry technologies and many actions from the government; the general population just does not analyze their daily risks in that same, dry rundown of statistics and data. In an article on risks, Dr. Gregory Benford, a physicist, astronomer, and noted author at University of California, Irvine, points out the difference between public perception of risk and actual risk as measured by researchers (see Table 6.2).

**Table 6.2**
**Ordering of Perceived Risk for 10 Activities and Technologies**[11]

| Activity or Technology | League of Women Voters | College Students | Experts |
|---|---|---|---|
| Nuclear Power | 1 | 1 | 20 |
| Motor Vehicles | 2 | 5 | 1 |
| Handguns | 3 | 2 | 4 |
| Smoking | 4 | 3 | 2 |
| Motorcycles | 5 | 6 | 6 |
| Alcoholic Beverages | 6 | 7 | 3 |
| General (private aviator) | 7 | 15 | 12 |
| Police Work | 8 | 8 | 17 |
| Pesticides | 9 | 4 | 8 |
| Surgery | 10 | 11 | 5 |

What is interesting here is how nuclear power is clearly regarded as most dangerous, when, in fact, the current safety protocols and licensing requirements have made this a very risk-free enterprise. No one in the United States has died of the effects of nuclear power generation, the case of Three Mile Island included. Police work is not as risky as Hollywood and video games portend because police take extraordinary precautions not to get shot on or off the job. Conversely, people may feel that doctors know what they are doing in surgery and therefore they do not worry about it. Yet by the numbers, this is a high-risk situation for patients who go under the knife.

The public agrees with the experts on the relative risk poised by handguns and smoking by this study, perhaps showing why recent court cases have successfully litigated against the manufacturers of those products. This case does not seem to have been made for alcohol, which experts rate as very risky but which the public seems to downgrade as not so bad. All this demonstrates is that the public does not think like the experts, preferring the five-minute news clip to official calculations of risk and probability.

Other examples are the risk comparisons of air travel to automotive travel. In one year in the United States, there may be a few hundred deaths caused by a plane crash during 1 billion passenger miles. Compare that to 150 deaths per day caused by automobile accidents or 100 deaths per day caused by smoking in the United States alone. Why do people worry more about flying than driving (other than seeing vivid crash pictures on the evening news)? This may be the case because, as passengers, we are helpless to control the airplane, while we think we can control the consequences of driving a car, smoking, or drinking.

Benford suggests that this public perception is based on a combination of control and technology. This is why, for instance, the public fears nuclear power plants that have a very good safety record and does not get excited about oil- and coal-burning furnaces that contribute to deaths caused by lung cancer and emphysema. We understand burning coal and oil; we do not understand nuclear fission. We do not get excited about the carcinogens in wine or beer or the carcinogens that inhabit the daily workplace or home, but what about the carcinogens in municipally delivered tap water? When you see the numbers as exposure per day, someone breathing the air in a new mobile home can intake up to 21,000 times the carcinogens as compared to someone drinking city tap water.[12] As a result of these public perceptions focusing on the wrong hazards, politicians are encouraged to spend funds on programs that are not reducing the more dangerous elements in our society.

Returning to the disposal program, the risk analysis would continue to plague the Army program throughout its efforts. As the disposal program's critics became increasingly vocal, questioning every step that the Army took and the emissions levels of the facilities, the Army continued to attempt to counter these allegations with science and quantitative risk and safety information. For instance, a PMCD report noted that if an adult were to breathe in the air from a deactivation furnace smokestack each day for an entire year, it would be equivalent in dioxin toxicity exposure to smoking one cigarette every three weeks. It fell on empty ears that citizens were being exposed daily to more dioxins in their normal living conditions than the expected emissions of the facilities.[13] In fact, the Sierra Club acknowledged that it was not the level of emissions that mattered as much as that these facilities would add to the already high (in their estimate) potentially harmful emissions from other natural and man-made sources. It did not matter that the quantity being added was, in fact, inconsequential to the health of the community.

The reformists (concerned citizens and critics) focused on this risk assessment to make the case that the Army should continue storage until a technology came along that would ensure that there were no cases of "maximum fatalities" or "person-years at risk." They were also disturbed that the Army had chosen incineration based on tests that the public had not had time to evaluate or participate in. The logic that there would never be alternative disposal technologies without some degree of risk fell on deaf ears. The technicians (PMCD office) had made a critical misstep by stating that the risk assessment was the primary driver for recommending the on-site disposal option, rather than explaining that the decision also included control options, legal considerations, and political necessity. The EIS focused on demonstrating that the risk of disposal operations could be mitigated to a degree that ensured that the environment, workers, and public were much better protected than just letting the munitions sit in storage.

The disposal program was not simply addressing the risks of storing an aging and leaking chemical stockpile; the Army had been doing this for decades, without incident. The risk of an incident as a result of continued storage was relatively insignificant compared to many other public risks, but it was growing and could be reduced to zero only by disposal. What drove the program's timeline was the congressional directive to destroy the unitary weapons prior to procuring binary chemical weapons; the Army leadership was driving the clock on that issue. The question should have been, What is the best approach to execute given the allotted time and resources from both cost and safety issues? If the program could be executed more quickly without a great increase in risk, that option should have been chosen. The use of an engineer control methodology intended for industry risk management was not the best choice for telling the public how the PMCD had arrived at the best disposal option. The decision, communicated as primarily based on this risk assessment, had not been communicated effectively.

The rationalists (OSD and Army leadership) and incrementalists (congressional representatives) were watching with interest but were not active participants in the PMCD's (the technician) evaluation and recommendations. They would abide by what the subject-matter experts told them was the right course, as long as it was developed within legal parameters and would not get them into trouble. The many questions from the public, state officials, and special interest groups would give cause to greater involvement among the DOD leadership, Congress, and the PMCD. As these groups continued to examine the programmatic EIS risk assessment, there would be more studies, more delays, and, ultimately, increased costs to execute the program.

Artillery projectiles are part of the chemical weapons stockpile at Tooele, Utah.

Aerial view of Tooele Chemical Agent Disposal Facility. The plant covers 27 acres and is located approximately 12 miles south of the town of Tooele.

Chemical weapons are stored in concrete igloos (left) until they are destroyed in the disposal facility (right).

On-site containers transport chemical weapons from storage igloos to the disposal facility.

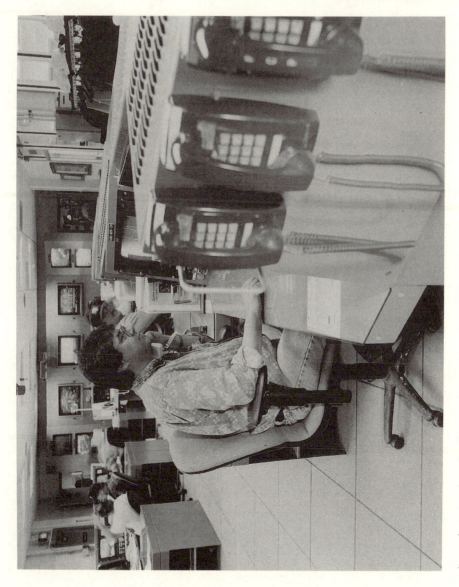

An engineer monitors the disposal process from the TOCDF control room.

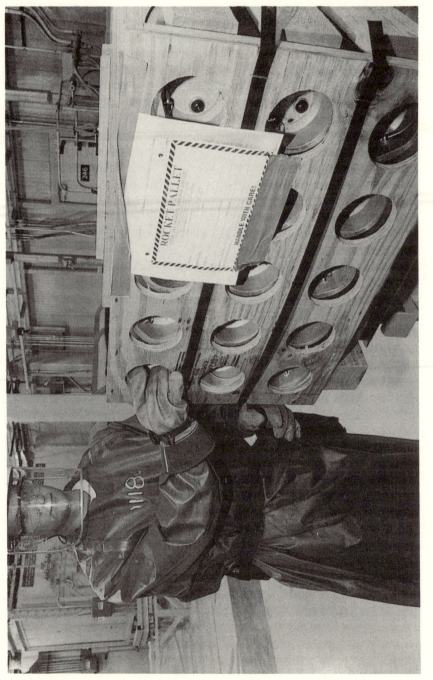

An unpack operator inspects M55 rockets delivered from storage igloos. Following inspection, the rockets are fed into the disposal line for destruction.

An unpack operator performs a test of the ACAMS, one of the more than 100 that test the air inside the plant to verify the absence of chemical agent.

Extra protection: carbon filter banks ensure that no agent is released through the stacks.

# 7

## Legitimating Incineration

Most critics address the national program that started in 1985 after Congress authorized the Army (through PL 99-145) to initiate its disposal of the entire chemical weapons stockpile, rather than addressing the Army's efforts that began in 1972. Only after 1985 did the four policy groups (rationalists, technicians, incrementalists, and reformists) begin frequent interactions on the concerns surrounding the chemical stockpile disposal program. News about construction of a disposal facility on Johnston Island demonstrated that the Army was sincere in its efforts to initiate and execute a national disposal program. People living near the stockpiles started paying more attention, since, if the Army was successful at Johnston Island, it meant that their communities would be hosting a disposal facility next. It was one thing for these communities had been living with the risk of stored chemical munitions for years; now these munitions would be removed from storage and incinerated near their homes. Their level of interest was raised.

As noted in Chapter 5, USATHAMA drafted the first chemical disposal PEIS for disposing of all chemical-filled M55 rockets in April 1985. This PEIS had been expanded to address disposal of additional types of chemical munitions and the potential risks involved in their transportation. The revised draft PEIS was released to federal and state officials and agencies (as well as to the general public) for review on July 1, 1986. The PEIS stated that the Army viewed incineration as the only sound disposal method available and had eliminated other alternatives from consideration, largely as a result of past research and with NRC concurrence.[1]

In April and May 1986, prior to the release of the draft PEIS, the Army held public scoping meetings at the eight stockpile sites and at several regional sites for those states that might host chemical weapons movements, based on the options entailing off-site transportation. The initial discussions were of mixed enthusiasm. Citizens at most of the stockpile sites generally supported the on-site disposal option, but those at Aberdeen and Blue Grass were vehemently opposed and pushed for moving the chemicals somewhere else, opting for disposal anywhere else other than near their crowded communities. On the other hand, there was considerable opposition to moving these munitions through Illinois, Ohio, West

Virginia, and Tennessee from the concerned citizens and public officials of those states. This "not in my back yard" attitude was perhaps not hard to predict.

The final PEIS would be over three inches thick, presented in three volumes. Volume 1 included the main report identifying the program, the alternatives that were studied, description of existing environments, analysis of health and environmental consequences and mitigation measures, and a list of the preparers and their professional qualifications. Volume 2 included all the written comments from the public and agencies responding to the draft PEIS, the PMCD's responses to the written comments, and responses to questions taken from public hearings. The third volume included much of the raw data and in-depth analyses that had been used to develop the report, such as the characterization of the stockpile, agent toxicity, transportation concepts, risk analysis supporting the EIS concepts, and cultural and socioeconomic impacts.

The research and responses to the public comments had to be thorough and consistent, demonstrating how the Army was going to develop and execute a safe and responsible program in response to congressional direction. The final PEIS would document the concerns and recommendations of the major influential players—the states and federal agencies that would have to work with the Army on executing the program—as well as allow the public to examine in detail and comment on how the Army was planning to execute the chemical demilitarization program.

The DOD Explosives Safety Board, as the expert in ordnance disposal, fully supported on-site disposal and opposed any movement of munitions to outside sites. The HHS Toxic Substances and Disease Registry had no favored alternative but noted that the "gravity of potential health hazards involved in transportation has not been adequately staffed." The HHS office in Portland, Oregon, saw on-site disposal as the most reasonable option and suggested that the Indian tribes around Umatilla should be given full consideration as a stakeholder. The Department of Interior supported an on-site destruction strategy, as did the Department of Transportation, noting "serious concerns about transportation of these materiels in commerce." The EPA, notably one of the more involved decision makers, had concluded "that the alternative selected, on-site disposal, appears to be the best." The EPA's Office of Federal Activities suggested that the Army might wish to consider one or more combinations of the alternatives, but whatever was environmentally preferable was the key. They also noted the extremely technical nature of the report.

At the state level, Governor George Wallace of Alabama noted that the "only logical alternative to select would be disposal of the materiels on-site . . . transportation is not in the best interest." He was vigorously opposed to any alternatives that would involve transportation of any stockpiles into or through Alabama for disposal. The state of Arkansas and mayor of Pine Bluff supported the on-site disposal option. California saw on-site disposal as the best available alternative, as did Indiana and the city mayor of Clinton, Indiana, (adjacent to

Newport Army Ammunition Plant) also echoed by Colorado and Pueblo's mayor. Oregon saw on-site disposal as the best option, but not necessarily by incineration, asking for more details on alternative technologies. Kentucky stressed the desire to transport munitions to less densely populated areas. Nevada's, Wyoming's, and Utah's state governments all preferred on-site disposal as the best alternative, opposing shipments that would increase the potential for an agent release. Governor Bob Kerry of Nebraska also wanted to "avoid the risk of transportation by destroying the nerve gas stocks on site."[2]

From the general public, there were considerable suspicions that the Army had not considered all the possibilities and approaches that could be developed for complete risk mitigation, not that this was based on any rational logic. The 1985 methyl isocyanate spill at Bhopal, India, killing thousands and injuring tens of thousands, and the January 1986 Challenger space shuttle explosion had stunned the public into not trusting that companies could safely design and operate high-technology projects. The Sierra Club (Cumberland Charter) in particular summarized this sentiment, noting that new, sophisticated technologies were "inherently dangerous." Not only did it not support incineration as the chosen technology, but it saw transportation of the stocks to a more remote area as much wiser than on-site disposal.[3]  One extreme example of this line of thought was Pastor Richard Wilson of Muskegon, Michigan, who suggested packaging the waste into a rocket and sending it into the sun.

One letter referenced a GAO fact sheet that had noted Army plans to move the U.S. chemical weapons from Europe to Johnston Island and questioned that if the Army could move those munitions, why not the ones in the states? Many public comments questioned whether the on-site disposal selection was a political convenience or one that seriously addressed health and safety factors. To a large degree, most just did not understand the technical writ of the PEIS and were not inclined to trust the Army's proposals. After all, this was the Chemical Corps, which had conducted secret biological weapons tests in the 1950s and 1960s, developed tear gas and napalm for use during the Korean and Vietnam conflicts, produced a Superfund site at RMA, and never admitted guilt to the alleged sheep kill near Dugway Proving Ground.

The respondents also questioned the vulnerability of chemical munitions to sabotage or terrorism while being transported through the states, whether the Army had developed emergency planning and evacuation options for the sites during disposal operations, who would be liable in the event of an accident, the adequacy of the disposal technology and the environmental assessments, and the understanding of the risk and hazard analysis. They questioned why Congress had set the deadline of September 1994 and why the Army had conducted a programmatic and not site-specific EIS. Many opposed the program for their own agendas, either not trusting the Army or not seeing the answer they wanted. In short, they questioned every aspect of the disposal program that they did not fully understand, and given the very technical features of this program, that was most of the report.

D. J. Shearin, a retired Chemical Corps colonel living in Bel Air, Maryland, while not representative of the norm, made interesting comments in the PEIS on the disposal concept. He observed that the military had shipped war gases including nerve agents all over the United States and Europe without incident for years and that the probabilities for an accident were so low that "the primary concern should be one of economics, not whether or not the one-in-a-million accident may occur." He suggested using Tooele's CAMDS as the sole site, as the Army had invested several million dollars in that facility, and there had to be a hundred other national security projects all requiring money rather than wasting funds on building duplicate facilities across the country. At the least, he noted, the low volatility of mustard agent and the potential risk to nearby people living around Aberdeen should make the case for transportation for those ton containers. Shearin noted (rather presciently) the need for a public affairs strategy, keeping a "continuous barrage of factual articles" in the local media to allay the public's fears on whatever alternative was chosen.

Unfortunately, this was an idea whose time had not yet come. After the first public scoping meeting, USTHAMA hired a company to provide advice on public relations efforts and to develop a plan of action to execute. Colonel Hidalgo had taken this plan forward, but the Army leadership responded that they did not execute programs that way. The Army wanted to be seen as above board in all its efforts and did not want the impression that they were influencing public opinion.

Following the release of the draft PEIS, the Army continued informal public hearings at the eight stockpile sites (mostly in August 1986) in an effort to better explain its rationale. These discussions did not necessarily convince the public that the Army's option was right, but they did cause the public to ask more questions to the PM's office and to their congressional representatives. Some wanted other disposal options examined, such as moving all the munitions to Johnston Island or some other remote area where the Army could dispose of the munitions without any environmental impact or hazard to humans. The large number of comments and requests for additional clarification would cause the Army to take 18 months to complete the final report (the normal period of time to incorporate comments and release a final EIS report was 6 months). The PM's office called for more studies, 13 of which would be conducted in 1987. These included:

- A risk analysis of the continued storage of chemical munitions and risk analyses of the disposal at national and regional sites and on-site. These reports revisited the initial calculations and substantially revised the draft PEIS risk analyses based on public comments and various options in disposal.
- An upgraded transportation plan for the chemical agents and munitions, which included the use of a panel of hazardous material transportation experts.
- Conceptual designs for a new chemical munitions transport system and on-site transportation package for chemical munitions.

- An emergency response concept plan for the disposal program, as a basis for Army and local officials to develop site-specific emergency planning, preparations, and response plans.
- A chemical stockpile disposal monitoring concept study, outlining basic concepts and logic relevant to developing monitoring plans for all disposal alternatives.
- A study on mitigation of public safety risks, identifying mitigation measures for all disposal alternatives that would reduce the probability and/or magnitude of an accidental chemical release.
- Review of transportation of chemical munitions at reduced temperatures, which concluded that there were definite advantages of moving mustard and GB agents at reduced temperatures.
- A historical summary of the Army's experience in chemical agent and munitions disposal, documenting the Army's past experience in destroying chemical agents by neutralization and incineration technologies.
- A historical compilation of the Army's chemical weapons movements from 1945 to 1986, identifying past movements and events and noting that there had been no fatalities that arose from the movement of agents due to agent exposure.
- An evaluation of multiple incinerator air quality impacts, addressing whether or not chemical disposal facility's incinerator outputs, added to the outputs of other trash incinerators on post, would have any potential adverse health impacts.
- A classified analysis of the vulnerability of the chemical disposal process to terrorism or sabotage.
- An integrated summary of all risk analyses of the alternatives, to portray the final results in a more understandable format.
- A methodology for selecting the most environmentally preferred alternative, including consideration of impacts on human health, cultural and socioeconomic resources, and the ecosystem.

In the months following the release of the draft PEIS, Congress added a few requirements of its own. In PL 99-661 (NDA Act for FY87, November 1986), Kentucky's congressional delegation inserted language to prohibit the shipment of any chemical munitions or agents to Blue Grass Army Depot and, following disposal of the current stockpile, prohibit the future construction, storage, or disposal of chemical weapons at that site. Congress also called for a new report outlining alternative disposal methods to optimize safety and cost-effectiveness measures and not considering the deadline of September 1994.

## NEW PROGRAM COSTS

As the PMCD continued to staff the programmatic EIS, work continued at Johnston Island, whose disposal operations were not addressed under that document. Facility construction had been initiated in 1986, with the Army awarding contracts for staging and shipping the equipment to the island. About half the work would be completed during 1986, and all the major equipment contracts had been awarded. The Army released additional funds to procure the remaining processing equipment (to dispose of munitions other than the M55s) and selected a contractor for operating the disposal facility. While the facility was not expected to start operations until 1988, this early contract would permit advance planning and training for the contractors that would conduct the day-to-day operations.

The Army finalized the design of the baseline technology and received an endorsement of the process from the NRC in 1984. The process began by operators' unpacking the munitions, draining the agent, disassembling the weapons, and channeling the parts into a four-stream incineration process (see Figure 7.1). The dunnage (packing materiels), energetics (explosives and propellants), metal parts, and chemical agents would all be processed in separate incinerators. Each incinerator had its own afterburner and pollution abatement system to clean the exhaust gases prior to the release of the air through a common stack. The internal air was forced from areas of lower potential contamination toward higher potential contamination, through the furnace rooms and a bank of charcoal filters, before being released to the environment.

The chemical agents would be fed into an incinerator running 2,600–2,700 degrees Fahrenheit, about 500–600 degrees hotter than any commercial hazardous waste incinerator. The gases would quickly move to the afterburner, where a 2,000-degree wall of fire would bake the gases. This treatment would be hot enough to destroy the agent in less than half a second; in the process, the agent would be exposed to these extremes for two seconds. This gave the Army its proven efficiencies of nearly 100 percent. The dunnage incinerator also performed well above commercial standards, and the metal parts furnace cooked all metals for 15 minutes at over 1000 degrees Fahrenheit to meet the 5X standards, allowing the release of metals for recycling.[4] All waste streams would be processed in accordance with EPA regulations.

A chemical incident at CAMDS on January 29, 1987, drew public attention as the Army was publically staffing the PEIS. The detectors registered a small amount of nerve agent in an incinerator stack. While no one had been exposed and no injuries reported, it caught the attention of the news media and local community. The Army suspended operations pending a full investigation and modified its procedures on reporting incidents to the public.[5] It ended up that the agent had leaked through the valves and gaskets following the completion of a disposal run and was released into the atmosphere. This incident shut down CAMDS for about a year.

About this time, citizens groups and environmentalists started to closely examine the Army's plan. They had not yet developed their own conclusions, in part because they had few technical experts who could translate the Army's plans. They had heard horror stories about state and local hazardous waste treatments, landfill problems, and sloppy incinerator regulation and wanted to go over the Army's proposal in fine detail. They petitioned the Army for time and funds to review the draft PEIS, resulting in Under Secretary Ambrose providing funds for five contracts to allow citizens groups at Aberdeen, Blue Grass, Newport, Pine Bluff, and Umatilla to hire experts to analyze the report. Each group would develop

**Figure 7.1**
**Processing Chemical Munitions Through the Baseline Process**

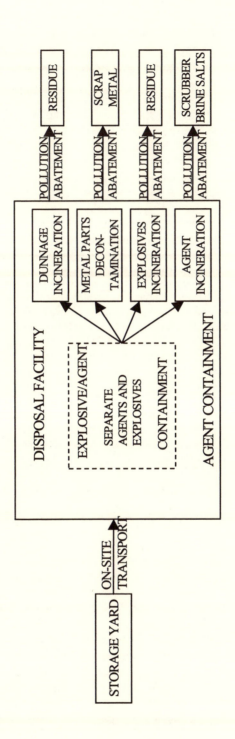

its own review, the results of which would go into the final PEIS. The Army hosted a public CAMDS tour in March 1987 to allow a better understanding of the disposal process and program's goals. About 30 people from Newport, Edgewood, and Pueblo attended.

To answer the congressional language in PL 99-661 calling for alternative approaches for destroying the chemical stockpile, optimizing safety and cost-effectiveness, and not being held to a deadline of September 1994, the Army developed six options. These included:

- A modified baseline program, where the Army would redesign the CONUS disposal facilities based upon proposed improvements identified during the JACADS performance.
- A JACADS operational testing program, where the Army would run the plant at full scale for 18 months to verify safety and operability issues. The eight CONUS disposal facilities would be constructed after this period and operated simultaneously.
- A similar JACADS operational testing program, where the Army would run the plant at full scale for 18 months to verify safety and operability issues, and the eight CONUS disposal facilities would be constructed after this period and operated sequentially. The same construction and operating crews would be used at each disposal facility.
- A dual-technology evaluation, where a cryofracture/thermal destruction facility would be built at Tooele, while the JACADS plant operated as planned. After both technologies were evaluated, a final decision would be made for remaining chemical stockpile sites.
- A similar dual-technology evaluation, by which the superior technology would be implemented at the remaining sites in sequence, using the same construction and operating crews at each disposal facility.
- A hybrid approach, where the Army would continue to develop cryofracture technologies and design and build disposal facilities based on cryofracture, while still operating some of the disposal facilities using the baseline technology.

The Army estimated that the effect of implementing these options would mean a slip of 1 to 12 years in the schedule, with increases in programmatic costs ranging from $200 million to $1.1 billion. The Army recommended in July 1987 that, in the event that Congress allowed a slip in the stockpile destruction deadline beyond September 1994, it implement the first option, modifying the following disposal facilities based on JACADS' performance and slipping the stockpile elimination date from 1994 to 1996. PMCD developed an operational verification testing plan to give Congress hard data that the process was safe and efficient and could be replicated at the CONUS sites.

Another challenge was how the PMCD worked with the commanders of the stockpile sites. There were no centralized Army control over the eight stockpile sites and the PMCD office was not authorized or permitted to exert any control exerted on the sites. The U.S. Army Depot Systems Command directed operations at Anniston Army Depot, Blue Grass Army Depot, Tooele Army Depot, and the Umatilla and Pueblo Depot Activities. The U.S. Army Munitions and Chemical

Command controlled Pine Bluff Arsenal and Newport Army Ammunition Plant, and the U.S. Army Test and Evaluation Command owned Aberdeen Proving Ground and Dugway Proving Ground. Each one of these commands had a two-star general officer with whom Brigadier General Nydam had to communicate on stockpile issues. This complicated issues, not the least to the local communities that did not understand that the PMCD did not have the power to direct anything other than disposal operations. To them, the Army was the Army; distinctions of different commands with different responsibilities meant little to them.[6]

The Army had completed construction of the facilities for the BZ disposal at Pine Bluff Arsenal in September 1986, with installation of the processing equipment following closely behind the construction. Costs to complete the construction and equipment installation would run nearly $24 million. Steps to shake out the facility's process and train an operating crew would take up much of 1987, leading the Army to plan for beginning plant operations in late 1987 or early 1988. On the plus side, the townsfolk outside Pine Bluff's front gates had a fairly good, long relationship with their Army colleagues at the arsenal and were not picketing the site.

The binary munitions program was not running as smoothly as the OSD and Army leadership would have preferred. The initial plan was to have the 155-mm binary projectiles fielded by December 1987, the Bigeye chemical bomb fielded by September 1988, and the MLRS binary chemical warhead fielded by December 1990. The company contracted to produce canisters for the 155-mm projectile was running late on its deliveries, creating a backlog for half of the weapon system. The Army needed to construct a chemical plant at Pine Bluff to produce the chemical required for one of the two binary components, a facility that would not be ready to produce on a full-scale basis until 1990.

The Navy was evaluating the Bigeye bomb's performance in operational testing, observing less than stellar results. During 1987 operational testing, the Navy and Army tested 58 binary bombs, with very inconsistent results. Problems included excessive pressure buildup, questionable efficiencies on how much lethal agent was generated, unpredictable agent flashing (burning), and an overall reliability concern of the bomb's performance. The delays in developing and producing binary munitions were unfortunate, but the slips in implementing the chemical demilitarization efforts allowed some allowances. On the other hand, it focused more controversy on the general issue of chemical weapons, which increased public attention and media focus on the proposed disposal program.[7]

Congress desired to keep a lockstep relationship between the two national programs, despite the earlier separation of the two program manager offices from under the Program Manager for Chemical Munitions. The passage of PL 100-180 (NDA Act for FY 1988–1989, December 1987) called for the Army to develop binary weapons to replace the unitary chemical weapons in Europe; otherwise, the Army could not withdraw the unitary chemical weapons for disposal operations.

The bill also included language directing the Army to ensure that its final PEIS include an evaluation of alternative technologies, to develop an outline for full-scale operational verification testing of the JACADS facility (taking the PMCD up on its initiative), and (again) to ensure maximum protection for public health and the environment. The binary weapons program was hostage to the results of the chemical demilitarization program.

## EVALUATING THE ARMY'S FINAL PEIS

It is hard to accuse the Army leadership of making the wrong decision in selecting the on-site disposal option, using incineration as the chosen technology. It developed a program agenda that was endorsed by OSD and Army leadership and that was supportive of a concurrent binary weapons program, a major component of the national security strategy. The Army had decades of experience evaluating and testing various lab scale and pilot plant disposal efforts, and was convinced that it had selected the right technology. It conducted a thorough risk analysis identifying the various hazards and completed an exhaustive environmental program assessment. The Army identified a disposal recommendation with which every federal agency, every state agency, and every governor that had a stake in the plan concurred. The plan met every regulation in the NEPA legislation and HHS and DOT guidance and followed every legal clause to the "T." The desired binary chemical munitions program was intimately tied with the disposal program, with similar technical issues, discussed together as public and international concerns, and tied together for the time line of obtaining a modern retaliatory capability. It was a sure bet and a conservatively safe option, based on a well-researched plan that could be executed to meet the congressional intent to design and execute a safe and efficient process.

What the Army had failed to do was to foresee the impact of the citizen groups' fears and desires, discontent that would boil up through the state legislators back to Congress. While the majority of the public was not concerned about the Army's disposal plans (most were probably unaware of the effort), the mass media and several politicians focused on the strident cries of a minority that would not accept any disposal process that did not guarantee zero risk to the environment and the people's health. The fact that the chemical munitions represented a higher risk remaining in storage than through a disposal process was, in the author's opinion, deliberately overlooked by newspapers, news anchors looking to boost their ratings, and politicians looking for a hot campaign line.

The PM's office had focused on answering the letter of congressional language, which is to say, efficient disposal of the munitions while considering maximum protection and minimum risk, as engineers defined protection and acceptable risk. There was no planned, coordinated outreach program to identify the public's issues, to work with the true, knowledgeable stakeholders (state and federal politicians), and to develop an executable, safe, and cost-effective solution that could be accepted by the public. But then again, perhaps nothing short of a presidential declaration that there would be a single national disposal facility would have worked.[8]

The Army leadership made a fundamental error in allowing the perception that its recommendation for on-site disposal was a result of its overall risk assessment alone. The PMCD was communicating that the need to minimjze risk and the need to have rapid emergency response capabilities were the primary measures, when these factors really were not major discriminators between the PEIS alternatives. In reviewing the many options, the overall risk and total cost estimates between a national, regional, and on-site selection were very close. The assumption that any transportation option would require an extensive (and perhaps unaffordable) emergency response capability all along the routes of travel also wrote that option out as impractical. Yet it was demonstrated years later that the Army could transport chemical weapons safely on public roads and railways. In November 1990, the U.S. Army safely moved tons of chemical weapons (largely artillery projectiles, no rockets or mines) through heavily-populated areas in Germany to Johnston Island. This included moving chemical munitions over rail, road, and sea-lanes. Clearly, transporting chemical weapons could be safe and was executable; it just was not politically acceptable and, years later, it was not even legal due to congressional directives prohibiting any studies as to the feasibility of transporting chemical agents or munitions. It came down to politics as the determining factor, the concern being that if the Army chose off-site transportation to a national or regional site, governors of the states through which the chemical weapons were passing would have sued to stop the Army, potentially holding up the disposal program (and, by association, the binary munitions program) for years.

If transportation were ever an option, moving the rockets remained the largest risk factor. To mitigate this risk, the Army might have considered moving all the munitions and bulk agent except the rockets and perhaps the mines. It could have developed a transportable disposal facility, as had been intended by USATHAMA, to travel to the five sites and eliminate the M55 rockets and mines. This may have significantly reduced the costs and risk of the national or regional disposal facilities or even made the partial relocation a less risky and more viable option. Given the five alternatives, the risk assessments, lack of any realistic cost analysis, and initial public reaction, the regional disposal facility could have been an executable option. It would have permitted the Army to focus on building two, rather than eight, disposal facilities.

At the very least, the Army could have examined a combination of transportation and on-site disposal, moving the least hazardous munitions and agents (mustard munitions and bulk agent at Pueblo and Aberdeen) to Tooele, eliminating the need for two disposal sites, and saving literally billions of dollars. The bulk agent at Newport could have been safely moved, given the lack of energetics, and the limited number of munitions and agent at Blue Grass Army Depot could have been easily and safely moved to Anniston (had Governor Wallace been talked into supporting this option) or Pine Bluff Arsenal. The Army could have built the railroads and applied enough security and emergency response forces to safely execute such a move. This option would have required more work with the state governors and federal agencies, not to mention assistance from the Reagan administration, but it could have resulted in a more streamlined and cost-effective alternative that was just as safe as the on-site disposal option and one that would have been much more palatable in the end.

On the other hand, this line of thought may be naive and without consideration of the considerable safety and environmental requirements imposed on the Army's disposal facilities. The Army knew that it could move chemical munitions safely; it had been doing so for years, safety was never in question. The cost was not the issue, politics were the killer—bottom line, nobody wanted to see chemical munitions transported through their states regardless of the safety measures taken. The political costs did not warrant the limited engineering or financial benefits of centralizing the disposal effort. Even the transportable disposal facility was not realistic. The main reason why the original plan in 1972 had devolved into CAMDS and DATS was the severe demands of the disposal facility engineering designs and required safety features. The explosives containment vessel used in the disposal facility, for instance, had to be three feet thick, which was unfeasible in the creation and employment of a transportable disposal facility.

Part of the public's adverse reaction to the plan was that it had no input as to the selection of the technology, development, and evaluation of the alternatives and no sense of the Army's decades of experience in chemical weapons disposal. Many citizens accused the Army of rushing to judgment to curry favor with Congress, to satisfy defense contractors, or to ensure future business for the Chemical Corps, rather than recognize that the Army had done this for decades on a smaller scale. In addition to the complaints over the selection of on-site disposal as the path ahead, many disliked the entire concept of using incineration as the baseline technology, basing this view on the perception of the safety of less regulated commercial and private medical incinerators. The decades of testing conducted at Rocky Mountain Arsenal and Tooele, comparing neutralization and incineration technologies, was done behind closed doors and without public forums or academic involvement; therefore, to the public, it was all questionable data. It was just too difficult for the average citizen to translate and understand the risk assessments or technical discussions in the EIS to make a rational decision. The citizen groups refused to accept the NAS accreditation of the baseline technology or its observation that it was 45 times more dangerous to continue storing the weapons as opposed to disposing of them.

At this stage in the program, the PMCD office and Army leadership had underestimated the impact of the public's perception. While the public's negative perception of incineration was unfounded, nonetheless it shaped the position of many political leaders. Had the Army's top military leadership worked to inform the congressional delegations of eleven states, congressional committees, and those state governors on the alternatives, costs of execution, and program risks, maybe the program would have gotten started on a different path. Getting these influential representatives to voice their informed statements on a particular alternative would have had much greater impact on winning the citizens over. While OSD and the Army civilian leadership and the NRC committees had talked to Congress on the technical aspects of demilitarization and the logic of on-site disposal, the Congress and state elected officials were very focused on the perceptions of their constituents. Uninformed as the public may have been, they drove the federal and state political reaction to the Army's program.

Of course, thinking that the Army military leadership would talk to Congress was not really a practical option. The Army military leadership was not inclined to discuss any of its internal program management issues with Congress. As mentioned, there was no Chemical Corps general officer in the Pentagon to act as an active advocate in the DC area. Under Secretary Ambrose was personally and heavily involved and the military leadership just did not want to get involved if the civilian leadership was handling the issue. The chemical demilitarization program was not seen as critical to the Army's warfighting priorities, and it was a distraction to these priorities. It was absolutely in the Army and OSD leadership's interests to ensure that the best and most affordable option was chosen and that the political leadership would back the program, yet one does not see much leadership involvement (outside of the PMCD) after 1987 and prior to 2000.

To be fair to the Army, much of this criticism is hindsight. The PMCD was locked into a particular direction, based on its experience, its assessments, its indications from state and federal agencies, and the lack of any negative feedback from OSD leadership and Congress. The PMCD recommended what it honestly believed was the best option, one that answered congressional intent and offered the least chance of accidents. It had gotten the state governors and federal agencies to approve the on-site disposal alternative. It knew with utmost certainty that the safest and most efficient technology was incineration, that the least risky approach was not to move any munitions, and that it could eliminate the stockpile without risk to the local citizens. It was not merely a gut feeling of the particular technical and programmatic issues involved, but was based on solid science as well as years of experience and testing. Having said all that, the Army's chemical demilitarization program would continue to face significant resistance.

# 8

## Implementing the Disposal Program

The Army's final PEIS, released in January 1988, was followed by Under Secretary Ambrose's record of decision in February approving the on-site disposal alternative. This option was chosen as the most environmentally preferred, risk-adverse, and executable solution for the chemical stockpile disposal program. The period between 1987 and 1990 would be difficult years as the Army dealt with the many challenges of starting up its national chemical disposal program. Actually executing the disposal program would be a much greater effort than developing a plan that satisfactorily met all the national and state regulatory demands.

As public attention increased on the chemical disposal program, congressional legislators hotly debated the pros and cons of the U.S. binary munitions program; the execution of the demilitarization program was seen as merely a process step toward the modernization of an important weapon system. Plans to initiate operations at the JACADS facility, as the pilot program for the chemical disposal program, had not drawn much notice but would soon become the focus of attention. The Army had been planning the construction and operation of this facility for some years and was eager to demonstrate its ability. The sooner this effort began, the sooner the Army could begin constructing the following disposal facilities.

The Army awarded four contracts to cover testing and integration, plant operations and maintenance, and closure operations between August 1986 and July 1994. Ralph M. Parsons Company had the job to design the facility based on CAMDS. The Army Corps of Engineers hired a Honolulu-based firm called Black and Veetch Construction to build facilities on Johnston Island. Bechtel National would procure the control room equipment, with United Engineering and Constructors (a subsidiary of Raytheon) in Denver, Colorado, purchased the major common disposal facility items. The contractors had completed construction of the disposal facility by November 1987 and continued installing the processing equipment through most of 1988.[1] Since the facility was going to dispose of more than just M55 rockets, the Army developed a supplemental EIS to cover the larger disposal task and examined additional waste disposal alternatives. These alternatives included dropping the waste in a deepwater site 13 to 19 miles south of the atoll, discharging the waste into the ocean through an outfall pipe, transporting the waste to an authorized landfill in the United States, or storing the waste on Johnston Island indefinitely. Greenpeace (and many other critics) weighed in heavily with comments, which delayed completion of the record of decision on the supplemental EIS to 1990.

After the construction of JACADS had begun, Congress added additional guidance (PL 100-456, September 1988) extending the disposal program deadline to April 30, 1997, and requiring the Army to successfully complete the PMCD's proposed operational verification testing (OVT) at JACADS before starting a systems test at any new chemical disposal facilities. This language essentially accepted the Army's recommendation in adopting an alternative approach to its original disposal program plan, and would (the PMCD hoped) assist in convincing Congress to approve funding for construction at the other sites if the JACADS had proved itself. The series of OVT would cause a schedule shift, moving the beginning of full-scale operations from February 1989 to December 1990. The OVT would include four disposal trials to examine the safety and efficiency of its personnel, equipment, and operating procedures. The trials would include M55 rockets filled with GB, M55 rockets filled with VX, one-ton mustard containers, and mortar rounds filled with mustard.

This was the first official slip in the disposal program's schedule, with Congress linking the success of JACADS to the further construction of U.S.-based disposal facilities. The Army would have to incorporate any required improvements into future disposal facilities; therefore, there could be no construction until the OVTs were completed (with the exception of TOCDF, as funds for starting its construction had already been approved). While these tests would permit the Army to develop more data to assure Congress on the safety and efficiency of incineration, it would also mean a delay in schedule and a big increase in program costs.

The BZ disposal facility at Pine Bluff Arsenal began its disposal operations in May 1988. It had undergone a lengthy effort to test and prove out each of the processing systems prior to initiating operations. Once all the environmental documentation was complete, the plant was ready to start operations. Once initiated, the actual disposal effort would take under two years, continuing through January 1990. The stockpile of 95,000 pounds in bulk agent drums and 85,000 pounds of filled munitions was disassembled and incinerated and the waste removed, with no off-post exposure threats to the local populace and no threat to the environment.

This successful elimination of the entire BZ stockpile in 1990 received very little notice, since the disposal operations ran without incident. Following the operations, the Army reevaluated its plan to use the same facility to dispose of the chemical munitions stored at Pine Bluff. Because the new guidance was to observe JACADS for efficiency and safety issues and improve upon the design in subsequent disposal facilities, it would be difficult and expensive to implement these new designs upon the older BZ disposal facility. While some of the support buildings at Pine Bluff could be used, a new disassembly and incineration facility would have to be constructed. These new costs were not, of course, in the original planned budget.

## EMERGENCY RESPONSE PREPAREDNESS

One of the unintended consequences of the final PEIS was the public acknowledgment that the chemical stockpile sites were a potential health risk to the public. The Army had acknowledged that this risk existed through the PEIS, stressing that disposing of the chemical weapons would be much safer than letting them remain in storage. While there had not been an incident at any stockpile site since the CW agents were stored and the overall risk was low, the Army leadership interpreted the congressional direction for maximum protection to include an obligation to ensure the public's safety during the chemical munitions' time in storage as well as during disposal operations. The solution was to implement an emergency response preparedness effort at each stockpile storage location to enhance the community's emergency response capabilities to a potential chemical incident. This would lead to the creation of a new program, titled the Chemical Stockpile Emergency Preparedness Program (CSEPP).

CSEPP's basic goal was to develop tools and procedures to mitigate the effects of a chemical accident or incident. This program was not intended to address accidents or leaks that occurred during the demilitarization process; those would be manageable and not seen as an off-post danger because of engineering designs and risk management measures. CSEPP had two objectives: first, to establish and enhance emergency preparedness in nearby communities, including a community alert and warning system and hazard mitigation strategies. It would provide for planning, training, coordination, and improvements for state and local emergency response and public education to the citizens within the potential hazard area on necessary protection measures. The focus of the attention was to provide warning to the roughly 100,000 personnel within six miles of the stockpile sites, who would receive less than one hour for warning purposes in the event of a major accident. This was called the immediate response zone (IRZ). Each county within the IRZ would receive an emergency operations center and funds to staff and train the personnel manning the emergency operations center. Those personnel who would have at least one hour's warning but might be in the plume of a maximum credible event were in the protective action zone (PAZ).

The second objective of the program was to institute protective measures at the chemical stockpile site to lessen the susceptibility of the bunkers and their contents to any internally or externally generated accidents. This included enhanced monitoring (both physical security and chemical agent detectors), munition overpack containers for the leakers, fire retardation systems, and software tools to monitor, track, and predict the movement of any leaks or incidents that might result in potential agent exposure. For instance, between 1984 and 2000, Umatilla Chemical Depot detected and repackaged about 185 leakers and moved them to one of two storage igloos designated for holding overpacked leakers. The program began as an Army-funded effort, but FEMA became the executing agency coordinating the off-post effort, given its role supporting state and local response to natural or man-made disaster incidents. This relationship was consummated in a memorandum of agreement in 1988. The PM's office would fund CSEPP but would not oversee the program itself, as these safety measures would be applied to the installations and surrounding communities, not the disposal facilities themselves. The ASA(IL&E) would have oversight of the CSEPP effort, and the U.S. Army Chemical Research, Development and Engineering Center (CRDEC) would execute the Army's portion of the program.[2]

An Emergency Preparedness Steering Committee, co-chaired by the Army and FEMA, became the policy maker for the program. It established six subcommittees to execute the bulk of the coordination, one each for planning, exercises, training, computer applications (e.g., hazard predictions and communications), public awareness, and recovery/reentry operations. The program assisted in the development of response zones and emergency operations plans for each stockpile storage location and surrounding community. It would procure warning sirens, tone alert radios, and emergency communications systems. Over the following years, the program would upgrade each community's emergency response capability and procure additional equipment for the local emergency responders.

Difficulties would arise later when questions arose as to where the funds were going, who was tracking the Army funds funneled through FEMA to the state and local agencies, how the money was spent, and whether the efforts surrounding the stockpile location were truly beneficial or not. The measure of success for this program was very arbitrary. In a signed memorandum between the Army and FEMA, the CSEPP's definition of "maximum protection" had two measures identified: one was to measure the benefit and cost associated with the design and implementation of the protective measure, and the other had to measure the acceptance of the protective action or preventive measure by the affected community.[3] That is, while the first measure was more important, if the community did not believe that it was safe despite precautions, the program had failed.

The program began modestly in 1988 with a few million dollars and was expected to cost $114 million in total life-cycle costs, running through 1994. The true costs of implementing this effort would grow many-fold, due to poor communication between the local, state and federal agencies, problems in implementing the response measures, an extended stockpile disposal deadline that required the response capability for a longer period than anticipated, and unconstrained state and county demands for more preparations. In addition to the eight states with stockpile sites, two neighboring states received funding (Washington and Illinois) because of the location of two of the storage sites and potential plume length extending over state boundaries.

Each community sought different levels and types of aid from CSEPP, depending on what emergency response services it currently had and what its emergency response managers (or local politicians) thought was required. While all·counties would receive the same basic equipment, each would identify how many schools in the hazard zones would need to be protected with filtration systems and overpressure fans, which highways would be identified as evacuation routes, and if citizens should receive shelter-in-place kits to create a "safe room" within their house. Each community would train and exercise its emergency operations center (paid for by federal funds) with state and federal coordinators to prepare for that worst-case scenario, a plume of agent that might threaten thousands of their fellow citizens. The CSEPP officials negotiated with the states and local communities through integrated process teams to determine what could be procured. As Table 8.1 indicates, the amount of money invested is a factor of both the number of personnel around the stockpile and the amount of agent stored at the site, modified by that state's political clout and perceived needs (the latter two factors being unquantifiable variables).

**Table 8.1**
**CSEPP Costs by State**

| Stockpile Site | No. Personnel w/in 10 km of stockpile site (circa 1994) | Percentage of Munitions within the Total Stockpile | CSEPP Funding to States (in millions),* 1989-2000 | Percentage of Total CSEPP Funding |
|---|---|---|---|---|
| Aberdeen, MD | 44,054 | 5.0 | $22.5 | 6.1 |
| Anniston, AL | 22,249 | 7.1 | 107.8 | 29.3 |
| Blue Grass, KY | 26,849 | 1.6 | 35.3 | 9.5 |
| Newport, IN | 4,499 | 3.9 | 24.2 | 6.6 |
| Illinois (no site) | N/A | N/A | 6.2 | 1.7 |
| Pine Bluff, AR | 6,584 | 12.0 | 31.5 | 8.5 |
| Pueblo, CO | 414 | 9.9 | 19.3 | 5.2 |
| Tooele, UT | 101 | 42.3 | 48.3 | 13.1 |
| Umatilla, OR | 4,035 | 11.6 | 49.5 | 13.4 |
| Washington (no site) | N/A | N/A | 24.3 | 6.6 |
| **Total** | **108,785** | **93.4** | **$368.9** | **100** |

* Funding does not include Army on-post efforts ($270.2 million) or FEMA support costs ($122.6 million)

The real challenge was getting the state officials to agree to how the money was intended to be allocated and what represented an adequate emergency response capability. The states and counties were not staffed with personnel familiar with responding to potential chemical warfare agent incidents. Many thought that the money should be invested in more conventional emergency response vehicles and assets, not necessarily dedicated to responses to the chemical stockpile. After all, the stockpile had sat there for decades, but there were real (non-chemical event) emergencies every day, and here was Uncle Sam with a big check. There was a constant turnover of emergency responders, not to mention the mayoral and local elections, requiring time and resources to train and inform new personnel. Of course, the longer it took to get the disposal facility operational to dispose of the chemical agents and munitions, the more money had to be invested in training and resources. When the locals did not get what they thought they should have received, many accused FEMA and the Army of keeping the money within the DC beltway instead of giving it to the states and counties as the law intended. Yet when one looks at the books, the money was mostly spent resourcing the state and county agencies or enhancing protective measures at the stockpile sites as it was intended.

## CONTINUED GROWING PROGRAM COSTS

Other emerging demilitarization efforts would require funding and direction; for instance, what about the chemical munitions that were not stored at one of the eight state-side stockpile sites? These are technically called non-stockpile munitions. How should the Army dispose of chemical warfare materiels that the military had buried decades ago in compliance with contemporary federal and state regulations but now unearthed by farmers and home developers? Each state with a stockpile site was already developing regulations to bar the arrival of any additional chemical munitions. In April 1989, the commanding general of AMC informed the Under Secretary of the Army that the PM's office would also assume the costs of constructing and operating the BZ facility at Pine Bluff, continued testing at CAMDS, and continued management of the leakers through DATS. Operating CAMDS cost an average of $20 million per year between 1985 and 1990, while DATS was a much lower scale operation, costing between $1 million and $3 million each year. The PMCD decided that they needed to focus on constructing and operating disposal facilities at the eight stockpile sites, naming this particular effort the Chemical Stockpile Disposal Program (CSDP).

The JACADS OVT also would add to the original costs and schedule of the program. The OVT consisted of four separate campaigns, processing certain classes of munitions and agents through the disposal facility to identify the efficiencies and safety features of the equipment. The original estimate was that it would take an additional 16 months to conduct the testing. In addition to the campaigns, the facility would conduct three four-hour trial burns to identify the concentrations of potential EPA-regulated emissions. The Army saw these data as required both to refine and validate the prototype facility's operations and to convince Congress that the facility was indeed safe and efficient in all disposal situations.

JACADS' planned start of full-scale operations had slipped an additional 10 months due to several unexpected problems that arose between 1988 and 1989. They included personnel issues in addition to technical challenges. Raytheon faced difficulties recruiting personnel to staff the remote island for two reasons. First, it had underestimated the number of personnel required to train its personnel and to operate the control room. It had also underestimated the number of personnel required to keep the equipment operational in a saltwater environment through the period of performance. Many of these personnel shortages occurred in critical positions, such as control engineers installing process equipment, control operators debugging the software, and the personnel trainers, all of which meant schedule slips as the work was not getting done. Living conditions on the island, designated by the military as adequate for military personnel, were not capable of handling an influx of hundreds of civilians. The crowded housing conditions, poor quality food, lack of recreation, and being isolated from their family members (who were not allowed to live on the island) all translated into higher bonuses and salaries to compensate the civilian personnel.

Technical challenges also caused considerable slips, not the least of which was the need to redesign portions of the facility to guard against the saltwater corrosion. The liquid incinerator and deactivation furnace required redesign and rebuilding due to design flaws discovered during installation. The rocket-processing equipment was not chopping the rockets into the right size lengths. The heating, ventilation, and air conditioning systems required adjustments to ensure that the ducts and air pressure would not spread chemical agents throughout the facility in the event of an accidental spill or explosion. These challenges would increase the total costs of JACADS by more than $190 million, of which $123 million could be attributed to the operational verification testing. The 10-month delay due to installing equipment and staffing the facility also contributed to the higher than anticipated operating costs.[4]

Undeterred, the Army drove forward with tests of the furnaces through 1990. JACADS successfully initiated its trial burns for its liquid incinerator in late 1990, fulfilling a critical step in the EPA's certification of the facility's environmental compliance and operating permit. The development of an air monitoring system would also enhance the facility's ability to safely operate. A study conducted in 1988–1989 verified that a perimeter monitoring system could ensure that any permissible agent exposure concentrations could be detected with a 95 percent confidence. The major complication would be the saltwater spray, which was creating havoc with equipment mounted outside the facility.

There were two agent monitoring systems selected for employment at JACADS. The first was called the Automated Continuous Agent Monitoring System (ACAMS), capable of detecting agent concentrations at 20 percent of the permissible exposure level for workers (see Table 3.4), which would cause an automatic shutdown of operations, with a three- to eight-minute response time. These systems were not foolproof; because of their extreme sensitivity, they were prone to false alarms due to chemical interferrents such as fuel oil vapors, diesel exhaust, and antifreeze. This is a common problem with military chemical detectors as well; the more sensitive the detector and the shorter the response time required, the more prone they are to false positive responses to chemicals that have a similar organic structure. The Army could have set the agent detection level at a higher concentration to reduce the false alarms, but the pressure was to err on the side of extreme safety.

Each ACAMS could detect one agent at a time, so they had to be used in lots of three. More than 70 detectors were emplaced on Johnston Island. During the fourth OVT campaign, ACAMS detectors within the pollution abatement stacks generated 55 alarms in more than 151 days of testing, but all were determined to be false alarms. If one considers the number of samples per day for each detector, averaging one sample every five minutes, this works out to more than 20,000 samples per day. Fifty-five false alarms out of more than 3 million samples in that time frame are a very insignificant fraction, but still one has to counter the potential complacency (cry-wolf syndrome) of workers upon hearing an ACAMS alarm. This resulted in development of a more sensitive and thorough monitor that would permit the technicians to determine if there truly had been an agent release or if it had been a false alarm.

The Depot Area Air Monitoring System, or DAAMS, collected samples of air over a 45-minute period. These collection tubes were then taken to a gas chromatograph equipped with a flame photometric detector cell, allowing the sample to be monitored down to the general population limits. The DAAMS detectors would confirm or counter the ACAMS detection of agent concentrations and also serve as a permanent record of agent concentrations at much lower concentrations than the ACAMS detected.[5]

Both of these detectors would be upgraded over the years, detecting lower concentrations with increased reliability. In addition, other detectors designed to warn personnel of low-level agent leaks, such as mini-CAMs, were added to the facilities. The fact that these alarms were meant to warn the workers of chemical agent leaks measuring in the amounts of thousandths of a milligram is something to keep in mind when one hears accusations that the disposal facilities were "dangerous" simply because a leak was detected. These detectors ensured that leaks were identified prior to the creation of hazardous conditions to either the on-site workers or the general population.

Given the extremely technical nature of the chemical demilitarization program, Congress had been increasingly turning to the NRC for its objective reviews of the program. In 1987, the Under Secretary of the Army formally requested that the NRC establish a permanent committee to monitor the disposal program and to review and comment on relevant technical issues as an independent oversight board. This committee was titled the Committee on Review and Evaluation of the Army Chemical Stockpile Disposal Program, or Stockpile Committee for short, and included 18 high-level industry, academe, and government advisers. It was chaired by Dr. Norton Zinder of Rockefeller University. During 1988, the Stockpile Committee traveled to Johnston Island to review the JACADS' construction and the baseline technology and to Tooele to evaluate the CAMDS program and whether there was a good transfer of technology across the many disposal programs.

In 1989, the Stockpile Committee reviewed the JACADS OVT program, discussed the ongoing arms control efforts under way (the Chemical Weapons Convention), and released two technical reports. The first was a recommendation that the Army change handling responsibilities for the chemical munitions as they were moved from the igloos to the disposal facilities (this would become the responsibility of the chemical stockpile personnel, not of the disposal facility operators). The second was that DOD should not continue its development of cryofracture as an alternative technology, citing the lack of any real advantage over the baseline system. Both used incineration as a final process to eliminate the chemical agents and to thermally decontaminate the metal munitions. Cryofracture, however, would not so easily leave the stage, given special interests talking to Congress to keep it a viable disposal alternative.

The Army had spent $20 million in 1988 specifically on the cryofracture/ incineration process testing at CAMDS, examining the treatment and fracturing system and testing the press that would be used to crack open the munitions. While data analysis would be ongoing, the results did not impress the Army engineers; while there were potential risk reductions in handling the munitions, it still meant increased complexity and expenses due to the introduction of an untested technology into the disposal process. The Army decided to stop further research on the cryofracture approach. Congress insisted that the Army continue its cryo-fracture research, specifically identifying $16.3 million in FY 1989 for this purpose in PL 101-165 (DOD Appropriations Act for FY 1990, November 1989). This was quickly followed by language in PL 101-189 (NDA Act for FY 1990–1991, November 1989), calling for the Army to develop an operational cryofracture facility at Tooele Army Depot. General Atomics, the contractor developing cryofracture technology, had continued its own testing at its facility in La Jolla, California, in the intervening years. The Army would conduct its own design, engineering, and environmental work leading to construction plans for a full-scale cryofracture demonstration plant at Dugway Proving Ground.

PL 101-189 also restricted the Army from obligating funds for the European retrograde operation until the Secretary of Defense testified that there was an adequate binary munition stockpile and that the retrograde program was based on the minimum technical and operational risk and assured maximum protection to the public. The Army had been planning for this move to take place during the latter part of 1990. Some in the Bush administration were pushing to start the retrograde operation in 1989, with or without a signed bilateral agreement with the Soviets.

## GETTING THE DISPOSAL PROGRAM RUNNING

The PMCD office had decided to build a Chemical Demilitarization Training Facility (CDTF) at Edgewood, Maryland, starting in 1988. As it could turn out that a different contractor would build and operate each disposal facility, there was a strong desire to ensure that a uniform and consistent level of training existed for all personnel operating the disposal facilities. The facility would replicate each function of the disposal facility's equipment and operations center, allowing the operators to gain valuable experience in the process and to test their ability to respond to incidents. Eventually, this five-building complex would cost $17 million to build and open for business.

After the PMCD office developed and completed an EIS and obtained a clean air permit for the CDTF, General Physics of Columbia, Maryland, received the contract to build the facility in June 1989. It would not actually use any chemical agents or munitions but would utilize training devices to simulate the process. The facility would begin training operators in 1991, in anticipation of disposal operations starting at Tooele Army Depot.

Because the Army's original schedule had identified construction of TOCDF starting in 1987, the PM's office became increasingly concerned that this effort should be started as soon as possible. The development of a site-specific EIS and state environmental regulatory documentation (clean air and RCRA permits) would be extensive and controversial, as the first of eight CONUS disposal facilities to be built. Because of the criticism arising from the use of a programmatic EIS, each disposal facility would undertake its own site-specific EIS and appropriate state permits for the Clean Air Act and RCRA.[6] To stay on track, the TOCDF EIS had to be published and a record of decision made in 1989. Applications for a Utah Clean Air permit also had to be completed for the construction to start. These documents were all submitted between September and December 1988. The Utah permits would finally be awarded on June 30, 1989, but had the provision that the disposal facility would have to periodically operate at 50 percent capacity as a precautionary measure.[7]

Tooele's final EIS was published in July, and the Army's record of decision was published in August 1989, clearing the way for a $212 million contract for building, equipping, operating, and closing TOCDF. EG&G Defense of Falls Church, Virginia, would receive the contract in September 1989, nine months after the PM's office released the proposal for the work. The contract called for construction to be completed in two years, with operations beginning in July 1992. In addition to the disposal facility, the PM planned to build several other buildings (to include a laundry facility and maintenance building) and to initiate road improvements to Tooele Army Depot, reducing the risk of on-site transportation of the munitions.

These new buildings and additional enhancements were ending up as a necessary cost for all eight proposed disposal sites, instead of the exception. As part of the risk management efforts, the PM's office had to ensure that all steps would be taken to reduce any chance of a chemical accident or incident. Site-specific analyses at Anniston, Umatilla, and Pine Bluff were initiated in 1988 and 1989. The PMCD had already identified necessary infrastructure improvements for the disposal facility at ANCDF, which would start construction in 1991. In 1990, the Army Corps of Engineers assessed the total cost of building the eight disposal facilities at $351 million, an increase of about $66 million since 1988. Total equipment acquisition and installation costs for the eight facilities had risen about $197 million since the 1988 estimate. These additional programs and their costs would end up doubling the PM's estimates of the program's life-cycle cost.

Brigadier General Nydam reassessed the potential life-cycle program cost following the approval of the PEIS and the new initiatives that were considered above and beyond the 1984 estimate of $1.7 billion. Considering the projected costs from CAMDS, CSEPP, the BZ facility, and JACADS, the program's cost estimate rose to $3.4 billion. The program's cost growth resulted from the Army's initial optimistic estimates and assumptions and had not accounted for the unexpected challenges of building a large-scale disposal facility to process and destroy a large volume of chemical munitions in a very short period of time. The Army had built its 1984 cost estimate of $1.7 billion for a program based on destroying the munitions at eight sites simultaneously with Johnston Island's operations, on reusing the BZ disposal facilities at Pine Bluff, and on the use of a single programmatic EIS. In addition to all these assumptions being reversed, the Army now had to fund the OVTs, the development of an emergency response program, the application and approval of site-specific EISs and clean air and RCRA permits in eight states, the evaluation of cryofracture as an alternative technology, the building and operation of a training facility, and a retrograde of chemical munitions from Germany. The Army leadership accepted this increase without comment, recognizing that the $1.7 billion had been only an initial estimate that had not been based on actual experience.

Brigadier General Nydam departed the PMCD position in December 1989 to become the commander of the U.S. Army CRDEC, where he would lead the center through the Persian Gulf War and the urgent demands for chemical-biological defense equipment. Brigadier General Walter Busbee, who had been in charge of developing the binary chemical munition production facility at Pine Bluff, would be assuming the position of PMCD. As both generals were stationed together at Aberdeen Proving Ground, Brigadier General Busbee had the time to become intimately familiar with the program.

The program lost its main agenda-driver in the summer of 1990. As a result of the Army's limited success in starting production of the 155-mm binary projectiles, the Soviet Union had increased its negotiations with the United States, meeting several times between 1986 and 1989 to discuss efforts to stem the increasing chemical weapons proliferation within each country. In September 1989, the two governments formally agreed to exchange data on their stockpiles and to continue negotiations toward a bilateral destruction agreement in a document called the Wyoming Memorandum of Understanding. Despite the memorandum, it was still the Army's (and Joint Chiefs of Staff's) opinion that the U.S. military still should develop and retain a modern chemical munitions retaliatory capability.[8] The Bush administration was determined to remove the U.S. chemical munitions from Germany in 1990 as scheduled, despite the limited chemical munition retaliatory capability available at that time (only the artillery projectiles were being produced), over the objections of Defense Secretary Dick Cheney and General Carl Vuono, Chairman of the Joint Chiefs of Staff.

In 1990, a series of negotiations between the two superpowers resulted in a summit meeting between President George Bush and Premier Mikhail Gorbachev on June 1, 1990. Together, they signed the U.S./Soviet Agreement on Destruction and Non-Production of Chemical Weapons and on Measures to Facilitate the Multilateral Chemical Weapons Convention, or U.S./Soviet Bilateral Destruction Agreement for short. The Soviet Union's agreement was based on the understanding that the U.S. binary chemical munitions program would be canceled. The accord called for the cessation of chemical weapons production and destruction of national stocks to begin by 1992, with a goal of reducing stocks to 5,000 metric tons by 2002. The accord included provisions for on-site inspections during and after the destruction process and the development of "environmentally sound methods of destruction."[9]

On July 12, 1990, the Defense Department formally stopped its binary chemical munitions program. Production of the 155-mm binary projectile ceased, as did all testing of the Bigeye chemical bomb and MLRS binary chemical warhead. Nearly $200 million in test and production was pulled from the 1991 budget, which was already in peril from congressional desires to eliminate the controversial binary program. The end result of this exercise was that the chemical demilitarization program no longer had the binary chemical munitions program as a driver requiring a strict schedule of eliminating the current stockpile.

With the cancellation of the binary chemical munitions program, the critics of the demilitarization program immediately began calls to reexamine the choice of incineration as the baseline technology. There was no need to rush the disposal effort if its intent was to make room for the binaries. This clamor would inevitably cause Congress to call for additional tests and evaluations, further delaying TOCDF's start of operations and further continuing arguments over whether the Army was providing the "maximum protection" to the populace and the environment. What the critics refused to acknowledge was that as long as the stockpile remained, the higher risk that a potential chemical incident could endanger the local communities also continued.

That same month, the JACADS furnaces opened full throttle to begin its OVT trials, completing the destruction of 600 GB-filled M55 rockets by the end of July as their initial "certification." By the end of the year, JACADS destroyed more than 5,200 rockets and nearly 50,000 pounds of GB agent. In early December 1990, trace amounts of GB were detected in the stacks as the incinerators were being shut down. While the amounts were a fraction of the Surgeon General's maximum allowable exposure level, there was an immediate shutdown to assess the problem. Weeks later, after a full investigation, the operations would resume.

The Army executed the European retrograde operation, dubbed Operation Steel Box, between July and November 1990. The U.S. Army depot near Clausen, Germany, had stored over 100,000 GB and VX-filled 155-mm and 8-in artillery projectiles. The plan called for repacking of munitions into secondary steel containers, and transport of these containers from the storage bunkers to military trucks, which traveled a short distance to a railhead at the town of Miesau. From the railhead, two specially configured ammunition trains moved the cargo to the port of Nordenham, where the Army's Technical Escort Unit loaded the munition containers onto two specially modified ships. The movement had been well publicized in advance, and despite ardent protests from the Green Party, it was executed swiftly and safely. More than 80 U.S. Army and West German army and police vehicles escorted the movement, with over two-thirds of the vehicles designated for security and emergency response. Air traffic was restricted over the convoy's path, and decontamination teams, medical teams, and firefighting units remained on standby along the entire land movement. The German public had access to a 24-hour telephone hot line before and during the operation.

The two ships left Nordenham on September 22, sailing around South America (avoiding the Suez Canal for security reasons) and escorted by Navy cruisers. With Desert Shield operations ongoing and Desert Storm in the works, the route had to go to the west, avoiding the traffic flowing into the Middle East. On November 6, the ships arrived at Johnston Island. The governor of Hawaii had protested this movement, noting that JACADS had not completed its OVT, so it was unclear if the disposal facility would be approved for full-scale operations. Representatives from governments throughout the Pacific had voiced similar concerns over the safety of the operation and the increase in chemical munitions that JACADS would be called on to destroy (potentially increasing the environmental risk to the area). They were also concerned that this movement would represent a precedent to transport chemical munitions from the other stockpile sites to Johnston Island.

The ships were loaded with collective protection shelters and mini-CAMs, and there were no chemical leaks throughout the two-week journey. On November 18, the ships unloaded their last containers, officially ending the U.S. military's overseas CW retaliatory capability. It would be more than a decade, however, before these stocks would be completely eliminated. The total cost of the retrograde operation was $53 million, only $11 million over budget (a 26 percent increase in costs, fairly good for government estimates).[10]

The success of this transportation effort was not without risk, but after all, the Army had executed a similar overseas movement of chemical munitions in 1971. This operation, while successful, would cause additional controversy for the program. The program's critics believed that the Army had obviously overstated the risks of transporting chemical munitions, given the successful completion of Operation Steel Box. Given that nearly every citizens group at each stockpile site had raised the idea of moving the chemical munitions to someone else's backyard, it now appeared that the Army had not given adequate thought to the transportation option. Unfortunately, Congress was the insurmountable obstacle preventing any studies of transportation as an option. A representative from the PMCD office would note in a 1994 interview that the Army never said that the transportation option was unsafe; the fact that the German operation went smoothly only demonstrated that this particular operation had been smoothly executed. The transportation option was not a technical challenge, in his opinion, inasmuch as it was a political challenge.[11] Of course, that could be said about the entire chemical demilitarization program.

# 9

## Managing the Disposal Program

The 1990s saw a paradigm shift in how people viewed the chemical demilitarization program, in that the Army and OSD policymakers could no longer state that
the destruction of chemical munitions and agents was a preparatory step to the
manufacture of binary chemical weapons. The loss of the binary chemical
munitions agenda meant a new ball game. Much of the military and political
leadership lost interest in the demil program, which meant that the policy offices
would have a tougher time justifying the program's objectives and costs against
those of other defense efforts. Public critics and citizens groups moved in with
increased energy, armed with legal and environmental statutes aimed at stopping
what they perceived as a dangerous technology. Congressional legislators and state
governors knew that they had committed to the Army's disposal effort and that it
was in their interest to get rid of the weapons but were in no hurry to rush to
completion, now that their constituents and the mass media were getting more
concerned about environmental issues. This left the PM's office increasingly under
fire, without a new agenda, without top cover, and scrambling to stay on course.

The first half of the 1990s saw most of the Army's focus on maintaining its
forward momentum against unexpected operating challenges, with TOCDF in
particular coming under heavy fire from the citizen groups. As the Army submitted
draft EISs and requests for RCRA and clean air permits for disposal facilities at
Anniston, Pine Bluff, and Umatilla, they engaged a heavy counterreaction from
state regulatory agencies. Increasing state involvement and new federal policies
and programs further raised program costs and shift schedules. The latter half of
the 1990s saw the Army finally begin to implement a public policy approach of
sorts, resulting in some improvements in executing the disposal program. The
construction of five more disposal facilities was initiated, but not completed, prior
to 2000. The Senate began its deliberations on ratification of the CWC in the early
1990s. This would not affect the execution of the program as much as how the
Army developed its new agenda would.

Congress took steps to extend the disposal deadline from April 30, 1997, to
July 31, 1999, through PL 102-190 (NDA Act for FY 1992–1993, December

1991). This was primarily the result of three actions; first, the longer-than-anticipated time taken to get JACADS on-line (due to the extended OVT campaign) meant at least a two-year delay to permit the transfer of lessons learned from the pilot disposal facility to the construction and equipping of the remaining disposal facilities. Second, Congress had cut FY 1991 equipment procurement funds, which would cause delays, leading to the estimated 1999 completion date. The PMCD had doubled the total life-cycle costs from $3.4 billion to $6.5 billion in April 1991, causing a fierce backlash from Deputy Secretary of Defense Donald Atwood against the Corps of Engineers and the Army leadership. Last, the federal and state environmental regulation process was taking longer than anticipated, which in turn put the already tenuous disposal schedule at further risk.

Public opposition to the program had already caused Kentucky and Indiana state legislators to require the Army to demonstrate the absence of any acute or chronic health or environmental effects as a result of incineration operations as part of the states' conditions of granting an environmental permit. Oregon modified its state statue recently to declare the Pueblo stockpile as "waste," bringing its operations under RCRA oversight. Under RCRA, it was within the states' prerogative to establish environmental regulations more stringent than those of the federal government. Groups in Maryland and Colorado had been contemplating similar actions, calling for more studies on potential adverse effects of hazardous waste incinerators on people and animals. According to the Centers for Disease Control (CDC), a proper epidemiological study to prove no long-term health effects could take up to 30 years, which would indefinitely stall the program.

This public groundswell was a minority view in the eight states but a vocal one, especially in Maryland, Kentucky, and, increasingly, Alabama.[1] It should be clarified that the overwhelming majority of average citizens living in a state that had a chemical stockpile was (and remains) unaware of the chemical disposal process or believed that the government could do the job safely.[2] The lack of a strong public opinion gave the few vocal critics a stronger voice in political offices. In addition, courts were allowing any and all parties to challenge the government on environmental issues, not merely those individuals that could potentially be affected by government actions. This increased the amount of litigation that the Army faced, as the Chemical Weapons Working Group (CWWG), based in Kentucky, and other national groups brought suits into the courts.

The result of these public objections caused the state agencies in Alabama and Arkansas to take longer in approving the environmental permits than the Army had anticipated. Instead of an 18-month approval process, it appeared that it would be anywhere from two to three years until the Army received its state environmental permits. While the state could issue a temporary permit authorization for site preparations, under RCRA, the incineration operator had to have a state permit in hand prior to construction of any incinerator. These delays would impact the expected start of disposal operations accordingly.

Congress formally canceled the requirement to destroy unitary chemical munitions in conjunction with procuring binary chemical munitions in PL 102-484 (NDA Act for FY 1993, October 1992) and outlined a number of specified changes to the disposal program. In less than a year's time, the stockpile deadline moved from July 31, 1999, to December 31, 2004.[3] This date was planned to ensure that the U.S. government would meet the CWC deadline, which was thought to be entering into force in 2005. This relatively long five-year extension would allow the Army to examine alternative technologies (again) using the NRC's analysis, including comparisons of each alternative technology to incineration on the points of safety, environmental protection, and cost-effectiveness. It had been more than seven years since the Army examined alternative technologies other than cryofracture. The citizen groups held out the hope that industry, now attracted to the large sums invested in the program, might have a solution that was more amenable than incineration. If the Army found an alternative process that was significantly safer and equal or more cost-effective than the incineration program, Congress wanted it to switch to that process, at least for the "low-volume" sites. The "low-volume" sites were defined as those sites holding less than 5 percent of the national stockpile (Aberdeen, Newport, and Blue Grass). To ensure that the Army would retain that option, Congress called for a stop to any new construction starts; this also stopped any work from occurring at Pueblo and Blue Grass until the alternative technology assessment was completed. This law also stopped the approved funding for construction at Anniston.

Under continued congressional pressure to invest in a cryofracture/incineration process, in particular from the House Appropriations Committee, the Army leadership proposed building a cryofracture disposal facility at Pueblo Army Depot instead of Tooele, as the buildings at TOCDF were more than 70 percent constructed. Congress accepted this compromise. The PM's office began drawing up process and facility designs for a full-scale cryofracture demonstration plant, to be completed in late 1993–early 1994. The PMCD would first construct a cryofracture pilot plant at Dugway Proving Grounds to develop and evaluate operating processes for the facility.

The legislation also identified a new responsibility; the recovery and disposal of nonstockpile chemical material. To date, Congress had outlined very specific guidance on how to dispose of the existing unitary chemical stockpile. The Army had always known, and had advised accordingly, on the knowledge that there were chemical materials not covered under the legislation (and therefore the Army could not legally fund the disposal of these items). These items included the binary chemical agents and munitions, buried chemical munitions (a practice that had been legal up through the 1950s), chemical munitions recovered from test ranges, chemical weapons production facilities, and miscellaneous items such as unfilled munitions and empty ton containers, chemical identification kits, and agent samples drawn from munitions or from laboratories. An example of non-stockpile munitions was the required movement of 109 World War II mustard-filled munitions from Solomon Islands to Johnston Island in 1991, or the ten Honest John warhead bomblets found at RMA in 2000.

Buried chemical munitions in the United States, if they stayed buried, were not the problem as much as the chemical munitions that suddenly and unexpectedly surfaced as a result of urban growth and a lack of institutional knowledge as to where all the buried chemical munitions were.[4] If the munitions were unstable, they were supposed to be destroyed in place, using a field process that used five times the weight of explosives to agent, ensuring that the chemical agent would be destroyed by the heat of the detonation and not become an airborne hazard. If the munitions could be moved, they would be repackaged, and transported to the nearest federal installation that could hold them. The states with stockpile sites were very unreceptive to the idea of these new chemical materials being added to their site, seeing this as a potentially endless incineration effort. There had to be a specific program and associated funding to address the non-stockpile chemical munitions and materials. The Army was tasked to develop a plan to address these non-stockpile chemical materials by February 1993. The first step was to create a provisional office for a Project Manager for Non-stockpile Chemical Materials (PM NSCM) in 1992.

Congress also directed the formal establishment of Citizen Advisory Commissions (CACs), 12-person advisory boards, appointed by the governor, that would interface with the PM's office to review issues related to the disposal program. The ASA(IL&E) office would also send a representative, often from the Corps of Engineers, to meet with the commissions. At the least, the three "low-volume" sites would have a CAC, and the other five states with a stockpile site could request a similar commission. These CACs had differing levels of energy, based on the local community's level of involvement. The members of the Colorado and Indiana CACs provided no formal comments. Utah's and Alabama's CACs agreed with the baseline technology approach but did not want any new chemical agent-related materials coming into their stockpiles. Arkansas did not establish a CAC until 1994 and met once before declaring that it was satisfied with the disposal plan. Most of the time, five of the CACs were hard-pressed to get any public involvement at their meetings. On the other hand, the Kentucky, Oregon, and Maryland CACs strongly rejected the incineration technology and vocally stated their preference to wait for alternative technologies.

In addition to the CSDP, the Army now had to coordinate alternative technology research efforts, CAMDS, and the non-stockpile chemical materials project and communicate frequently with the respective state CACs. These efforts resulted in a congressional directive to organize an overall chemical disposal program with responsibility for all CW agent destruction activities residing in one office.[5] The Army decided to create a new agency, designated as the U.S. Army Chemical Materiel Destruction Agency (CMDA) on October 1, 1992. Both PMCD and PM NSCM would fall under this agency. This change would permit the agency to hire additional staff and technical contract support (SAIC Inc. won the contract) to execute the major technical, regulatory, and public communication issues associated with the program.

In May 1993, the Army took steps to improve management of the stockpile sites by delegating authority to run operations of all eight sites to the U.S. Army Chemical and Biological Defense Command (CBDCOM, the former CRDEC). CBDCOM's Commanding General Major General George Friel created chemical activities at the eight stockpile sites, each under command of an Army Chemical Corps major or lieutenant colonel, to consolidate and coordinate stockpile operations at the disparate sites. The actual changes in command would take place in late 1994 and through 1995. This step would reduce the need for CBDCOM to coordinate with three other Army major commands on issues relating to the stockpile, but still allow each stockpile commander considerable leeway to exercise his or her own command environment. Rocky Mountain Arsenal, Pine Bluff Arsenal, and Deseret Chemical Depot would also come under direct command of CBDCOM as part of this change.

The Secretary of the Army announced the successful completion of JACADS OVT to Congress on August 25, 1993, clearing a critical legislative hurdle to allow continued funding of planning and construction of disposal facilities and initiation of pre-operations testing at TOCDF. The original 16-month campaign plan ended up stretching over two and a half years, destroying nearly 180 tons of agent.

| Campaign | Munitions | Duration | Agent Processed |
|----------|-----------|----------|-----------------|
| 1 | 7,490 GB-filled M55 rockets | 7/90 - 2/91 | 75,000 pounds |
| 2 | 13,899 VX-filled M55 rockets | 11/91 - 3/92 | 134,961 pounds |
| 3 | 67 mustard-filled ton containers | 7/92 - 8/92 | 113,031 pounds |
| 4 | 18,949 mustard-filled 105-mm M60 projectiles | 10/92 - 3/93 | 35,485 pounds |
| **TOTAL** | | | 358,477 pounds |

The good news was that the incineration equipment operated safely and with no adverse impact on the environment. EPA representatives monitored the trial burn tests, and they were in accordance with environmental permit requirements. The process proved that incineration would destroy the minute quantities of PCBs in the M55 rockets to 99.9999 percent and that the liquid incinerator could handle up to 750 pounds of agent per hour without any dangerous emissions. The operators did not detect any chemical agent in the exhaust stacks, with estimates showing that at least 99.99 percent of the chemical agent was destroyed. The EPA noted that the particulate emissions were all below allowable concentration levels. Not only did the incinerator fully meet EPA compliance on emission standards, but it far surpassed the destruction and removal efficiency of any commercial hazardous waste incinerators.

The bad news was that the rate of destruction was not as high as the Army had hoped to operate at full rate. They were aiming for a goal of 24 rockets per hour and maintaining incineration operations at 7.5 hours of a 10-hour working day; the actual rate was an average of 17 rockets per hour while operating at 6.5 hours of a 10-hour working day.[6] Unexpected maintenance downtime (in part caused by insufficient operator training) had significantly reduced their original predictions, which in turn would result in a longer disposal schedule and higher disposal costs.

The NRC's Stockpile Committee assessed the JACADS OVT as a success, based on reports from MITRE (an independent research group), its own many trips to the island and other disposal sites, and its long-term study of the incineration process. The reports were not without criticisms; certainly, many technical, operating, and managerial challenges had emerged as requiring correction. The lining of the liquid agent incinerator had deteriorated more rapidly than expected, requiring replacement with a more durable firebrick. The operators had to manually remove the glassy slag remaining after munitions were incinerated, requiring periodic (and unplanned) shutdowns. Failures of the munitions tracking system resulted in improperly processed munitions being fed into the furnaces. The mustard in the ton containers had polymerized to such a consistency that it had to be manually scraped out rather than being drained bay an automated system.

There were incidents of operator errors, safety protocol violations, and poor record keeping. The Army had not been able to process munitions at the rates that it had previously assumed, which meant that, barring the development of new procedures or introduction of better processing equipment, the time to complete disposal operations at Johnston Island would be much longer than anticipated. All of these issues would be addressed, with many solutions being integrated into the TOCDF design.[7] The NRC committee's final recommendation on the OVT campaign was that it had "judged the baseline system capable of safe disposal of the chemical stockpile."[8] The committee was satisfied that if the improvements were incorporated into future disposal facilities, the program would support safe and efficient disposal operations.

Congress would continue to press the Army to find ways to reduce the costs of demilitarization, to find alternatives to incineration, and to continue working with the NRC. What Congress did not permit (by public law direction) was any study on transporting chemical munitions from one stockpile site to another stockpile site. This effectively limited the PM's cost reduction options to finding a new technology vice moving any of the low-volume stockpiles to one of the larger chemical stockpile sites, for instance. These acts guaranteed that millions of dollars would be squandered for reviewing and testing various alternative technologies to meet the letter of the law. The Army and OSD leadership knew that there was no alternative technology that could be developed, tested, and safely implemented in time to meet the stockpile destruction schedule. This fact was not of interest to the political leadership.

The solution was obvious to the reformers—extend the schedule to allow for alternative technologies to be developed. They felt that Congress could waive international treaty commitments to ensure that there was "maximum protection." The question was, With new leakers being discovered every year, wasn't it risky to postpone disposal operations? The Army maintained that there was more risk in letting the stockpile sit for years while unproven technologies were evaluated, while the reformers charged (with some validity) that the Army cared more about meeting cost and schedule than safeguarding public lives. Congress called for the Army to report on the physical and chemical integrity of the stockpile in PL 102-484 (NDA Act for FY 1993, October 1992), which the Army completed through a contract with MITRE Corporation in August 1993. The report concluded three main points: the chemical weapons stockpile storage efforts had exhibited a high safety record of no fatalities and no public exposure to CW agents; through the year 2004, the chemical weapons stockpile should be safe for continued storage; and for the long term (beyond 2004), the safety was more uncertain due to factors such as continued aging and leaking of munitions and unknown interactions between the agents, propellants, explosives, fuzes, and decontaminants. Among the Army's Chemical Personnel Reliability Program (a screening process for personnel involved in agent work), its munitions surveillance efforts, and employment of newer, more sensitive chemical agent monitors called real-time analytical platforms, they could keep the risk manageable through at least 2004.

The program's critics assailed the Army over what they termed the Army's convenient reshaping of the facts. The Army had always claimed that the stockpile's instability was a key factor in the disposal process, and here was the Army now stating that it really would be stable to 2004 at the least, maybe longer. This became instant fodder to call for a continued investigation into alternative technologies and to further disregard the international CWC treaty deadline. The Army's rebuttal was that it never said that the risk was eliminated, only that the risk could be controlled until the demilitarization operations were completed by 2004; the risk associated with continued storage would only increase the longer the chemical munitions remained.

## NON-STOCKPILE CHEMICAL MATERIAL PROJECT

Congress authorized the Army to begin planning for the obligation and expenditure of funds for "destruction of chemical warfare material not covered by PL 99-145," otherwise known as the non-stockpile chemical munitions, under PL 103-160 (NDA Act for FY 1994, November 1993). Congress also called for a special report in which DOD would detail locations, types, and quantities of non-stockpile material; an explanation of disposal methods; estimates of destruction costs and a schedule; and transportation alternatives. This legislation also contained a special amendment from Representative Glen Browder (R-AL) calling for the suspension of funds for building a new chemical disposal facility at Anniston until the Secretary of Defense certified that JACADS had been proven operationally effective for over six months.

The Army released two reports in 1993, the first defining the different non-stockpile categories and locations, types, and quantities, along with some initial disposal concepts. The final survey and analysis report, released in November 1993, included cost and schedule estimates for the proposed non-stockpile chemical materials project. In all, the Army estimated that it had more than 215 burial sites at 82 locations, spread out among 33 states, the U.S. Virgin Islands, and the District of Columbia. The CWC, signed (in January 1993) but not ratified at the time of this Army report, specified the destruction of binary chemical weapons, recovered chemical weapons, former production sites, and miscellaneous CW materiel. This was not a problem; the PM NSCM estimated that it could dispose of these materiels by 2004 for about $1.1 billion. The issue was the buried CW munitions and materials at "formerly used defense sites," which the CWC didn't mandate had to be destroyed until they were "recovered." These represented the bulk of the challenge and could take up to 40 years and over $12 billion to recover and destroy. Then there was the basic cost of running the program for that time frame, which was estimated at $4.7 billion. None of these costs had been factored into the original program.

While Congress did not buy into the initial costs, the literature search on these formerly used defense sites was very thorough.[9] Among the first sites identified for cleanup were Raritan Arsenal, New Jersey; Fort Segarra, Virgin Islands; Ogden Defense Depot, Utah; Camp Lejeune, North Carolina; Fort Richardson, Alaska; England Air Force Base, Louisiana; and former Camp American University, otherwise known as Spring Valley, District of Columbia. The last site would become a national news item featuring the Army's execution of the disposal process in an upscale neighborhood and would take several years longer than initially estimated, largely based on the local community's reaction to the munitions and chemical materiels discovered.[10]

The Army and OSD leadership also went to Congress to emphasize the need to vigorously execute this program. Congress was not immune to the need to remove these materiels from their constituents' backyards and took action to accommodate this special category. PL 103-337 (NDA Act for FY 1995, October 1994) prohibited the Army from transporting any chemical munitions from any stockpiles out of the hosting state, as well as prohibiting the entry of any chemical munitions not located in a state into that respective state. This specifically did not apply to the non-stockpile munitions unearthed, which would require transportation and storage to the nearest DOD chemical storage facility. This would permit the Army some latitude, with careful conditions, on what it could and could not transport and to where these materiels could be stored.

Given the obvious challenges from political leaders in regard to bringing additional chemical materiels to the stockpile sites, the PM NSCM decided to develop transportable on-site destruction technologies. These munition management devices had to be portable closed systems capable of receiving, containing, accessing, and treating nonexplosive and explosively configured chemical munitions and containers. It would not be until 1999 that these transportable munition-handling systems would be available. Until these devices were developed, it would be up to the Technical Escort Unit to identify the munitions, and if they were stable, move them to the nearest federal installation capable of storing these munitions. The Army Corps of Engineers would be responsible for overseeing remediation operations and unearthing the munitions. Pine Bluff Arsenal, Aberdeen Proving Ground, Anniston Army Depot, Dugway Proving Ground, and Tooele Army Depot became the main sites for storing recovered non-stockpile materiels.

## ALTERNATIVE TECHNOLOGY APPROACHES

The NRC's 1993 report, titled "Alternative Technologies for the Destruction of Chemical Agents and Munitions," examined the JACADS OVT campaigns and other nations' disposal efforts (including Germany, the Soviet Union, the United Kingdom, Canada, and France) in addition to a number of proposed alternative technologies. In making their assessment, the group developed a set of screening criteria for the technologies. This included the level of development (conceptual, laboratory stage, pilot plant stage, in commercial operations, and if it had ever been used in destroying chemical warfare agents), its functional performance (ability to treat liquid agent, metal parts, propellants and explosives, dunnage and air streams, and waste stream requirements), and engineering factors (such as pressure, temperature, corrosion, stability of operation, explosive potential, inventory requirements, and potential for human error).[11]

The report broke down the alternative technologies into three main sections: thermal treatment and improvements to preprocessing and postprocessing operations; low-temperature, liquid-phase processes; and medium-to-high temperature processes. Thermal treatments included the incineration and cryofracture technologies, with a focus on variations to the current baseline process. These variants included the use of indirect heating and an oxidation process (to reduce the release of exhaust gases), changing the treatment of waste streams to minimize risks of leakage, controlling the generation of nitrogen oxides (to ensure compliance with federal regulations), water recycling, use of gas-holding tanks as a safety measure, and adding activated carbon adsorption systems to the pollution abatement systems.

In the area of low-temperature, liquid-phase processes, the NRC examined detoxification (chemical neutralization and ionizing radiation), oxidation of organic residue, and biological processes. These processes generally would require specific chemical or biological reactions, requiring several processes to manage all their reaction products. In general, these processes would not be applicable to decontamination of metal parts or for disposing of associated dunnage. This meant that other processes would be required in addition to low-temperature, liquid-phase processes. The NRC thought that GB and VX could be detoxified by enzyme reactions, but probably not mustard agent. Alternative low-temperature technologies were not deemed to be useful at the time of the report.

Medium- and high-temperature processes included wet air and supercritical water oxidation, molten metal and plasma arc, catalytic fluidized-bed systems, molten salt, catalytic oxidation, and a hydrogenation process. The medium-temperature processes (wet air and supercritical water oxidation) could treat chemical agents but might not completely treat energetic residues. Neither of these processes had ever been tested outside a laboratory and would require a pilot plant to work out any challenging engineering issues. The high-temperature processes (molten metals and salts, plasma arcs) had direct potential to treat the chemical agents and metal parts. All these processes would require an afterburner to complete the process, and all would require further development and demonstration prior to committing to construction of a disposal facility.

In all cases of examining alternative technologies, the NRC committee pointed out that any disposal system must satisfy congressionally mandated and international treaty demilitarization and timing requirements (irreversible treatment and completed by 10 years after treaty ratification), minimize risks of agent release to nearby communities, ensure the reduction of gaseous toxic materiels to acceptable levels, and minimize final disposal problems (treatment of solid and liquid waste streams). The challenge in moving to a new technology is that it would likely require 5 to 12 years of research and development for incorporation into a disposal facility, literally another JACADS-like operational verification test process. Some risk could be eliminated by disassembling the weapons and treating and storing the chemical warfare agents until complete oxidation processes could be developed.

The NRC alternative technology report was released on June 10, 1993. The next assessment would be a comparison of the baseline technology against the alternative technologies, assessing the relative measures of safety, environmental protection, and cost-effectiveness in addition to the practical challenges of implementing a new technology. Of the report's 21 findings and recommendations, the most important was its endorsement to continue with incineration technology as a proven safe and effective process. Given the time required to test, demonstrate, and prove a new technology's effectiveness, the committee felt that the emphasis should be on reducing the total cumulative risk created by the stockpile. This would not be accomplished by continuing to experiment with new technologies that might have potential for other hazardous materiels but not for chemical demilitarization. The process demonstrated through the JACADS OVT could be improved, but none of the proposed alternative technologies were seen as significantly reducing disposal risks. They would not reduce costs or allow the Army to stay on its current disposal schedule. The NRC recommended that the baseline process should continue in parallel with further analyses of new technologies.[12]

The GAO echoed the NRC's views, noting that to implement any of the alternative technologies would require a rigorous and lengthy EPA technical review and analysis, a demonstration that the technology could meet EPA standards for protecting the public health and environment, and then gaining the respective state's environmental permit approval. The development of multiple alternative technologies, which might not perform any better than incineration, could significantly add to the chemical demilitarization program's schedule and overall costs if any developmental problems or delays resulted.[13]

The sole technology that the NRC did like was a neutralization approach that could be employed at Aberdeen and Newport, where there were ton containers holding bulk agent and no energetics or associated dunnage. Any neutralization process would still require secondary treatment of the waste streams and thermal decontamination of the ton containers, but it was a far more feasible approach than any that existed for the other six stockpile sites. While the Army had proven that neutralization was not as efficient as incineration, the question was not overall efficiency as much as the perception of increased safety (by reducing air emissions) and ability to execute the option in a timely manner.

The PMCD accepted the NRC's recommendations and initiated a new research project, titled the Alternative Technologies Assessment Product (ATAP). This effort, executed by CBDCOM, focused on defining criteria for accepting a new technology, testing the new technologies and evaluating them against the criteria, and making a final recommendation on the suitability of these new technologies. One major change was a heavy emphasis on public involvement within the project, including bringing in professional consultants trained in interactions with the public to facilitate the group's efforts. "The public" that participated included the CWWG, which would continue to advocate any technology that did not include open-air emissions. What the CWWG was not telling the public was that this decision would require swapping an incinerator for a chemical processing factory, potentially generating much more waste than the baseline technology.

The Army leadership decided to reject construction of a cryofracture facility in October 1993, identifying the baseline technology as the preferred approach. The pilot facility at Dugway Proving Ground had been tested with simulant-filled munitions, and there had been two major incidents with 105-mm artillery projectiles. The automated process had been intended to lessen the human–munition interface and to increase safety measures, but the artillery projectiles with fuzes were an issue. One blew up in the rotary kiln, and a second blew up in the press that was designed to crack open the munition and release the frozen agent and energetics (the technical term was "low-order detonations"). In releasing the Army's decision, the leadership cited the increased complexity and costs of the cryofracture process without any real improvements in environmental or personal safety. Congress was notified of this decision in March 1994.

## THE SHOW MUST GO ON

On October 1, 1994, the U.S. Army CMDA was formally renamed as the U.S. Army Chemical Demilitarization and Remediation Activity (CDRA) and merged with its neighboring tenant CBDCOM. Colonel James Coverstone had assumed the Director's position after Brigadier General Walt Busbee left in September to assume the position of director of the Joint Program Office for Biological Defense. The stated intent of the merger was to share resources, control costs, and leverage CBDCOM's environmental and occupational health expertise. Those within the chemical demilitarization program did not welcome this move. Some cynically suspected that CBDCOM was looking to either steal demilitarization funds or foist excess scientists and engineers onto the agency.

At any rate, the cost of business was growing. With the addition of ATAP and the non-stockpile program, the PMCD had come to the Army and OSD leadership looking for a $1.8 billion increase in total life-cycle costs, increasing the costs to $10.2 billion as of 1994. On December 26, 1994, the USD(AT&L), based on direction from Defense Deputy Secretary John Deutsch, designated the chemical demilitarization program as an Acquisition Category (ACAT) 1D, a major defense acquisition program, comparable in oversight and costs to DOD weapon systems such as the Joint Strike Fighter project. This change in program status, from a strictly remediation-focused effort to an acquisition program, meant that OSD would play a much larger role in the oversight and execution of the program. It also called for a change in Army oversight, moving the program under the ASA(RDA), then the newly appointed Honorable Gil Decker, rather than the ASA(IL&E). Part of the rationale was that the demilitarization program was increasingly looking like a research and development program, and Deutsch believed it should be run by acquisition experts instead of managers of installation and environmental remediation projects.

The Army leadership initially fought this decision, as it meant taking funds out of its direct control. The ACAT-1D designation strengthened OSD oversight, exercised by the Deputy Assistant to the Secretary of Defense for Chemical and Biological Matters (DATSD(CBM)) and the Director for Operational Test and Evaluation.[14] Dr. Ted Prociv filled the DATSD(CBM) position and reported to Dr. Harold Smith, the Assistant to the Secretary of Defense for Atomic Energy (ATSD(AE) (subsequently renamed ATSD for Nuclear and Chemical and Biological Matters (NCB) in 1996).[15] There were strict rules on how to execute an ACAT-1D program, and ASA(RDA) had to manage a DOD acquisition program that would never give the Army a completed product (thus diverting its attention from other projects). The program was enthusiastically attacked by Assistant Secretary of the Army Decker, but was literally an unwelcome dead albatross around the Army leadership's neck. For the most part, policy direction would remain unchanged, because the Army's overall management philosophy had not changed. The goal was still the safe and efficient destruction of chemical agents and materiels, using incineration as the proven baseline technology. This management change created a duplicate review process by OSD and the Army, which created opportunities for disposal opponents to pit the one against the other.

With the successful completion of the OVTs and completion of upgrades to the liquid incinerator and deactivation furnace system, JACADS was clear to start full-scale operations. These operations began in January 1994 but were halted in March due to a detected agent release in the stack monitoring system. This was only the second leak detected in four years, with no injuries or agent exposure to the workers given the very small amount of agent recorded as being present in the stack. Indeed, none of the perimeter detectors noted any chemical agent exposure releases outside the facility. Following an Army investigation showing that operator errors and an instrument failure were the causes, operations resumed in July. At the end of the first year of full-scale operations, the Army had destroyed all the VX-filled M55 rockets (seen as the highest risk) and HD- and GB-filled ton containers previously stored at Johnston Island.

A third chemical agent leak in March 1995 caused the Army to replace all the door seals on access doors in the air filtration system; again, there had been no agent exposure to the workers or leak outside the facility. In December 1995, the Secretary of Defense officially certified that JACADS had been in operation for over six months and had met all environmental and safety standards. This certification of operational efficiency would permit construction to resume at Anniston Army Depot. By the summer of 1996, JACADS had processed over 50 percent of its chemical stockpile, over 1,000 tons of chemical agents.

Construction at TOCDF had finally been completed in December 1993, with systemization testing proceeding through 1994. The disposal facility had incorporated a number of improvements over JACADS, including a redesigned purge system for agent feeding into the liquid incinerator (ensuring agent would not get hung up in the line), an improved heated discharge conveyor (reducing any chance of agent remaining on metal), and a thicker shell on the deactivation furnace (reducing the chance that any burster detonation could create a hole in the furnace). What stopped the process was a whistle-blower's charge, in September 1994, that the facility was unsafe to begin operations. Steve Jones, the contractor's safety manager, claimed that EG&G had fired him upon his refusal to sign a safety report accepting hazards identified in a MITRE report. Brigadier General Tom Konitzer of the Army Safety Center conducted an independent investigation of the 119 specific complaints. The report, released in November 1994, noted that all personnel (inside and outside the facility) had adequate protection from any operational hazards, that no live chemical agent had been processed (this was a pre-operational safety survey that took place without using live agent), and that the team was satisfied that a safe work environment existed. The Army Corps of Engineers, HHS, EPA, Utah state officials, and other federal agencies conducted their own safety reviews resulting in similar findings.

Trial burns of the incinerators using surrogate chemicals (not live agents) took place in June 1995, but longer than expected review periods for several regulatory documents (environmental permit modifications, facility construction certifications, and a health risk assessment) delayed the start of toxic operations until early 1996. Given the delay, the Army began separating the propellants from the agent-filled artillery and mortar projectiles, which would improve safety concerns about the stockpile. In May 1996, a group of organizations filed suit in federal court to prevent TOCDF from initiating disposal operations. The CWWG was joined by the National Sierra Club and the Vietnam Veterans of America Foundation (not to be confused with the Vietnam Veterans of America) in claiming that the disposal facility caused an undue threat to the workers and people living around the facility. Of interest was that none of these organizations were local and that no local suits had ever been brought against the Army.

In early July 1996, U.S. District Court Judge Tena Campbell threw out 7 of the 11 charges in preliminary hearings, noting that the majority of the claims, based on environmental challenges, had been addressed under the RCRA permit process or similar environmental permitting processes. On August 13, she dismissed the remaining charges, noting that the plaintiffs had failed to prove that the initial trial burns of CW agents would cause "irreparable harm" to the workers and local populace. She also discounted much of the testimony of Steve Jones, a major witness for the plaintiffs, noting that much of his testimony had been based on hearsay or involved problems that the Army had already corrected.[16] This judgment, along with payment of impact fees to Tooele County,[17] allowed the Army to finally initiate its first live agent incineration operation on August 22, starting the destruction of GB-filled M55 rockets. By November 1996, the facility had disposed of more than 7,200 M55 rockets and 74,500 pounds of GB agent.

The PMCD continued to report the number of chemical weapon leakers in their annual reports, although their agency did not directly deal with resolving the issue. The stockpile commanders monitored the status of their respective munitions and containers and, when faced with a leaker, took the necessary steps to overpack and move the munition to another bunker with technical support from CBDCOM. There had been about 1,700 leakers prior to 1983, when USATHAMA had initiated its stockpile surveillance program. Between 1983 and 1996, another 2,025 leaking munitions, over half of them being M55 rockets, had been identified and addressed (see Table 9.1). Considering there was more than 3 million chemical munitions and containers in the stockpile, these numbers were not excessive, but of course they represented hazards to the stockpile site workers. At no time did a leaker pose a threat to the community outside the gates, although the Army was never sure if a M55 leaker would cause that dreaded "worse-case" chain reaction incident. In 1993, Tooele had a ton container leak 75 gallons of mustard agent onto the yard, caused by abnormal pressure inside the container forcing agent to leak through the plug. This incident was cleaned up without hazard to the workers or local community, in large measure due to the low volatility of mustard agent. Citizen groups would accuse the Army of overstating the hazard from the leakers as another reason that the disposal process could not wait for alternative technologies.

**Table 9.1**
**Incidents of Leakers from 1983 to 1996**

| Munition Type | Leaker Incidents | Percent of Munition Type |
|---|---|---|
| GB M55 rocket | 1,321 | 0.4 |
| VX M55 rocket | 7 | 0.008 |
| HD 105-mm projectile | 3 | 0.0008 |
| GB 105-mm projectile | 25 | 0.004 |
| H/HD 155-mm projectile | 176 | 0.04 |
| GB 155-mm projectile | 195 | 0.08 |
| VX 155-mm projectile | 30 | 0.008 |
| GB 8-in projectile | 6 | 0.008 |
| VX 8-in projectile | 0 | 0.0 |
| VX land mine | 29 | 0.03 |
| VX spray tank | 0 | 0.0 |
| GB 500-lb bomb, MK-94 | 72 | 2.9 |
| GB 750-lb bomb, MC-1 | 42 | 0.4 |
| GB Weteye bomb, MK-116 | 0 | 0.0 |
| HD 105-mm cartridge | 28 | 0.006 |
| GB 105-mm cartridge | 5 | 0.002 |
| HD/H/HT 4.2-in mortar | 48 | 0.01 |
| GB ton container | 88 | 1.5 |
| VX ton container | 11 | 0.5 |
| H/HD ton container | 29 | 0.2 |
| **TOTAL** | **2,115** | |

Source: Department of Defense's Interim Status Assessment for the Chemical Demilitarization Program, April 15, 1996. Does not include 444 leakers from drilled or tapped holes in munitions used for chemical agent sampling in the surveillance program. Another 900-plus leakers have been identified and packed up to September 2000.

If one thing was constant in this program, it was change. The Army leadership separated CMRA from CBDCOM and resumed the program under the PMCD banner, with Major General Bob Orton assigned as the Program Manager on June 5, 1995. The PMCD had overall responsibility for the CSDP, NSCM, CSEPP, and ATAP. The Army Corps of Engineers would execute Army military construction funds to initiate construction of disposal facilities at Anniston, Pine Bluff, and Umatilla. FEMA and CBDCOM executed CSEPP efforts at the disposal sites, and the EPA, HHS, and CDC were working with the state regulatory agencies. There were continued challenges to coordinate with all the local, state and federal agencies, which would make it a challenge to avoid further schedule slips in the construction, testing, and operation of the disposal facilities.

Congress finally let the Army off the leash for developing a cryofracture facility through PL 104-106 (NDA Act for FY 1996, February 1996). In addition to the Army's tests identifying safety concerns, public critics viewed this technology as essentially the same as incineration and therefore undesirable. There remained a continued reliance on incineration for agent and energetics destruction, metal decontamination, and dunnage disposal, which left most convinced that, while it might reduce handling risks, it was not an acceptable alternative to incineration. The funding for this research and development program was spiraling only upward, and some in Congress saw that it was time to cap costs wherever possible. The PM's office was tasked to complete an assessment of the entire program to identify those measures that would reduce the total cost of the program (while still ensuring maximum protection) by March 1996. This interim assessment was released to Congress in April.

There were more productive events upon which the PMCD would focus. Tooele was ready to start full-scale operations, and with the release of the NRC's alternative technology report, it was time to push forward with the long-delayed construction at Anniston, Umatilla, and Pine Bluff. Regardless of what new alternative technologies were discovered, these three sites would employ the disassembly/incineration process, a technology proven at two sites without any injuries or deaths in more than a decade of operations.

# 10

## The Impact of Public Outreach

The PMCD office had always understood the need to communicate with the public and the mass media; the problem was that it just was not getting good results with its methods. Its outreach efforts had started with town hall meetings at the local communities, which the local media covered as if they were Yankee carpetbaggers coming into town to sell a nonnegotiable Washington "deal" to the locals.[1] In 1991, the PMCD initiated national and local Intergovernmental Consultation and Coordination Boards (ICCBs), which focused on providing program updates to the state governors, the governors' staffs, and other invited attendees. The governors were invited to visit Johnston Island to inspect JACADS; no governors attended, but their scientific advisors and most of the state representatives to the national ICCB participated. In 1992, the national ICCB held its meeting in Salt Lake City to allow the attendees to tour the TOCDF construction site. Local ICCBs at the stockpile sites focused primarily on emergency preparedness and environmental documentation. The ICCBs were later replaced by the CACs.

The state CACs, also appointed by the state governors, gave the PM's office a relatively stable set of representatives with whom to meet and to discuss aspects of the chemical disposal program. Very often, these meetings became mired in technical discussions of the baseline technology, the equipment being purchased and environmental documentation and later included more talks about alternative technologies and why the Army was not supporting these approaches. Army and OSD policymakers also attended these meetings to answer questions from the public. As mentioned earlier, these meetings were very often poorly attended; outside of a few repeat hecklers and the state CAC representatives, not many of the public took part in this program. Of course, the PMCD annual investment of $600,000 into an outreach effort, supported by a total of three public affairs officers, did not go far, either.

In a 1994 report, the NRC recommended that the Army should increase its interaction with the public and the CACs with greater community involvement in decisions regarding the technology selection, oversight of operations, and decommissioning plans. In 1995, Dr. Ted Prociv, the DATSD(CBM), directed that the PMCD create outreach offices in the local community outside the stockpile sites. The annual public affairs budget increased from $600,000 to $2.3 million; in 1997, this sum increased to $5.5 million and to more than $6 million in the following years. The PMCD hired community members to staff these outreach offices, hand out brochures, and answer questions of those citizens curious about the program. In 1996, PMCD hired Booz-Allen & Hamilton to execute a more robust public outreach program. Interestingly, the CWWG responded by accusing the government of spending millions on spin doctors, using the term "marketing" in a derogatory sense rather than welcoming the government's attempts to better dialogue and distribute information to the public.

Starting in the late 1990s, the PMCD's information campaign plan was very well crafted to provide a framework educating the workforce, to share information with the local community, to set conditions to clearly reflect the hazards and actions taken to mitigate these risks, and to make the public "part of the solution." Agencies other than the Army fulfilled a public outreach role, although perhaps not as visible. The NRC members were the honest brokers for the public, often holding public meetings and testifying to Congress on demilitarization issues. The CDC held meetings and published results of its assessments of the demilitarization program's health and safety standards. The EPA also told the Army's story to the public as it announced the results of its evaluations of how the disposal process met environmental regulations. As a result, the majority of the population at the local communities are often very supportive to the Army (with the possible exceptions of those at Lexington and Aberdeen).

In January 1996, OSD formally declassified the exact numbers of chemical munitions held in each stockpile site. This information had been previously classified, as it would reveal to the Soviet Union what and where the United States' chemical weapons retaliatory capability was. Withholding this information from state and local officials, let alone the public, had always been a point of contention for those trying to better understand the risk assessments and health hazard evaluations.[2] After September 2001, this information was removed from the PMCD's internet site and its literature due to security considerations.

Despite interaction with the CACs, the town hall meetings, the outreach offices, news bulletins, a robust web page, fact sheets, and surveys after surveys, the PMCD outreach message has not significantly changed the overall public opinion of how the Army is executing this program. The question was (and remains), Was the PMCD really going after the right target audience? A 1999 independent study conducted through the University of Arizona noted that government officials often view activists as representative of the public, whereas these groups' views really represent only a small fraction of a very diverse population.[3] If government interaction with the public focuses on these citizen groups as opposed to the larger public, the government will make decisions that do not reflect what the majority want. Concurrently, when the public finds out these decisions and are dissatisfied, the mass media jumps on the controversy, making it appear that the government is not responsive to the public's needs. Clearly, the government cannot afford to make the assumption that the public is of one mind on public policy issues or that these activist groups represent the public in general.

Yet how does the government choose to interact with the public on sensitive issues? Frequently, the forum for public involvement is through town hall meetings or speaking events with either the top agency officials or technical experts trying to explain the elements of their program. While this informs the public, this often does not satisfy citizen groups' desires to participate in the decision-making process. Conversely, the government's involvement with activist groups in its decision-making processes can be detrimental to moving the program forward, given that these groups' agendas are not in concert with those of the government. Trying to capture the larger public's frame of mind is often frustrating due to the public's lack of willingness to get involved and (of those who do attempt to get involved) a lack of knowledge on technical issues.

## CATEGORIZING THE PUBLIC

The University of Arizona's 1999 study surveyed over 8,300 individuals living in 10 states and 40 counties surrounding the stockpile sites, of whom about 80 percent participated. The purpose of the study was to investigate public involvement through three questions. To what extent did the respondents participate in civic activities, and to what extent did they intend to participate in site-related decisions? To what extent did physiological, social, economic, and programmatic factors influence the respondents' participation in civic activities and site-related decisions? To what extent was the respondents' civic participation or personal intent to participate individually or contextually determined?

This study indicated that the people living around stockpile sites were actually more inclined to participate in civic activities than those around hazardous waste or nuclear disposal sites. The majority of the respondents (more than 65 percent) indicated that they wanted to participate in site-related decisions, but they did not know how. While many were aware of the outreach offices, less than half of the survey respondents accepted the local outreach office's phone number, and less than 1 percent actually called the office after the survey. The study's author suggested that survey respondents can often exaggerate their desire or intent to be involved, thus over reporting socially desirable behaviors such as their local civic participation.

Contrary to expectations, the study indicated that local residents were more apt to want to participate on site-related issues as a result of positive, not negative, beliefs about the disposal site. These data seemed to suggest that public outreach did have a potential to directly influence public participation. The desire to participate was also influenced by whether the respondent had a strong belief that either incineration or neutralization technology was potentially more effective. Those without strong opinions were not as interested in participation.

Over 80 percent of the respondents indicated that they were confident in the Army's ability to operate safely, but many still felt that a high degree of risk remained in the Army's disposal program. In part, this was felt to be linked to the Army's inability to promise that there would be no risks when the Army could not control all factors responsible for risk reduction. The federal, state, and county emergency services have large roles, in part supported through CSEPP, but the public was not knowledgeable of these other agencies and their roles.

These findings are similar to other public policy analyses. In a recent article in *Public Affairs Review,*[4] Alan Rosenthal (director, Eagleton Institute of Politics, Rutgers University) noted that most Americans were actually satisfied with representative democracy, just not the way it was working on a practical level. The legislative system has improved over the past 35 years, with increased participation of women and minorities, more independent representatives, more competitive races for congressional and state seats, and increased responsibilities, responsiveness, and openness to the public. He noted that the overwhelming number of legislators and lobbyists do have integrity and are trying to do the right thing for the public, even in the course of partisan politics.

The challenge has been with the layperson's observing the issues but not knowing how to influence the system. Individuals look at our representatives hotly contesting issues and think, What's wrong with them? Don't they see the obvious answer? The challenge is that they reflect society too well—just as the American society is a collection of individuals with different backgrounds, education, interests, and varied points of view, the legislators also mirror these different perspectives. While the legislative process is not orderly or predictive to those unfamiliar with that culture, there is a process to resolve differences of opinion, to compromise and resolve issues within a large body. People who do not like the outcomes—because they were not in line with their viewpoint—think that the process is "broke" or that the politicians are all corrupt or that the interest groups have too much control.

The media add to this lack of education in areas of public policy and complex political issues. Rosenthal notes, "And for the media, the very definition of news is a negative one. Controversy, conflict, and deadlock are newsworthy. . . the media goes for the jugular, seeking out the most sensational stories of scandal and corruption."[5] This is especially true in the chemical demilitarization program; all too often, CBS will send Dan Rather to Umatilla not to evaluate the citizens' or local politicians' perceptions of the stockpile and successful preparations of the upcoming disposal operation but rather to stress that an accident could mean the death of tens of thousands of surrounding citizens. Journals such as *Time*, *Newsweek*, and *U.S. News and World Report* have all parroted inaccurate stories about the Army's culpability in the Dugway Proving Ground's 1968 sheep kill incident as "historical background" as to why the Army can not be trusted to tell the truth in today's chemical disposal program. As an example, years later in 1976, when a herd of wild horses died of dehydration on Dugway property, the press was peppering the public with videos of dying sheep and speculating that the herd's death was the result of "secret testing" gone awry.

While the PMCD was interested in interfacing with and involving the public in the decision-making process, it had been talking to the wrong audience. The PMCD had not engaged representatives of the majority's views, nor had the majority of citizens voiced their views to their government representatives. The public's indifference meant that radical activists would carry their message as the accepted public's concern, even if it seemed intuitive to national policymakers and the PMCD that the activist message of "no emissions is good emissions" was without merit. Additionally, the PMCD's insistence on centralized control of information (from Edgewood, Maryland) prevented direct dialogue between the media and public with knowledgeable local PMCD representatives at the sites. The mass media would continue portraying the program as unresponsive based on the Army's troubled interactions with activists, which is one reason that the Army's program has so often been portrayed as problematic and its leaders combative.

A 1995 study conducted by Innovative Emergency Management for the PMCD reviewed the public's views of the program around Anniston, Alabama.[6] Their survey of more than 1,000 local residents was undertaken to improve communication between the PMCD and the public. Their findings suggested that the public could be identified into specific statistically significant groups. First, the overall public could be divided into those that were aware of the program and those that were unaware of the program. While this may seem intuitive, their survey findings indicated that slightly more than half of the public around Anniston were not aware of the stockpile or the demilitarization program.

Of the aware survey participants, the survey findings suggested four identifiable groups: the believers, who trust the Army and do not desire participation or some control; the participants, who trust the Army and do desire participation or some control; the cynics, who do not trust the Army and do not desire participation or control; and the watchdogs, who do not trust the Army and do desire participation or some control. Within the context of this book, the reformists (citizen groups and activists) are essentially the same group as the watchdogs. At Anniston, the two low trust groups (cynics and watchdogs) comprised nearly two-thirds of the aware population. This survey has not been completed at other sites, so it is difficult to state if these results are representative of the public as a whole.

The watchdogs are the least likely group to support destroying the weapons on-site and to transport the weapons elsewhere, with the believers as the group most willing to support on-site disposal and least willing to support transportation alternatives. All four groups trusted emergency response officials, the CDC, and doctors and health officials as information sources more than the Army, with the believers and participants trusting the Army nearly as much as these agencies. The four groups rated the news media in their bottom three trusted information sources and, with the exception of the believers, state and local governments. Additionally, the believers and participants did not trust environmental groups for information, and the cynics and watchdogs did not (surprisingly) trust citizens and civic groups as information sources.

These results substantiate the University of Arizona study and the Rosenthal article, in that it demonstrates that the public is not of one mind and that the watchdogs, or reformists, do not hold views that mirror the majority of the public. This is the heart of the PMCD's challenge, in that the watchdogs are the ones that are talking to their political representatives and the media about how the Army is not executing the disposal program safely or effectively. If the PMCD could increase the number of aware citizens and better communicate its efforts to the public, increasing the number of believers and participants, it is possible that their efforts would be viewed more sympathetically by the local, state and federal politicians and perhaps even the mass media.

The number of activists has grown over the years. In addition to the Sierra Club, the Vietnam Veterans Foundation of America, and CWWG (a project of the Kentucky Environmental Federation), there is the Oregon-based Group Against Social Predation (GASP), the Oregon Wildlife Foundation, the Indiana Citizens Against Incineration in Newport (CAIN), the Utah Families Against Incineration Risk (FAIR), and the Alabama groups Serving Alabama's Future Environment (SAFE) and Families Concerned About Nerve Gas Incineration. These activists often use the regulatory process as a vehicle to bring the Army to court, where federal judges would have to review the charges, further delaying a particular disposal facility's construction or operations. The overwhelming majority of the charges were often thrown out as having no legal or scientific basis, but they did result in delaying the Army's progress, which was often the main goal anyway.[7]

## ALTERNATIVE TECHNOLOGIES BECOME INSTITUTIONALIZED

The ATAP effort had moved from bench chemistry to pilot program status. In August 1995, the PMCD announced its plans to investigate alternative disposal technologies in addition to the two neutralization technologies identified by the NRC in 1993. The Army narrowed down 23 proposals to three commercial approaches: electrochemical oxidation, high temperature gas phase reduction, and molten metal catalytic extraction process. The NRC evaluated these five concepts in 1996 and recommended disposing of mustard agent through aqueous neutralization followed by biodegradation of the waste streams at an off-site treatment, storage, and disposal facility as the best alternative technology option. For the bulk VX containers stored at Newport, the NRC recommended neutralization with sodium hydroxide followed by treatment of the waste streams at an off-site disposal facility.[8] Following the release of the NRC report, OSD and the Army asked the Maryland and Indiana CACs to review the reports and provide their recommendations, and both CACs endorsed the neutralization approaches. In November 1996, the Army Acquisition Executive formally concurred with PMCD on the recommendation to implement neutralization-based, pilot plant operations at Aberdeen and Newport. These facilities would be full-scale operations; the term "pilot plant" was a term to note that, as these disposal technologies had never been executed on a large scale, this was a considered an extended research and development effort.

In January 1997, Paul Kaminsky, the USD(AT&L), directed the Army to begin development of environmental impact assessments at Aberdeen and Newport, to begin programming funds to build disposal facilities, and to initiate the RCRA paperwork based on the alternative technologies. In February 1999, the Aberdeen environmental permit was approved, and the Army began its construction effort under Bechtel with a formal groundbreaking in June. The Army began construction of Newport's disposal facility in April 2000, following the successful completion of its environmental permits in December 1999. Parsons/Honeywell would be responsible for constructing and running the pilot plant. Both plants expected to start their systemization testing in 2003, with operations starting in 2004 (barring any technical challenges with the "alternative technologies").

In PL 104-201 (NDA Act for FY 1997, September 1996), Congress requested that the NRC assess techniques of destroying assembled chemical weapons through alternative technologies other than incineration. This was different from the previous alternative technology efforts as they had addressed only bulk agents. The neutralization technologies did not offer an alternative for the citizens groups at Blue Grass or Pueblo; Congress intended that the Army should continue its research for technologies for the agent-filled munitions. The Assembled Chemical Weapons Assessment (ACWA) program was initiated as a result of PL 104-208 (DOD Appropriations Act for 1997, September 1996), identifying $40 million to construct a pilot program to identify and demonstrate no fewer than two alternative destruction technologies.

Congress directed that the ACWA program could not be run under the PM's office, to ensure that an objective and independent assessment could be developed separate from the agency that favored incineration. This program would be run by the PM's neighbor, the U.S. Army Soldier and Biological-Chemical Command (SBCCOM, formerly CBDCOM), with heavy participation from representatives of citizens groups. The USD(AT&L) appointed Mike Parker, the executive director of SBCCOM and a former Rocky Mountain Arsenal employee, would assume the program manager role. Until this program was completed and the Secretary of Defense had submitted its results to Congress (expected in 2002), the Army could not continue to obligate any construction funds for disposal facility at Blue Grass or Pueblo Army Depots. This effectively threw the completion date of 2004 out the window, requiring yet another extension.

The ACWA program had three broad phases. SBCCOM would develop evaluation criteria to publish in a broad agency announcement to which industry would respond. SBCCOM would evaluate the technologies and select the best two candidates. SBCCOM had to demonstrate that the technologies would indeed be effective and yet ensure maximum protection to the population and to the environment. Following the USD(AT&L) approval, the PMCD would then take the approved technologies and incorporate them into the chosen disposal facilities.[9] While this may sound like a straightforward and logical process, it would become very political and contentious.

A partnership was developed by the government and the citizen groups. Taking the advice to "team" with the public, the SBCCOM scientists and the Keystone Center, a neutral facilitator specializing in environmental and health policy issues, joined forces with the states' citizen groups, the state EPAs, the U.S. EPA, the Sierra Club, and the CWWG to discuss the measures by which they would screen technologies and select the promising candidates for further tests. The CWWG's aim of teaming consisted of telling the SBCCOM scientists that a disposal efficiency of 99.9999 percent was not good enough, that "other measures" would be required to convince "the people" that the technology was safe and effective. The engineers and scientists were perplexed; what technical measure was good enough, if not the standard measure of "six 9s" was not good enough?[10]

The technological debate was partially solved when PM ACWA agreed to pay for independent technical consultants for the citizen group representatives. This clash between ideologic environmental goals and science and engineering is not uncommon in other federal–public forums. Despite the best efforts of the facilitators, the groups would remain cautious partners. The PM ACWA's annual reports refer to these discussions as "the Dialogue." In a sense, the efforts of ACWA could not fail because those wanting a change from the baseline technology were essentially in charge of this effort.

Out of an initial field of 12 proposals, the ACWA program chose 6 candidates for testing, but the budget only allowed for three. As the budget had already been submitted, the Army was forced to re-program monies from their existing baseline program. At the completion of the testing, the NRC reviewed all approaches and determined that none of the technologies were mature enough to be safely implemented. Despite this, SBCCOM and the CWWG petitioned Senator Mitch McConnell (R-KY) to write legislation (PL 106-52, Military Construction Appropriations for 2000, August 1999) keeping the program alive at the expense of the disposal program.

After three years of discussions and testing, the ACWA program had narrowed their selection down four technologies with merit: Parson/ Honeywell's neutralization followed by biological treatment; General Atomic's chemical neutralization followed by supercritical water oxidation (SCWO) treatment; Teledyne-Commodore's solvated electron technology; and AEA's silver II electrochemical oxidation process.[11] The neutralization/biotreatment option would work with blister agents, but not nerve, and was being put into place at Aberdeen. The remaining three could treat either nerve or blister agents; General Atomic's process was investigated simultaneously for Newport. In 2002, the neutralization/ biotreatment process was selected to destroy the munitions at Pueblo Army Depot. One of the continuing challenges would be the disposal of the dunnage and miscellaneous equipment; by public law, all waste created by the chemical disposal program was to be treated on-site. Since the alternative technologies could not dispose of energetics or dunnage contaminated with CW agents, these materiels would have to be disposed of, perhaps by . . . you guessed it, incineration.

One might think that the Army had unjustly ignored potential neutralization technologies, since the ACWA program had, over time, identified these processes as potential candidates. This naive impression should be countered with the hard facts that the Army had earlier considered and rejected these technologies in the late 1970's simply because they were not as efficient or as cost-effective as incineration, they had never been evaluated in a large-scale disposal operation, and they were still not notably more safe than incineration. The three neutralization technologies would require between 7 and 18 million gallons of process water per year and another 6.5 million gallons of potable water per year. The neutralization processes would create a considerably heavy waste stream that would require further treatment and disposal, similar to the ATAP efforts at Aberdeen and Newport, costing millions more to complete than the incineration process. The original cost of ACWA was $40 million; it is now projected at costing more than ten times that figure by the time the program is completed. These reasons were why the decision was made to move from neutralization to the "alternative technology" of incineration, as it was described in 1978.

The Army leadership was not ignoring these facts; the issue came back to Congress demanding that the Army invest in the development of these untested technologies, and the Army and OSD leadership insisted that the PMCD employ these technologies at one or more of the stockpile sites. The idea of a cost-effective and safe program had been overridden by activist demands for "no emissions" technologies. Cost and efficiencies were no longer important factors, and Congress would keep funding this effort by specific language in the defense appropriations bills until the Army came up with the "right" answer. Once again, the schedule for completing destruction of the stockpile was no longer executable. In a FY 1999 report to Congress, the ACWA team reported that if the Army moved out immediately, it estimated that Pueblo and Blue Grass could dispose of their stockpile sites by 2011 and 2012, respectively.[12]

## GETTING THE PROGRAM BACK ON TRACK

Congressional ratification of the CWC on April 24, 1997, established the new stockpile disposal date, identified as 10 years after the Senate ratification, September 2007 (as the end of the fiscal year). There is a 5-year extension permitted under the CWC, which both the U.S. and Russian government will request. This ratification started the clock for the U.S. government to begin counting its destruction efforts; by the treaty's guidelines, the U.S. government would have to destroy 1 percent of its stockpile within three years of entry into force and 40 percent within five years. The roughly 5 percent of the chemical stockpile destroyed prior to the CWC's entry of force "officially" did not count toward measuring the U.S. government's progress. That was not a great concern, however, with TOCDF ready to begin disposal operations. As the largest chemical stockpile, disposing of the munitions there would put the U.S. government well on track for compliance.

The PMCD was prepared to meet CWC directives, having had over four years to study the signed, but not ratified, treaty. They had anticipated having to address CWC issues in 1995, but Senator Jesse Helms (R-NC) had held the treaty hostage for two years while the Senate debated the implications of having to live up to its requirements. The CWC created the Organization for the Prohibition of Chemical Weapons (OPCW), based in the Netherlands, which would send its inspectors to national disposal facilities and stockpile sites to verify government compliance.

The PMCD would also support the Russian demilitarization effort through the Cooperative Threat Reduction (CTR) bilateral arms agreement. This agreement, originally designed to facilitate the destruction of aging nuclear weapons, was adapted to allow the U.S. government to aid in technical evaluations and to fund the design and construction of demilitarization sites in the former Soviet Union.[13] The Russian government had declared seven stockpile sites and roughly 40,000 tons of CW agents. This cooperative exchange would enhance an international effort to demilitarize chemical weapons as well as increase the United States own security by disposing of the world's largest chemical weapons stockpile. Given the new Russian government's fragile state, it ended up taking years longer to negotiate who in the Russian government and industry would actually take charge of the effort. Congress accused the Russian government of mishandling the funds intended for setting up the demilitarization program and withheld the bulk of the funds. Meanwhile, Russia claimed that it did not have the funding or time to destroy its weapons by the CWC-imposed deadline and would have to ask for a five-year extension (which was allowed in the CWC). Ironically, because of the ACWA program, the United States would also have to ask for a similar extension.

In 1998, Defense Secretary William Cohen's Defense Reform Initiative (DRI) formally transferred control of the chemical demilitarization program to the Army, revising the program's acquisition status to ACAT 1C (still a major defense acquisition program but under the Army's direct control). The DRI was an attempt to reduce OSD management by transferring certain functions to more appropriate agencies or to consolidate similar defense functions from disparate groups to combined efforts.[14] The Army created a Deputy Assistant Secretary of the Army for Chemical Demilitarization under the Assistant to the Secretary of the Army for Acquisition, Logistics, and Technology (ASA[ALT], formerly ASA[RDA]). This new position, headed by Dr. Ted Prociv, would be the Army's primary policy advocate for the program. The PMCD still reported directly to the ASA(ALT), which placed the Deputy Assistant Secretary of the Army position as an advisor to the Army Acquisition Executive and as a coordinator with the Congress and other federal agencies rather than in the direct chain of command over the PMCD.

The CWWG disliked this change. It did not trust the Army to lead the program and did not like the chemical demilitarization program remaining as an acquisition program. The disposal schedule was still unchanged, which to the CWWG meant that the Army was more interested in a piece of paper (the CWC treaty) than the safety of the public. It immediately increased its vocal attacks against the Army and its pressure on Congress.

The CSEPP fell under increasing criticism for its lack of progress in developing adequate emergency response capabilities at the eight stockpile sites. By 1997, CSEPP had been budgeted for over $430 million, with about a third going to the Army stockpile sites and two-thirds to FEMA for off-post emergency response. The total life-cycle costs for CSEPP are now estimated to reach $1.2 billion by the stockpile disposal deadline of 2007. The GAO had commented that the Army–FEMA joint partnership had not worked particularly well.[15] SBCCOM and FEMA had agreed to create site-specific integrated process teams to ensure that the off-post and on-post efforts were coordinated, but FEMA's regional headquarters did not see the need for these teams. It recommended that the teams be disbanded, since once the Army and FEMA developed a site-specific plan, it really did not need the Army interfering in "its business."

The states and counties weren't particularly happy with the "teaming" arrangement either. They had the idea that the local officials would list what requirements they felt they needed, and the federal agencies were supposed to comply with the wish list. If they wanted additional patrol cars, ambulances, walkie-talkies, and (in one case) a road grader (to improve evacuation routes), FEMA should pay for the costs without question. Several counties wanted to develop a shelter-in-place capability for citizens living close to the stockpile sites, arguing that they would not have time to evacuate. This is standard procedure for hazardous material incidents, but for several years FEMA did not agree with the concept and refused to release funds for shelter-in-place kits for houses.

At an Alabama meeting, the CSEPP Integrated Process Team (IPT), composed of 12 state and county officials and three federal officials (FEMA HQ, FEMA's regional office, and the Army), discussed the desire for the counties to hire local public information officers with CSEPP funds. The vote was, predictably, 12–3 in favor of making the hires. FEMA did not see the IPT as an official decision-making body and refused, probably correctly assessing the hires as not really critical to the emergency response capability. This was not viewed favorably by the state and county officials.

A federal study released in 1997 suggested that there was a chance of liquid chemical agent deposition onto the ground and onto personnel as the result of a chemical accident or incident. While the overwhelming majority of off-post hazard cases would constitute strictly a vapor hazard, the results of this study caused demands to purchase military and commercial protective suits and masks, as well as decontaminants, for the police and firefighters who would have to respond to the incident and to control the evacuation process. The states and local counties continued to press for additional enhancements, such as real-time weather monitoring, software upgrades, and more sirens and detectors around the sites.

Issues such as these resulted in the GAO assessment that, after eight years of execution, only two chemical stockpile sites were adequately protected to the full measures identified as necessary.[16] It was not clear if this was a money management issue or an execution problem. FEMA did not track the Army funds once released to the states and counties, seeing it as beyond their responsibilities to identify where the money was going and if it was being appropriately spent. In some cases, the states and counties were slow to execute the funds and had different accounting methods that did not match federal records. Despite the difficulties, all was not dark. Most of the sites had fully operational emergency operations centers, automated information systems, and operational communication systems. Most of the alert and notification systems (sirens and tone-alert radios) were either operational or on schedule to be installed, and pressurization of selected buildings (in those counties that requested this capability) was on track. Not all the personal protective equipment and decontaminants were procured, but then again, it was not very clear that this was a real "must-have" requirement.

Despite the program's challenges, the CSEPP communities had an adequate response capability in nearly every critical area. The criticisms were largely a result of certain officials and critics who believed that the state and local communities deserved everything that they desired (under the poorly defined rubric of "maximum protection), rather than what they really required for an adequate operational capability. In a recent progress report, the GAO noted that three CSEPP states were fully prepared (Maryland, Utah, and Washington) and that four more states were nearly prepared, with only three (Alabama, Indiana, and Kentucky) with unresolved issues.[17] In 1997, the Army and FEMA leadership reassessed the program and signed a new memorandum of understanding that would result in a new management structure and a more explicit division of responsibilities. In essence, FEMA would have full responsibility and authority for emergency response off-post activities, and the Army would have total responsibility and authority for emergency response on-post activities. In addition, the ASA(IL&E) assumed oversight of CSEPP instead of PMCD and ASA(ALT).

In an effort to identify an eventual end to the response funds, PL 105-261 (NDA Act for FY 1999, October 1998) capped the obligation of CSEPP finds for each community as the completion of a site's destruction of its stockpile. It also called for a report from ACWA not later than September 30, 1997. If a technology had been found successful, as safe and as cost-efficient as incineration, capable of meeting the CWC deadline of 2007 and capable of meeting state and federal environmental and safety laws, the Army was to take action to implement a pilot facility for the technology. Finally, it seemed that the Army leadership and Congress were recognizing the need to place constraints on making drastic changes to the disposal program, changes that would inhibit or not benefit the final resolution of destroying the stockpile.

PL 106-65 (NDA Act for FY 2000, October 1999) called for another NRC program assessment, with Congress asking for advice on potential cost reductions yet reinforcing the call for destroying the disposal facilities upon completion of their tasks. This would preempt any ideas of regaining costs by using the chemical munition incinerators to address disposal of general trash or other hazardous materials after their original mission was completed. These recommendations were to be limited, however, to on-site disposal operations. PL 106-79 (DOD Appropriations for 2000, October 1999), prohibited any funds to transfer chemical munitions to Johnston Island for the purposes of either storage or demilitarization, excluding any non-stockpile chemical materials discovered in the Pacific Theater.[18]

TOCDF received permission from the state and EPA to go to full operations in September 1998, after over two years of agent tests and operations. Between 1996 and 1998, it had destroyed 10 percent of Deseret Chemical Depot's stockpile, over 22,000 munitions and over 2,300 tons of GB agent. While the CWWG continued to drag the Army into court on legal nuances and defenses built on advocacy science, it also continued to see its suits rejected by the judge. Operational delays and continued dialogues with state and federal agencies had limited TOCDF from meeting its disposal goal of 4,800 tons in 1998, but this was soon to change. The approval to begin full-rate operations meant that TOCDF could switch from GB-filled ton containers and projectiles to the more dangerous munitions, the nerve-agent filled M55 rockets.

Within one year, TOCDF was able to destroy another 15 percent of the stockpile, consisting of nearly 9,000 rockets and 245,000 GB-filled projectiles. There were also five chemical events, where very low levels of agent were detected where it should not have been, but no workers had been exposed, and no agent escaped from the facility.[19] By September 2000, TOCDF had disposed of more than 35 percent of the Deseret stockpile. This milestone was marred by a detection of GB agent in the facilities' common stack on May 8, 2000, following a maintenance operation in the deactivation incinerator. The amount of GB agent leaked was between 18 and 36 milligrams, the same size as a large drop of water, significant enough to shut down the facility but not enough to set off any of the perimeter alarms. Estimates were that it would have taken up to two gallons of agent to drift off-post and threaten off-site citizens.

Nonetheless, the reformers leaped to take advantage of the incident. The CWWG had just been handed another legal defeat in April 2000, when a federal judge gave a final ruling on its 1996 allegations, ruling for the Army in all counts. The facility was shut down for four months to allow for a full investigation, which resulted in Utah's approving the resumption of operation on September 18. This approval was rather timely for the Army, in that it was preparing to brief Congress on what had happened. The House Armed Services Committee's Military Procurement Subcommittee called the Army, EPA, state officials, EG&G, and other groups to testify about the incident on September 21, 2000.[20]

Representative James Hansen (R-UT) led the testimony, pragmatically noting that the Army had been safely executing the program for years, that no one had been killed, and that people shouldn't overreact about an incident that was correctly managed. While he noted that the incident was preventable, he had confidence in the Army's execution of the program. Representative (and later Governor) Bob Riley (R-AL) was not convinced, stating that the risk from a leak at Tooele was not the same as a leak in the more populated area of Anniston, Alabama. He wanted "zero tolerance" for his incinerator and was worried that the Tooele incident proved that the Army's methods weren't ready.

Senator Jeff Sessions (R-AL) also grasped this opportunity to voice his concerns about the soon-to-be completed incinerator at Anniston, commenting that "the unsafe operation of one chemical demilitarization plant ultimately impacts the credibility of the Army at the other chemical demilitarization plants." He directly challenged the Army's credibility, that if they did not have things under control at Tooele, why shouldn't the communities near the remaining seven stockpile sites feel a bit anxious? In addition to noting the Calhoun County officials' concerns about the execution of the CSEPP efforts, he brought up the issue of financial compensation to the local citizens for "socioeconomic impacts possibly associated with the Chemical Demilitarization Program."

The CDC, Director of Army Safety, and Utah's Department of Environmental Safety expressed their confidence in the disposal facility operations. Following a very technical discussion of the facility and exactly how the incident occurred, the head of the Utah CAC voiced his continued support of the disposal operations, noting that while the critics might be saying, "I told you so" in response to the leak, he was saying, "Nothing happened." He criticized Congress' continual interference with the Army as an obstacle for getting rid of the stockpile, largely due to Congress' listening to the critics instead of the public. The Tooele County Director of Emergency Management echoed this strong support.

Dr. Anna Johnson-Winegar, the Deputy Assistant to the Secretary of Defense for Chemical and Biological Defense (DATSD[CBD]), Dr. Gloria Patton, Deputy Assistant to the Secretary of the Army for Chemical Demilitarization, and Denzel Fisher, from ASA(IL&E), voiced their support of the program as the OSD and Army policy oversight agents. The subcommittee also heard testimony from the PMCD (Jim Bacon), SBCCOM (Dr. John Ferriter), and FEMA (Russ Salter). There were no follow-up actions directed by Congress. A cynic might observe that it appeared that Congress knew that the Army and OSD were doing the right thing, but had to hold the hearings to satisfy their constituents.

Construction had started at Anniston and Umatilla in the summer of 1997, and the Army held a groundbreaking ceremony at Pine Bluff in February 1999. Lengthy delays in final approval of its environmental regulatory documents had been the main reason for the late construction dates. Full operations at the Anniston and Umatilla facilities were scheduled to begin in 2003. While Umatilla's communities were relatively comfortable with the CSEPP efforts and construction schedule, Anniston's communities and the Alabama governor grew increasingly frustrated with obtaining the equipment and promises that they thought they required for assuring "maximum protection" prior to the disposal facility start-up. While the governor sought the CSEPP equipment for protection against the stored chemical weapons, the presence or absence of this equipment had nothing to do with the disposal facility operations. This issue would become a leverage point for the governor to force the Army and FEMA to give his state the equipment he wanted in exchange for allowing the start of operations.

Table 10.1 illustrates the increasing delays in approving the EIS and RCRA permit for the incineration facilities as compared to the relatively quick approvals for the alternative technology (Edgewood and Newport) sites. Ironically, the alternative technology efforts were the ones that were unproven, yet they faced less scrutiny from the regulators than the incineration technology had.

**Table 10.1**
**Schedule of Environmental Approvals and Construction Starts**

| Site | Environmental Impact Statement | | RCRA Permit | | Construction |
|------|-----------|-------------------|----------------|-------------------|---------|
|      | Announced | Final Approved | Draft Issued | Final Approved | Started |
| Johnston Island | Feb 83 | Nov 83 | Apr 84 | Aug 85 | Sep 85 |
| Tooele | Aug 88 | Jul 89 | Sep 86 | Jun 89 | Oct 89 |
| Anniston | Dec 88 | May 91 | Feb 94 | Jun 97 | Jun 97 |
| Umatilla | Feb 89 | Jun 96 | Sep 86 | Feb 97 | Jun 97 |
| Pine Bluff | Mar 89 | Nov 96 | Jul 95 | Jan 99 | Jan 99 |
| Edgewood | Jun 97 | Sep 98 | May 97 | Feb 99 | May 99 |
| Newport | Jun 97 | Dec 98 | Mar 98 | Dec 99 | Apr 00 |
| Blue Grass | N/A | N/A | N/A | N/A | N/A |
| Pueblo | N/A | N/A | N/A | N/A | N/A |

# 11

## Evaluating and Terminating the Disposal Program

In May 2001, Under Secretary of Defense "Pete" Aldridge made the decision to move the chemical demilitarization program to an ACAT 1D designation, taking back oversight of the program from the Army. The continued increasing costs, the alternative technology issues, and renewed congressional interest in what was going on at the facilities under construction all were factors in the decision to return control of this program at the DOD level. Senators Richard Shelby (R-AL) and Mitch McConnell (R-KY) had been calling Defense Secretary Donald Rumsfeld to investigate and restructure the chemical demilitarization program, citing local mistrust in their communities that had been fueled by what they considered misleading testimony and poor leadership.[1]

In December 2001, Secretary of the Army Tom White changed the Army oversight responsibility from Claude Bolton, the ASA(ALT), to Dr. Mario Fiori, ASA(I&E), essentially changing the program from being run as an acquisition program to an installation issue (as it originally had been). This consolidated PMCD and CSEPP efforts under the same Army oversight office. The CWWG crowed that this change in oversight had been the result of poor leadership in the Army acquisition community, and now they had the chance to work with new management that was focused on environmental rather than technical matters. This view was perhaps a bit overstated, seeing as the ASA(I&E) had always monitored the disposal program's environmental compliance and safety and occupational health program. The PMCD would remain in charge of the day-to-day management and execution of the overall program.

This management change may be very short-lived. In September 2002, an e-mail message from a Pentagon employee working under Dr. Fiori described an attempt to "take the offensive in Alabama and become proactive rather that reactive to the negative media coverage the last year." The discussion was focused on changing the reluctance of local officials to participate in emergency preparation exercises, despite the millions poured into the CSEPP effort. The plan was to improve the Army's image in Alabama by inviting local officials to participate in a series of emergency drills. If the local officials declined, as it was expected, the Army could go on the offensive by deriding their apparent lack of concern. News articles would portray the locals, not the Army, as unconcerned about emergency preparedness and the citizens' safety.[2] "When either the State or Calhoun County say 'no' [Fiori] wants a series of press releases directed at their 'no' telling the public [it] is their agencies, not the Army, that is unwilling to help improve emergency preparedness at the Anniston site," the e-mail ran.

Needless to say, there was a flurry of irate calls from Alabama's governor and congressional legislators as to the nature of the new leadership's oversight of the chemical disposal program. The Army leadership is now considering whether the program should return to ASA(ALT), with a new organization at Aberdeen assuming management of the PMCD and the stockpile sites.[3] Others have suggested that this may be the opportune time to consider taking the Army out of the picture altogether, and to let a defense agency such as the Defense Threat Reduction Agency (DTRA) take over the job. DTRA is currently overseeing the U.S. government's assistance to the Russian chemical demilitarization program, and so could provide another management option.

These constant adjustments of program management are based on periodic evaluations of the program's progress, which is why it is important to assess the PMCD's performance to date. The typical government review process takes the form of PMCD's annual reports to Congress, testimonies at congressional hearings, and evaluation of citizens' concerns. The GAO, of course, played a substantial role in the program's evaluation, releasing several reports critical of the chemical demilitarization program's execution of schedule and funds between 1991 and 2000. None of these evaluation methods assessed the costs of the program against the benefits that were being delivered, but that is the way public programs are often evaluated in Washington DC.

## EVALUATING THE PROGRAM

It may seem difficult to objectively assess the successes and failures of the chemical demilitarization program, since the two sides that are most impassioned about it (government versus activists) are polar opposites in their views. It is vital to accurately evaluate how well public programs perform; as the GAO has noted, "Program evaluation—when it is available and of high quality—provides sound information about what programs are actually delivering, how they are managed, and the extent to which they are cost-effective."[4] Of some use as a reality check are Harvard professor James Q. Wilson's two laws on program evaluations:

- Wilson's First Law: All policy interventions in social problems produce the intended effect—if the research is carried out by those implementing the policy or by their friends.

- Wilson's Second Law: No policy intervention in social problems produces the intended effect— if the research is carried out by independent third parties, especially those skeptical of the policy.[5]

If you ask the Army, you will note that it is successful in meeting the goals set by Congress: executing a national program that will dispose of chemical weapons and materiels at nine stockpile sites while taking measures toward maximum protection of the workers, local communities, and the environment. In April 2000, it reached the CWC's requirement for 1 percent disposal of the national stockpile and 40 percent destruction of its chemical weapons production capability two years in advance. By July 2001, it hit the 20 percent disposal mark, 10 months in advance of schedule (see Figure 11.1). It completed operations at JACADS in November 2000 after the successful elimination of more than 2,000 tons of chemical agents without any accidents and without any environmental impact. TOCDF has destroyed more than 880,000 munitions and 5,000 tons of agent by September 2001, and the Army has construction of five more disposal facilities under way. The non-stockpile program destroyed all the binary chemical munitions and associated materiels and is tackling major disposal areas and tearing down old CW production and testing facilities.

If one asks the CWWG or other citizen groups, they will say that the Army has never played straight with the public, that the Army has repeatedly ignored alternative technologies without adequate justification, and that the Army's risk management analyses have been flawed. They have stated that operation of the disposal facilities is inherently unsafe to the local communities, that the Army changes its interpretation of stockpile stability to meet its own needs, and that the Army continues to fail to meet its own schedules or meet its targeted costs.[6]

The GAO would probably fall somewhere in between, depending on which aspect of the demilitarization program it was evaluating. Its most frequent criticism is that the Army has trouble meeting its deadlines due to slower rates of disposal than anticipated and that obtaining required approval of environmental regulation documents is complicated due to poor coordination with the state and local officials (resulting in more delays). It have reported that the Army has repeatedly increased its program costs due to schedule and process issues and that the program has an overly complex management structure. The GAO has observed that the Army has always been fully compliant with EPA regulations. It has never observed the Army's practices as causing harm to any individual or that the Army was less than fully committed to disposing of the munitions and agents.

In measuring the impact, it does little good to measure outputs such as the number or rate of chemical munitions processed, how many town hall meetings were held, or the number of dollars invested in the CSEPP activities. These are ineffective measures that do not reflect the public benefits of the program. Public policy analysts can offer a more concrete examination of the disposal program's

Figure 11.1
Completion Against CWC Schedule

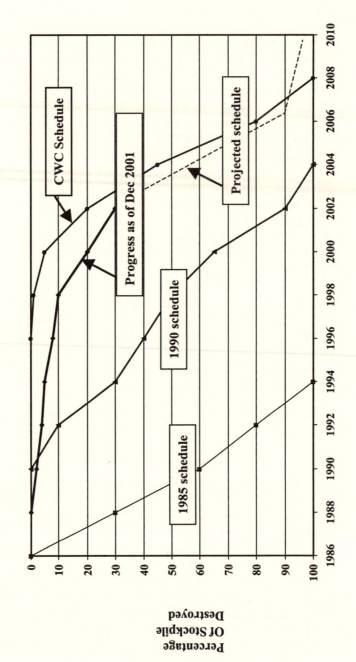

record instead of evolving into a diametrically opposed "he said, she said" argument. If one assesses the impact of the chemical demilitarization program based on its effects on real-world conditions, we could examine:

- Impact on the local communities living around the stockpile sites;
- Impact on the Army/DOD's military strategy and the U.S. government's national and foreign policies;
- Impact on future as well as immediate conditions;
- Direct costs in terms of resources devoted to the program; and
- Indirect costs, including the loss of opportunities to do other things.[7]

## IMPACT ON LOCAL COMMUNITIES

The de sired outcome for the local communities has been and continues to be their freedom from harm as the disposal operations eliminate the immediate hazard. There have been at least 80 chemical events (any incident associated with chemical demilitarization operations that resulted in an actual or potential release of chemical agent) of which nearly 20 chemical agent incidents occurred within the facilities of the two operating disposal facilities, but these incidents have never occurred during incineration operations. These leaks were apparently so minute that they dispersed into the atmosphere to undetectable levels that harmed no one; in fact, the monitors had alarmed at hazard levels that were many times lower than any state or federal emission standards. There have been zero chemical accidents that resulted in off-post exposures at any stockpile site in more than 40 years, really since the stockpiles were initiated during World War II. Thousands of munitions have leaked over the past 15 years at the nine stockpile sites, but guess what? Everything leaks.[8] The Final PEIS acknowledged back in 1985 that there would be minute leaks and that these leaks would not result in harm to anyone. This continues to be the case to this date.

The EPA, CDC, HHS, and other federal agencies have all confirmed that the Army has correctly disposed of its chemical munitions at Johnston Island and Tooele within very strict environmental standards. No one has been injured on-site, and no one off-post has been exposed to dangerous levels of incineration by-products. All the waste streams were treated well within EPA regulations. The Sierra Club's concerns about the disposal facilities operations adding to the levels of furans and dioxins already present across the country are, frankly, frivolous, given the nearly immeasurable levels emitted from these incinerators in comparison to existing levels. If anyone thinks that these standards are somehow not low enough or not being adequately enforced, they should take note of the many critics who decry the EPA's measures as excessive in the agency's establishment of environmental standards far below what is required to meet public health concerns.[9] An example of real environmental impact is the continued devastation of the Florida Everglades due to continued commercial and residential development, despite state and federal claims of the need to restore that wilderness. Of course, that's "what the public wants," or so the developers claim. The Army can claim success, then, in minimizing the impact of incidents as it eliminates the chemical weapons stockpile.

There are two potential, negative impacts on the local communities, but both are transient in nature. The heightened anxiety of living near a chemical stockpile site and worrying about disposal operations has caused increased stress to some citizens, while the majority have no doubt ignored the entire operation (given the lack of any tangible impacts to their lives). Some communities (notably in Anniston) are claiming that they should be compensated for a loss of property value as a result of living near the stockpiles. Similarly, American University and citizens in Spring Valley have suggested that financial reparations should take place as a result of the Army's unearthing of chemical munitions in their neighborhoods.[10] The quick elimination of the stockpile would have reduced that stress; as for the monetary compensation, that remains outside the Army's ability to execute both from a legal and legislative point of view.

Perhaps property values have temporarily dropped as a result of the perception of a hazard, but in both cases (Anniston and Spring Valley), property holders have not be able to prove that their land value has been permanently reduced as a result of accidental or deliberate malice on the part of the Army. Interestingly enough, during the claims that the chemical disposal plant in Anniston was preventing economic growth, a number of major corporations moved into the area (to include a Mercedes plant), resulting in unprecedented growth in the economy of the northern Alabama town. An independent report assessing the benefits and harm caused to the local communities in 2001 confirmed that, contrary to the arguments of local politicians and plantiffs' attorneys, all of the communities have benefitted with jobs and other economic infusions as a result of the disposal program rather than suffering economic loss. This report led to the Deputy Secretary of Defense Paul Wolfowitz's recommendation to Congress in September 2001 to not recommend economic assistance to the communities.

The towns and counties surrounding the sites have done well from the millions of federal dollars invested in their emergency response capabilities, but the real impact will be assessed once the chemical stockpile site disappears as a potential health and environmental hazard. If the states work quickly to get the chemical disposal facilities up and running to complete their very short period of operations, the property values will quickly return to normal. After TOCDF completes its operations in 2003, assuming that there is no catastrophic incident in the next year, the Army can complete its promise that there would be no health hazard to the citizens in Utah. The Army cannot promise that at seven other sites, but at least it has started construction efforts at five of the sites. After these facilities begin operations to dispose of their respective stockpiles, the chance of any incident will drop, but not until then. Anecdotally, the TOCDF workers held one-year "full-scale operations" anniversary last year, where they called the other stockpile sites, saying "if you had started on our schedule, you'd be done by now!"

## IMPACT ON NATIONAL STRATEGY

The first and most obvious benefit is that the U.S. government can demonstrate to the world that it meets international arms control agreements, such as the Chemical Weapons Convention. The U.S. government can encourage other nations to disband their chemical weapons stockpiles, not merely from a standpoint of morality but rather from a pragmatic view that the United States will not attack its enemies with chemical or biological weapons, so other adversaries have no basis for developing chemical weapons.[11] Many nations, having feared their neighbors' aggressive initiatives, have created these chemical and biological weapon stockpiles as countermeasures to any military actions. Now created, they may at some time desire to destroy these stockpiles upon a lessened degree of tension with their neighbors. The United States can offer proven technologies and processes to assist in any international disarmament tasks. Without U.S. government assistance or encouragement, these weapons could continue to represent a threat to U.S. military and civilian personnel operating in that region, to say nothing of the local populations that live there.

The Army benefits by being able to complete what appeared to be an ever-growing program effort once the stockpiles are eliminated. For example, now that Johnston Island is free of chemical munitions, the military can choose either to close it down or to maintain it for other operations. The option of restoring the atoll as a wildlife preserve may be impossible, given restrictive EPA standards calling for the return of a pristine standard that may be so cost-prohibitive that the military may not be able to afford to walk away from the island.[12] The non-stockpile effort will continue for decades, but this effort can be more carefully managed and executed in a financially responsible (as well as safety-conscious) fashion than managing the disposal of tons of chemical weapons.

An indirect benefit may be the opportunity for the U.S. government to address how it executes other disposal programs, such as the desire to create a national nuclear waste storage site at Yucca Mountain. It is not known whether the Department of Energy examined the chemical demilitarization program for comparison; it probably did not. Accounts are that the Department of Energy spent $4 billion over 25 years to assess the environmental and public health impact of storing nuclear waste for 10,000 years in Yucca Mountain prior to making the recommendation to move state-held nuclear waste there. Despite the obvious logic of moving the waste from hundreds of nuclear reactors to one centralized site that is miles from any town, President George Bush's decision in 2002 to approve this program met with intense public criticism. Many state representatives cannot look above the paranoid and unfounded fears of their uneducated constituents to do what is right for the country. One might hope that the administration would point to the chemical demilitarization program and ask Congress if the states really want to have "on-site storage and disposal" facilities, costing billions more and continuing to represent a hazard to local citizens for decades.

## IMPACT ON FUTURE CONDITIONS

It is unclear whether there are any short-term positive effects resulting from the implementation of the chemical demilitarization program up to this date. The OSD and Army leadership have still not recognized that this is a public policy effort and have largely resigned themselves to reacting to whatever the Congress and state officials want them to do, rather than fighting for what is required to successfully complete this program. Let me be clear: the OSD and Army leadership need to work with Congress and state and local officials to be successful. They do not, however, need to be held hostage to citizen groups' demands, especially when it is not in the public's best interests to accommodate every whim that these reformist agendas outline.

Each program manager who had to oversee the chemical demilitarization program, as well as every stockpile site commanders, would tell you that the Army leadership and PMCD have listened to the people who lived around the stockpiles, that they have worked closely with the governors and mayors (and, in most cases, the congressional legislators), and that they have responded positively to the public's desire for involvement. It has been the political overreaction to activist demands that caused the majority of cost and schedule slips and that have caused controversy to overshadow the successes of the program. Yet the question remains, How could the Army improve the future public debates on chemical and biological warfare issues?

Take the recent concern (following 9/11) that the stockpiles represent a potential terrorist target that, if attacked, could have major consequences for the local communities and that the Army needs to accelerate the program to reduce this risk. Let us ignore, for a moment, the fact that at six of the eight sites, the chemical weapons are stored in massive concrete igloos that would require a major amount of explosives to gain egress, let alone bypassing the security forces and alarm systems that are at each stockpile site. While a plane could deliberately crash into the bunkers, these bunkers are not the World Trade Towers—they are difficult to see from the sky and present very small targets. It is enough that the state and congressional delegations now want the Army to speed up what has been a very deliberate and bureaucratic process of ensuring the maximum safety to the public and environment. Now they want to accelerate the schedule? The Army is completely willing, but it will take millions of dollars, perhaps billions, to accomplish this process within federal and state regulations.

The Army should capitalize on the success of this program, if nothing else but to demonstrate that it has been a good steward of a public program, ensuring "maximum protection" that resulted in zero casualties. It should engage the Congress and OSD leadership to develop the bonds that were absent these past years, especially as the concerns about chemical and biological terrorism incidents within the United States continue to mount. The development of a homeland security program will require subject-matter experts to address these threats; while chemical and biological agents are not the most likely threats (compared to good old conventional and improvised explosives), the impact (real and psychological) of such weapons far exceeds the actual damage done. Effective response requires someone to develop executable and affordable plans. This will require not merely technical knowledge but savvy on how to work with Congress, other government agencies, and the public on a very frightening issue.

As the U.S. government has agreed never to produce chemical or biological munitions, the long-term positive effects for the Army acquisition program are as yet unclear. It is not as if the Army could apply any lessons learned to future chemical demilitarization programs, but it may have some impact on conventional ammunition demilitarization efforts, where the Army is considering more environmentally safe means of disposal than open-pit burning. Hopefully, the Army will consider the cost-benefits of any new approaches rather than blind obedience to a poorly defined "maximum protection" end state. It could be that someone in OSD has noticed this lesson; Deputy Secretary of Defense Wolfowitz released a DOD policy memorandum in September 2002 declaring that all civilians on military bases will have "appropriate protection" against chemical and biological hazards caused by terrorist incidents—much more reasonable and executable than a declaration for "maximum protection."

## DIRECT COSTS

Of course, the Army has overshot its original 1984 budget estimate of $1.7 billion, when all the Army was proposing to do was to dispose of chemical munitions at eight stockpile sites within a nine-year period. That was a parametric estimate without real experience building and operating a full-scale disposal plant and should not be considered the real baseline measure. Brigadier General Nydam's estimate of $3.4 billion following the release of the PEIS is a much more credible baseline, but that budget soon was eclipsed by additional program costs. That being said, most critics still point out costs exceeding a 5-fold increase and a schedule that has changed its end date at least six times already. Evaluating the Army's execution of the program in terms of cost and schedule would certainly drive one to conclude that the disposal program has been a failure. Congressional detractors such as Senator Mitch McConnell (R-KY) have stated that the Army has "made every mistake in the book: poorly run, behind schedule and deceptive on top of it. [The Pentagon] may need to clean that office out and start all over again."[13]

This is a dramatic overstatement and not considerate of other factors, not surprising given that the senator is stating his constituents' views rather than making a rational evaluation, yet understandable given the results of an OSD program review in September 2001. At this review, the Army estimated that the program could require $4.7 billion above the formerly estimated $15 billion to complete disposal efforts, not including the non-stockpile efforts addressing former DOD chemical munitions disposal sites. The OSD program review added another $2 billion to account for unanticipated risks that might cause additional delays. The

May 2002 record of decision to use water-based neutralization at Pueblo will certainly be part of that increased costs. Because of the alternative technologies chosen for the Pueblo and Blue Grass sites, the completion of all disposal efforts will not be completed by the CWC end date of 2007. Factors cited included the usual reasons: lower than expected disposal rates at current incineration facilities, delays in obtaining environmental permits, additional environmental safety measures and emergency preparedness measures taken in response to public concerns, higher costs for labor and equipment, untested alternative technologies, and the continued need to address leakers in the aging stockpiles. The Army's overly complex management structure may also be a factor in their continual failure to plan and program for funding and to anticipate schedule slips. The Army has been fairly criticized for the overly optimistic (some would say completely unrealistic) budgeting and schedule anticipation.

Congress is not without blame for this condition. Its incrementalist approach to addressing the program has resulted in poorly crafted legislation and indiscriminate funding cuts, focusing on immediate political benefits rather than addressing the total program costs and benefits. The constant search for alternative technologies added billions of dollars in unnecessary costs and years to the deadline schedule, even as the NRC and other reputable agencies gave Congress clear evidence that the technical immaturity of alternative technologies ruled them out as viable solutions. Certain congressional representatives had to show their constituents that they were ensuring the Army did its job correctly. This is not a blanket indictment of all members of Congress; recently, some congressmen, having seen TOCDF in action, have commented that the Army actually was doing the job well. Unfortunately, the mass media usually do not capture and broadcast those comments.

The Bush administration's FY 2003 budget request to Congress included a review of selected DoD programs and their effectiveness. The Army's chemical demilitarization program was noted as ineffective, with the following note: "The Army's program to destroy the U.S. stockpile of chemical weapons is behind schedule. Costs have increased over 60 percent, from $15 billion to $24 billion. These delays are the result of various difficulties, including unrealistic schedules, site safety and environmental concerns, and poor planning."[14]

The Bush administration's indictment is unduly harsh, not only because of the reasons just cited. It simplifies an extraordinarily complex issue and ignores the complete lack of focus of the national or military leadership on ways to get this program back on schedule. What is often not considered is that the early estimates in the late 1980s were parametric cost estimates that were not based on any actual experience. When the PMCD had the chance to rebaseline costs on JACADS' performance after the first OVT, its estimate was a more defendable $8.6 billion. This was before the many delays from the states, start of the non-stockpile program, CSEPP's ballooning costs, and the alternative technology efforts. The GAO has noted that many officials and other individuals have already identified numerous cost-saving measures. These suggestions would require decision makers to contemplate the takeoffs between costs and benefits and would require changes in existing legal requirements. The suggestions include stopping the alternative technology program, consolidating disposal operations at regional sites, destroying selected non-stockpile chemical warfare materiel at stockpile disposal facilities, establishing a centralized disposal facility for non-stockpile chemical warfare materiel, and modifying existing laws and regulations to standardize environmental requirements.[15]

The real kicker is that the same congressional committees and their staffers that criticize the Army are really not concerned about the overall program costs; in fact, when OSD leaders went to Congress with cost-reduction options, they were summarily thrown out as interfering with "Congress' budget and business." Under the current political system, it is impossible to reduce the size of a congressionally-directed program. Dr. Prociv made numerous enemies in congressional staff when he proposed a $800 million savings. One of the comments received was "Who are you to reduce the size of MY program?" Congress's calls for cost-saving alternatives are just a facade to demonstrate to their constituents that they are trying to be responsible managers of taxpayers' funds. This mind-set will be reviewed more in the next chapter.

## INDIRECT AND SYMBOLIC COSTS

Identifying what the government could have done with the $24 billion that will be spent on this program is probably too difficult to assess and subject to a great deal of conjecture. There are two aspects in reviewing the cost of implementing the demilitarization program: where the funds could have gone and what this effort cost the Army in terms of symbolic measures such as credibility and prestige. While Congress has asked the Army to identify ways to reduce costs in this program, let us not delude ourselves that it was that concerned about the bottom line. When the Citizens against Public Waste identify more than $20 billion in FY 2002 appropriations as potential pork projects—$20 billion in one year—spending $24 billion over a 25- to 30-year period is a drop in the proverbial bucket.[16] As another example, the EPA's Superfund program has skyrocketed from a modest $1.6 billion initial allocation in 1978 (a cost estimate that Congress and the EPA knew was way too low) to $28 billion for total life-cycle costs today.

Financially, this program has cost taxpayers, in broad terms, a little more than $650 million a year on average, which in government terms, is not much in military acquisition budgets (see Appendix A). In 1999, the chemical demilitarization program's $15 billion in life-cycle costs could be compared to other major defense programs such as the Abram tank upgrade ($8.1 billion), the Comanche helicopter program ($8.2 billion), the Titan IV rocket ($17.6 billion), and the Family of Medium Tactical Vehicles program ($18.1 billion). Essentially, funding the demilitarization program meant that the Army is not funding one of its major acquisition programs. In its recent decisions to stop several major acquisition programs to fund its future transformation efforts (the Interim Brigade Combat Team, Crusader, Comanche), an extra $650 million to $1 billion a year could have come in handy.

The Army as a whole will not lose any symbolic face with the eventual end of this program since, for the most part, the military leadership has not been engaged. Most of the general officers will just sigh and think, "Thank goodness, no more pokes in eye!" It has always been a Chemical Corps issue or, at best, the Secretary of the Army's concern and not a real military operations or acquisition issue. With the tight direction of congressional directives and OSD funding, the chemical demilitarization program has not directly sapped the Army's strength at all.

Symbolically, the Chemical Corps' difficulty in executing this program will continue to hurt its relations with the public. While there has never been an off-post exposure incident, critics will continue to point at the PMCD's relationships with the local and state officials and claim this as evidence of "big government" trying to drive the public into a bad decision. Overall, the public still trusts the Army to fight its conflicts, but executing programs that directly impact the public (such as Spring Valley) remains a point of contention. In addition to the inherent lack of trust that many citizens feel about government programs, the Army in general and Chemical Corps in particular have not done well in addressing issues relating to Agent Orange, the Gulf War illness issue, the anthrax vaccination program, and responding to potential CB terrorism incidents in the United States. Many of these are related to the chemical demilitarization issue and can be elaborated upon in the next chapter.

## ADJUSTING AND TERMINATING THE PROGRAM

As this book has identified, the PMCD has adjusted its program several times, based on the constant flood of public criticism, demands from Congress, and technical observations from the NRC and others. By the late 1990s, the Army and OSD leadership had capitulated to running the program any way that Congress wants, giving up the leadership role seen in earlier years in an effort to please Congress and keep the controversy to a minimum. In reality, all the hard decisions have been made, and all the PMCD really has to do is be a good steward and carry out its legal obligations as best it can. Unlike other public policy efforts, this program actually has an end, when the stockpile sites are eliminated, and the facilities will eventually complete their disposal operations. The program will terminate some time over the next 10 or 15 years, pending any additional direction from Senator McConnell or the CWWG.

TOCDF completed its disposal of GB munitions and containers in March 2002 and began preparing for its VX disposal campaign when it hit another pothole. Two workers were exposed to low levels of sarin on July 15, 2002, as they were providing routine maintenance on an agent purge line of the liquid incinerator primary room. When the alarms went off, the two donned masks and evacuated. One worker showed no symptoms of exposure, while the other did exhibit lowered cholinesterase levels. Operations at the facility have stopped until the investigation is completed (this investigation has not been completed as of December 2002).

The incineration facilities constructed at Anniston was to begin full operations in September 2002, but Alabama's governor continued his obstruction of the disposal start-up until $40 million in unnecessary emergency response gear arrived. The Army is offering $8 million in protective masks for 35,000 nearby citizens, a move that could blow up in their face if a poorly-trained civilian suffocates trying to don a mask (as has happened in Israel). As a result, incineration operations will not start until March 2003. If started on time and allowed to run without undue interference, the operations could conclude by 2007, 2008 at the latest.

Umatilla started its systemization tests in 2002 and Pine Bluff should start its tests in late 2003 unless it is delayed for some reason. These incineration-based facilities have observed JACADS and TOCDF as models to identify how to improve the processing equipment, run the operations, and interact with the emergency coordinators. Barring *60 Minutes* investigations (such as the November 10 segment that called Anniston "Toxic Town" and made unfounded allegations about hazardous leaks, there really should be no challenges in completing operations prior to the revised CWC treaty deadline of 2012. What could complicate this is the Army's recent proposal to Oregon officials to destroy the mustard-filled ton containers at Umatilla with the water-based neutralization process. The mustard stocks constitute nearly 63 percent of the Umatilla stockpile, which means that incineration would still be required for the rest of the munitions. If the Oregon officials accept this proposal, this would increase costs and the time to complete the disposal process to 2009, with some estimates going to 2011 for the least hazardous chemical warfare agent in that stockpile.

The good news about the Aberdeen and Newport facilities is that they were already on a glide path toward eliminating their stockpiles in the next few years. As noted in the first chapter, the proposal to quickly reduce the chemical agent stocks at Aberdeen to their major components was accepted, with the understanding that the liquid wastes would have to be treated a second time at an off-site commercial biological treatment facility to thoroughly eliminate any chance of reconstituting the chemical agents. Barring any problems with implementing the technologies (considering that neither technology had never been operated on this large scale), the two facilities should be able to dispose of their stocks and close operations prior to the deadline of 2007.

It is the Pueblo and Blue Grass stocks that prevent the United States from meeting the 2007 deadline, which is ironic given that Blue Grass is the smallest chemical stockpile and Pueblo holds only relatively safe mustard-filled munitions. Aldridge made the decision to use the same water-based neutralization process used at Aberdeen at Pueblo, and Senator McConnell is relatively sure his site will receive an alternative technology decision soon. The PM ACWA has technologies that could be employed at the two facilities, but these processes will still require a second disposal process for the dunnage and energetics and a decontamination process for the metal munitions, something like incineration. There are disputes between the PMCD and SBCCOM as to who should execute the disposal operations at the two sites; the ACWA program believes that it should continue its alternative technology efforts (funded through research and development dollars) instead of the PMCD taking over and funding the effort as at its other facilities (procurement and operations and maintenance dollars).

The terrorism watches since 9/11 and the focus not to worry about the waste products has played to ACWA's benefit. The biggest unknown, according to the NAS, was the quantity and consistency of the waste products resulting from these technologies (including those used at Aberdeen and Newport). The Army and OSD leadership could have unemotionally and logically assessed the ACWA technologies and found that they were not safer technologies, nor were they more cost-effective or efficient, and made a decision to continue with the construction of incineration facilities. They did not, probably fearing the howls from the congressional delegations of those states, however misguided those politicians and the "no-emissions" reformists are.

The Army and OSD leadership could have taken advantage of the emergency period in which we found ourselves following 9/11, where the common sense of doing the right thing seemed to overwhelm the political sensitivities of our elected officials. The Army could have proposed that DOD move the Pueblo stocks to Tooele, as the Pueblo stocks are all mustard-filled munitions and ton containers and are the least troublesome munitions to attempt to move. It could have proposed that DOD move the Blue Grass stocks to Pine Bluff Arsenal, the one East Coast disposal site whose community has a good relationship with the Army and actually trusts the Army to do the right thing. These are not simple measures, but the Army has proven that it can safely transport chemical munitions over long distances, it would make the local citizens in two states happy, the receiving states (in all likelihood) would not complain too loud if compensated properly, and the transit states could do the noble thing and work with the government to ensure that this transportation occurs safely. It would save literally billions of dollars and allow the completion of the chemical disposal program on time. That time window has passed, unfortunately, and business/politics as ususal seems to again prevail.

It is a practical and defendable concept to reduce the overall risk to the public and save taxpayers' money, but it makes entirely too much sense, so it will not happen. Every time the PMCD tries to do the right thing, something unexpected happens to delay the program further.[17] Part of the challenge is that, in the public sector, the costs of making a mistake are far greater than the potential reward for performing more efficiently. As long as the mass media promote scandal and waste over common sense and politicians remain highly partisan, Americans will not trust public officials, and these officials will not make the bold decisions to do what needs to be done. It appears that the few public officials who do attempt bold decisions in this program ultimately are punished.[18]

The CSEPP effort is designed, by public law, to cease following the end of disposal operations at each stockpile site. This insurance policy, which in all probability will never be used, will elapse after 2007 (except for those two sites), costing the taxpayer more than $1.2 billion. Once the program terminates, there will be several counties and states with state-of-the-art response equipment to their benefit. The program does have an unexpected benefit for those communities and military bases in the United States that are concerned about chemical and biological terrorism. Here is the perfect model for how to develop a local program for responding to unconventional terrorism, if your community or military base sees the need. More than likely, they will want the funds to augment underfunded police and firefighter capabilities that are not directly related to responding to chemical or biological terrorism incidents, if CSEPP is to be of any example.

The non-stockpile project is perhaps the one aspect of this program that will not die, at least not for several decades. While the PM NSCM has efficiently worked its way through the binary materiels and is moving onto former production facilities, potentially there are still buried chemical munitions and materiels all over the country. Estimates are that it could take up to 30 more years and another $12–15 billion to complete the investigation and remediation efforts. Nothing is free,[19] and if the "no emissions" crowd insists that the military erect massive collective protection globes over each unearthed munition, as done at Rocky Mountain Arsenal in November 2001, the costs will grow. Of course, this is small potatoes compared to the defense budget and is well worth the Army's effort to ensure the public's safety. Buried, these munitions and materiels will not pose any danger until they are unearthed. Since the total weight of CW materiels is often very small, the overall hazard to the public as a result of any one unearthing is correspondingly very small and manageable.

How did the chemical demilitarization program fail to succeed as a public policy issue? It really was a group effort; other than an Army culture that does not know how to deal with Congress or public policy issues, ideologic critics, local politicians pressing relentlessly to make the Army pay for their local issues, and congressional representatives dismissed legitimate questions and ignored the need for well-crafted legislation. In fact, the local and state politicians and Congressional delegations did their best to encumber the law with exceptions and special interests for their own benefit. There was a lack of accountability for results that could force Congress to assume responsibility to actually complete the disposal process safely and effectively, and the mass media refused to educate the public but often overdramatized accounts of the hazards at the stockpile sites and disposal facilities. When JACADS operations were completed, the focus on Tooele redoubled. As TOCDF passed three years of relatively smooth operations, the controversy erupted at Anniston. This program has had a massive Sisyphus complex since 1985. There has been literally no end to the struggle.

As a final note in the discussion about the Army's chemical demilitarization program, let us review the ultimate measure of success that so many people worry about. In 1998, the CDC's National Center for Injury Prevention and Control noted 724,859 deaths in the United States caused by heart disease. There were 541,532 malignant tumors (about two-thirds were individuals over 65), and 158,448 strokes that led to death. More than 42,000 deaths were caused by motor vehicles, nearly 11,000 by unintentional ingestion of poison, 4,400 drownings and 4,500 suffocations. Over 12,000 citizens died as a result of a homicide caused by a firearm, and another 17,400 ended their lives with a firearm. U.S. cases of HIV-related deaths in 1998 numbered 13,426.[20]

In 1998, that same year, the U.S. government allocated $551.7 million on chemical demilitarization efforts. No one died at or around the stockpile sites or disposal facilities as a result of a CW agent incident in that year; in fact, no one on- or off-post has died under the Army's stewardship of the chemical demilitarization program since 1972. How many American citizens' lives could the U.S. government have saved in 1998 if that half-billion dollars were allocated toward more immediate threats and hazards? The role of public policy advocates is to make the Congress aware of what their programs are doing (and not doing) for the people. It is even more important that the Army demonstrate the positive steps that it is taking for the American public.

# 12

## Reflecting on Public Policy

In a *Washington Post* article published in February 2002, political strategist Ralph Reed offered some philosophy about the services that he could provide Enron Corporation in the way of political lobbying. He wrote, "In public policy, it matters less who has the best arguments and more who gets heard—and by whom."[1] This simple statement summarizes the challenges faced by the Army's chemical demilitarization program in a nutshell. It did not matter that the Army had made good decisions based on a reasoned assessment of the overall risk and applied funding as directed by Congress in a responsible fashion. What mattered was that its message was not reaching the state and federal political leadership, while its critics' advocacy science-based arguments were.

I did not originally purport to offer any solutions to the Army chemical demilitarization program; in fact, I originally thought that it would be folly to suggest that any changes to the program be made at all. The intent of this book was to demonstrate that the chemical demilitarization program was indeed a public policy issue and, from that angle, that public policy could offer an approach to addressing the chemical demilitarization program and similar chemical and biological defense issues. That was until I heard about the ASA(IL&E)'s suggestion in 2002 to use alternative technologies for the mustard-filled munitions at Umatilla, in addition to the use of incineration for the nerve-agent munitions. Then the news came that the ASA(I&E) office was conspiring to make Anniston's local officials look bad. I thought to myself, "These guys just aren't getting it." It is not too late to correct how the program executes its congressionally-derived charter. The recommendations in this chapter will not surprise advocates of public policy, but, in that same light, they represent new thinking for the OSD and Army leadership and the PMCD office.

### ROLE OF THE ARMY

Going back to Stephen Scroggs' thought-provoking book *Army Relations with Congress*, it appears that the Army continues to struggle with thick armor, a dull sword, and a slow horse (paraphrasing his book's subtitle). His research concluded that the Congress wants more liaising with the Army, that congressional representatives view discussions with senior leadership as not only legitimate but vital. Despite this fact, the Army remains the least effective military service in discussing its needs with Congress, with its approach shaped by a culture that does not value the need to address critical issues on the Hill. The Navy, Air Force, and, in particular, the Marine Corps, figured out present their issues on the Hill and how to win friends there decades ago. Finally, the Army's lack of liaising has created the potential for more serious consequences, as its leadership fails to ensure that OSD and congressional policymakers understand its institutional interests as part of the nation's overall security.[2] Recent cancellations of the Crusader artillery program and congressional attacks on the Comanche helicopter and Stryker combat vehicle demonstrate that the Army does not know how to get its message across.

His conclusions, written across a larger perspective, are equally applicable to the Army's chemical demilitarization program. The Army leadership and the PMCD office have not engaged Congress effectively on the chemical demilitarization program, with the resulting loss of initiative to citizen groups and leading to an entirely reactive, rather than proactive, effort. The PMCD's actions mirror the larger Army in its efforts and failures in major defense issues. In the words of one OSD policy maker, the Army just seems to do it wrong. Scrogg's four recommendations, therefore, are as pertinent to the chemical demilitarization program as they were to the Army as a whole.[3]

First, the current Army leadership must dramatically increase its engagement with Congress. The PMCD, with two- and three-star Army generals leading the way, should directly engage a larger base of congressional leaders and committees and make their case, not merely those congressional districts and states that are home to the stockpile sites. After all, the non-stockpile program affects all states; as the Yucca Mountain nuclear stockpile issue has shown, the ultimate success rides on the majority of Congress supporting the initiative, not merely the state owning the site. Issues involving chemical and biological defense, chemical and biological terrorism, treaty issues, and chemical demilitarization programs (internationally as well as nationally) have only increased in significance in Washington. Right now, the Army is not engaging the Hill on these topics unless tasked to do so, and this lack of leadership is noticed by everyone inside the Beltway and exploited by those outside the Beltway.

Second, the Army needs to prepare its generals to serve more effectively in Washington. The Chemical Corps needs to mirror this by preparing future Army chemical depot commanders to serve more effectively in this new environment. While the Chemical Corps has been occasionally gifted with good leaders who have an instinctive knowledge of how to address potentially controversial topics, their current generation of officers was not raised with an innate knowledge of chemical weapons, stockpile issues, and liaising on the Hill. The Chemical Corps' future leaders are learning on the job, and this lack of preparation will doom them to failure. Many Chemical Corps officers do not know (or want to know) their own professional history, and in this failure, these future leaders do not understand the unique terrain that they are entering. In fairness, this may be endemic to the Army rank and file in general, but again, it is part of the overall challenge of communicating current, important issues to the Hill.

Third, the Army must strengthen its legislative liaison operations. The Chemical Corps does not have the power to convince senators, representatives, governors, or their staffs on the merits of this program. Congressional representatives are not convinced that a program is critical when they see colonels and lieutenant colonels coming in to talk to their staffs, and they are less than interested in hearing a technical proposal on the way things should run. In addition to more professional and engaged legislative liaison operation, the Army senior leadership must acknowledge that it needs to be personally engaged to complete this program. There has to be a dedicated interest on behalf of the Army to solve this program quickly and resolutely, if for no other reason than to stop hemorrhaging funds and traveling to Congress to testify on this issue.

Last, the Army must clarify to its own members why interactions with Congress are necessary and, in reality, based on the Army's own culture and ethos. Congress already knows and admires that the Army values duty, honor, and country; that the Army rank and file want to serve as the nation's protectors; and that the Army is willing to take on missions as tasked with reduced resources if it comes down to it. The Army leadership must make the case that these values are not incongruent with the need to liaise with Congress, and that discussing Army issues with major defense contractors and Congressional leaders is not an immoral act but a necessary price of getting business done and serving the nation.

Overall, the chemical demilitarization program is being executed along the right path, if the Army had the nerve to proactively address the challenges and if Congress would stop interfering with the Army's desire to get the job done on schedule and on cost, safely and efficiently. The NAS, CDC, HHS, EPA, and GAO have already stated that the program's technology and overall execution of the program are as safe as a large disposal process can be. If the Army had been left on its own to work within the legal constructs of environmental safety, this program would have been completed long ago. I identify recommendations for how the PMCD interfaces with the public and the public's representatives in the following paragraphs.

## ROLE OF THE OSD LEADERSHIP

Now that OSD has reaffirmed its control over the program, the question will be, What will it do to better direct the program's execution? Not a few OSD leaders have lost confidence in the Army's capability to finish this task, but at the end of the day, it is the Army's responsibility to close its stockpile sites. Now that the reassessed life-cycle costs are estimated to reach a potential $24 billion, it could be the time for OSD to direct how to cap the costs—or will they merely nod to Congress and say, "Whatever you want," just as the Army has done for years?

OSD's strengths have never been in management and execution of programs; these skills are just not its role or its strength. OSD leaders are supposed to set defense policy as per the administration's guidance and oversee (not directly manage) the Army's execution of the chemical demilitarization program. The most important roles that OSD can offer are that of policy development, interagency coordination, and congressional liaison. Perhaps the two most important roles of Dr. Prociv's five-and-a-half-year tour as an Assistant to the Secretary of the Army for Chemical Demilitarization was repairing the Army–FEMA disputes on executing CSEPP and his dialogues with state congressional delegations in an effort to educate the representatives and their staffs. His role was instrumental in guiding the Army to keeping to a $15 billion dollar life-cycle cost and in controlling costs that were spiraling in the alternative technology program. OSD should continue to drive the total costs down as much as possible while watching to ensure that the program is safely and efficiently managed.

On the other side, the Army leadership and PMCD have often resisted OSD oversight in this program and rarely implemented the recommendations coming from the Defense Acquisition Board when the program was reviewed. True to its culture, the Army decided that it could handle its own problems without assistance (or interference, as the Army saw it) from above. This was unfortunate; if the Army could handle the states and Congress, ignoring OSD might have been an option. In this setting, on this terrain, refusing OSD assistance is folly.

With the gyrations of the program oversight moving from OSD to Army and back to OSD, the program's inertia has lagged to a crawl, and its continuity has been disrupted. If OSD leadership wants to get the program back on track, it should develop and impose a six-year strategic plan, outlining the goals and actions expected of the involved Army and OSD agencies. This plan should contain specific goals for OSD to chair interagency meetings with EPA, HHS, and other government agencies to seek avenues to accelerate and bring the program to closure by 2007. It could be done if all the players were serious about meeting the treaty deadline and if Congress allows these leaders to execute a responsible and executable plan.

OSD should also proactively engage Congress, if nothing else but to ensure that the appropriate representatives remain knowledgeable about successes such as JACADS and TOCDF in particular and the non-stockpile program and alternative technology efforts in general. While some congressional representatives will no doubt continue to use the program as a scapegoat to show their constituents that they are forcefully dealing with the problem, a lack of engagement should not and cannot be accepted. A strategy to inform and educate congressional subcommittees and specific congressional delegations on the policy approach, rather than recitations of the technologies and interactions with the public, would go far to ensure that Congress does not hear only from the citizen groups.

## ROLE OF POLITICIANS

Congress is made up of very talented and qualified people; most of them have integrity and want to do the right thing for the public. Public policy analysts generally agree that the Congress is more responsive to public mandates today, that the openness of the process is greater than in any other branch of government or business, that there is more participation of these representatives with interest groups than ever before. The problem is the incremental approach that legislators apply to critical public policy issues, issues that are often poorly developed at their initiation and are too controversial to ignore later, especially in the environmentally related areas. This incremental approach is caused by two sources: poorly developed, "knee-jerk" legislation, sometimes written by other interest groups, with inadequate funding to address the desired outcome, and the natural partisan structure of American politics.

The fact that different branches of government, special interest groups, and constituents all try to influence their congressional representative results in an often conflicting patchwork of legislation that is more akin to a compromise than a strong initiative funded adequately to meet its intended objectives. For instance, direction to eliminate all traces of carcinogens or toxic chemicals from soil, water, or food, no matter how tiny, when the risk to humans is nonexistent makes no sense, especially when this direction is ordered irrespective of the cost involved. If Congress and federal agencies executed comparative risk assessments on courses of action and identified the costs and benefits within reasonable parameters, they might avoid actions by those who insist that every toxic site be cleaned to a "pristine state" at exorbitant costs for every additional life saved. The goal should be to allocate public funds in such a matter that the overall result is more lives saved as a result of wiser investments of scarce resources.[4]

The second reason, partisan politics, seems to be unavoidable. In our representative democracy, the people want to elect a politician who addresses their needs. That is natural; that is why they say that "all politics are local." Most representatives want to do what their constituency asks them to do, but the constituency of any politician is far from having one mind on any particular topic. In our very diverse population, the values, interests, and opinions vary enormously, resulting in a general lack of consensus on public policy issues. This is further reflected in the constant debates and discussions in democratic politics in state houses and the Congress; major policy discussions have so many people with different opinions that in the process of building consensus on a particular topic, compromises are the general solution. When these compromises do not solve the problem to a particular congressional representative's satisfaction, they come in with incremental "fixes" to what their constituents think is an issue.

One might question, in this particular area, why a congressman or governor would listen to (relatively) small fringe groups that protest against the chemical demilitarization program. When a dozen protesters come out to picket the start of a disposal plant operation, the governor, state legislators, and often congressional representatives start making statements about the need to investigate the Army's efforts. This act goes on as if they have not received personalized briefings from the Army leadership and the PMCD's office. The majority of the public, when advised of what the Army is doing, is often uninterested or goes away less concerned, despite the best efforts of the special interest groups. Why are politicians not addressing what the majority clearly wants, which is to dispose of these munitions?

The answer is actually in two parts. First is how the American public chooses its representatives. Because our democratic process supports a multiparty competition every two to four years, and because we have such a diverse voting population with different views and values, the politicians running for office are fighting for every vote up to Election Day. In attempts to differentiate their positions from each other, politicians would rather make extreme statements that are completely divorced from the facts, instead of trying to educate the public about the lack of evidence of any threat to human health or the environment. Can you blame them? That is the electoral system that we, the people, have in place, and no one has seriously attempted to change it, despite alleged dissatisfaction with fund-raising practices, smear campaigns, and "politics as usual."

Second, some politicians make the mistake of thinking that citizen groups represent the majority's view, no matter how idealistic the groups' claims are. This might be because the politician is not hearing anything from the majority of his or her constituents (more on that in the next section). As discussed in Chapter 10, there are clear indications that much of the public does not even know about this program. Given the lack of opposing views from other citizens or the Army, the politicians are going with the information that is available to them; unfortunately, this information is often from the reformists and not from the participants.

And then there is Senator Mitch McConnell. In a May 2001 article, he was quoted as stating: "The potential of harm to the public is enormous. . . . There's significant doubt that the deadlines will be met because the program has been mismanaged for so long. It doesn't lead you to have much confidence in anything they tell you. . . . What we would like is sound science applied to this review [of the chemical demilitarization program], and we'd like attention to this whole matter at the highest possible levels at the Department of Defense." As this book has attempted to articulate, his claims are without foundation. His office has done the most harm to the program in terms of bad publicity in the last decade, raising the level of controversy to new levels through the national media.[5] In a different role, Senator Wayne Allard (R-CO) has taken time to understand the Army's program, poll his constituents' views, and supported the national interest in eliminating the chemical stockpile.

If there were one thing to improve, it would be to ensure that the politicians at all levels understood that greater public involvement in the program was not solely executed through the participation of citizen groups that oppose the Army's incineration program for no reason other than "no emissions are good emissions."

The mass media love these groups' controversial sound bites; the appearance is that "the public" as a whole has issues with the program, so who are the politicians to disagree? If state politicians are truly concerned with the health and welfare of their constituents, they should invest the time to poll the public and place responsible citizens who want to help get rid of these weapons in the safest and most efficient manner on the right panels. If that method happens to be incineration, so be it; get on with it, declare victory, and get off the stage.

Ideally, we would like to think that politicians would do what is best for their constituents, irrespective of the polls, based on solid evidence, deliberation on the costs and benefits, and building strict procedures and increased accountability into the process. This is a goal for many public policy challenges and, as previously noted, is not different for the chemical demilitarization program. Some senators, it is sad to say, still enjoy beating on the Army's efforts rather than working with it to complete this program. The incrementalist approach by politicians remains the major influence on the cost and schedule of this program, not the Army's performance measured against its 1984 cost-schedule estimates.

As a quick word about the state governors and local politicians, it is a mixed bag. At the state level, many governors want to get rid of the stockpiles and sooner rather than later. Most governors do not want to be personally engaged and send their staffers instead to work the issues, but their intent is clear. If the Army can get rid of these munitions safely, they want it done, just at minimal risk and with minimal turmoil. They elect responsible citizens to the advisory committees, and most of these citizens are intent on representing the public's concerns. This is contrary to the ideology of many local mayors and county commissioners that seek more resources for their jurisdiction and more credit for themselves. These local politicians support the program as long as it means more money pouring into their coffers, and indeed, their emergency operations center rival the Houston Space Center as modern command and control centers as a result. The term "green-mail" is heard often from government civilians that have to work with these locals.

The most interesting thing has been to see how the political representatives' views have changed since September 11, 2001. Suddenly, the good representatives are concerned that the greatest threat is, indeed, continuing to store the chemical munitions and materiels, since the sites are seen as potential terrorist targets. This terrorist threat has eclipsed all other safety arguments, creating a very real sense of urgency that the Army get rid of this hazard quickly and efficiently. Newport and Aberdeen have seen their schedules accelerated, and maybe the remaining stockpiles will become operational with a shortened schedule. It is a shame that the politicians were unable to see this risk a decade ago; if they had, certainly there would be no hazard to worry about today. Again, this window of concern for the most part has passed, and political considerations will once again overcome real concerns. Note how the formation of the Homeland Defense Agency have caused partisan and bureaucratic fights, overwhelming the initial urgency to get a new organization in place addressing this terrorist threat.

## ROLE OF THE PUBLIC

When we examine the public's role, one has to refrain from assuming that the public is of one mind on this topic. Certainly, the citizens groups that criticize the program would like Congress and their state representatives to assume that their view is the one that the majority holds, but of course this is not so. There are many views on this program, and most of them are neutral or positive. This is not to denigrate the role of special interest groups; in many public policy areas, special interest groups and lobbyists perform a valuable service as they educate legislators and citizens on special topics that are often very complex. The disservice is when some citizen groups turn to advocacy science and verbal assassination to gain their objectives, which, in this program, have been to stall and block the Army's efforts at every turn.

Policy advocates such as Alan Rosenthal and Derek Bok have pointed out that the real shortfall is education of the masses on these public policy issues. Americans have been shown to be extremely cynical of the government's execution of public programs, despite the acknowledgment that the government is the only force that can truly influence issues such as maintaining education, reducing poverty, preventing crime, cleaning the environment, and so on. They feel shut out of the process and without input to change anything. Politicians are seen as appearing to be interested in people's opinions, only to manipulate these views for their own purposes. Yet given the opportunity to participate directly on ballot issues, for instance, people do not vote on local issues, let alone state and national issues.[6] There is a very real lack of public involvement in these important issues.

This same phenomenon has been seen in the chemical demilitarization program. Despite the presence of local offices, town hall meetings, web sites, and newsletters, very few people ask for more information about the program. More than half the population in the states that have stockpile sites are unaware of their existence. This apathy actually increases the power of special interest groups and the critics and increases political partisanship of those seeking to gain the support of the public. Therefore, most of the things that Americans dislike about government are actually increased by their own disinterest.[7]

The public interest is really the key to the program's successful conclusion. This should not be a surprise, as Congress, the Army, the states, and the special interest groups all claim that the public is the benefactor of the program, irrespective of the exact method of its execution. That is what makes this a public policy issue. If citizens in Kentucky, Alabama, Oregon, Indiana, Arkansas, Colorado, and the other states want to see this program resolved, they should carefully educate themselves on the issues, visit the offices, visit TOCDF and the other disposal facilities, and start calling their political representatives. I think they would find the Army more than willing to work with citizens who do not have an ax to grind; it would be refreshing, in fact. All too often, it seems that people would rather listen to an activist that, lacking any formal education, is spouting off about the evils of government than the government's spokesman, an individual with a doctoral degree in chemistry, over 15 years in industrial experience, and widely published in the area of chemical weapons destruction. If people develop an educated interest in this program, the politicians might get the feedback required to affirm the Army's direction.

Most citizens do not have an immediate interest in the program, given that the overwhelming majority do not live within ten miles of a stockpile site. They are even less likely to participate in this national program. Certainly, they are not the ones sending faxes to their representatives demanding a justification of where the $24-plus billion of their money is going (although maybe they should). That is unfortunate but expected. Their education is based on a much more immediate m medium—the mass media. That is the really bad news.

## ROLE OF THE MASS MEDIA

Again, many other public policy experts have already noted the media's desire to sensationalize issues rather than educate the public and its political representatives. The mass media have a tremendous power in determining what issues are seen in the national press, and millions of Americans tune in nightly to faces that they trust to tell them what is going on inside government. It is up to the news executives and editors to tell us what issues and events are newsworthy. Politicians, public relations officials, and special interest groups understand this implicitly and attempt to attract the media's attention by any means possible to get favorable coverage.[8] This is a business area, not a public service.

In the 1980s, gains in cable networks resulted in decreases in newspaper readership. In the 1990s, the Internet's profusion of news sources only accelerated this. Television producers responded in the only way that they knew to stop the decline: briefer sound bites from politicians, simpler presentations (less analysis), and more emphasis on visual presentation over substantive content. For newspapers, this translated into shorter stories, more human interest, more photographs, more sports and local news, less national politics, and less public affairs. While the public says that it thinks the news is oversensationalized, the sales are supported by hard circulation data and high ratings to the contrary. Studies continue to suggest that people want to see scandal and controversy and are not that interested in public issues and politics in general.[9]

This has been consistently true in regards to coverage of the chemical demilitarization program. It is not that the media are liberally biased against the military, but the drama of military ineptness makes for good news. CBS, in particular, loves to send Dan Rather to Umatilla (repeatedly) to talk about the continued threat of the stockpile to surrounding communities and the environment and the government's seeming inability to get the job done. He has yet to cover the NAS recommendations on incineration as the best option and the inability of alternative technologies to meet the challenges. He does not interview the locals who have no problems with the planned disposal facility but rather hunts down an out-of-state CWWG representative for a sound bite critical of the government's program. Is this objective reporting?

Similarly, the *Washington Post* has failed to educate its readership on the Spring Valley issues of long-buried chemical weapons. While it enjoys printing maps of the old burial grounds and raising local residents' feelings of panic about arsenic levels, the *Post* has yet to examine the American University's role in those chemical weapons tests or to discuss the utter absence of any hazards that the overwhelming majority of residents face, given that most of the chemicals were retained within the munitions and/or containers and were not leaking to the surface, endangering their children or pets. That does not sell papers in DC.

There is not much to recommend here, but it is constructive to understand why the media acts the way they do. It would be futile to ask the news stations and newspapers to "do the right thing," to actually investigate the program and get the facts in front of the public. Maybe public television might do this, but the national stations will not, not because they are wicked but because it does not get the ratings. Telling the news is big business, and if telling only one side of the story sells more papers and more commercial time, that is probably what will continue. The shame of it is that the Army has had to spend so much of its resources to address the allegations that there are health or environmental hazards as a result of its program, rather than focusing on executing the program safely and effectively. The fact that no citizen has ever been harmed at the chemical stockpile sites or disposal facilities as a result of an agent leak or incident will probably never be told by the media. Because the media are not about to help in this area, it is even more important that the Army and the Chemical Corps learn how to develop and manage public policy issues.

## LESSONS FOR THE DOD CHEMICAL AND BIOLOGICAL DEFENSE PROGRAM

When you peruse a library's collection of military history books, you usually see a lot of military hardware-oriented books showing the tanks, battleships, aircraft, and infantry weapons. There should be some general books on military history, many on the battles (especially Civil War and World War II battles) and leaders. Then there is the "weapons of mass destruction" collection: nuclear weapons and deterrence theories and the dangers posed by chemical and biological weapons. The Chemical Corps is perhaps the only military branch that is expressly identified as the villain in any military nonfiction book, largely because of the spin on issues such as offensive chemical and biological munitions, vaccination programs, Agent Orange, and the Gulf War illnesses. Isaac Asimov, the learned scientist and author, even commented once that scientists were seen as heros until the First World War and the use of chemical weapons changed this perception. This attitude, beyond any reason, is why the Chemical Corps needs to learn how to manage public policy issues correctly.

In all cases, the Chemical Corps must understand that it cannot take on these issues alone. The Army culture seems to mandate completing the mission without asking for more resources and whatever the cost, and this attitude has severely limited the Chemical Corps' chances of success. Take the Army's Anthrax Vaccination Immunization Program, for instance. Because this is seen as a medical acquisition issue, the Chemical Corps has not engaged in this area. The military medical specialists are the major players and, like many doctors, sometimes do not want "laymen" involved in their policy decisions. Yet clearly, this is an important issue to the Chemical Corps, being directly related to defense against biological warfare. For too long, the Chemical Corps and Medical Corps have been segregated in their approach to chemical and biological defense. The result is a beleaguered medical department struggling to articulate its views and trying to counter a vicious and vocal minority view that seeks to stop vaccinations without understanding the consequences—increased battlefield deaths as a result of inadequate medical countermeasures. We see members of Congress taking advantage of this controversy by grandstanding on the issue rather than assessing if the military's program is on the right track.

The DOD web site for its anthrax vaccine immunization program (http://www.anthrax.osd.mil) was a belated attempt to counter Internet sites that deliberately twisted the truth about the vaccine. It was a good first step, but not enough to counter the efforts of groups that continue to lobby congressional representatives in an effort to discredit the Army. The real concern is that, while anthrax vaccine has been the focus, the Army is developing vaccines for smallpox, plague, botulinum toxin, and other biological warfare agents. Anthrax vaccine is by far the safest of the lot, and it is approved by the FDA. When these new vaccines are used, the controversy will increase exponentially. Already we can see the controversy on use of vaccines for civilians exposed to biological terrorist incidents has increased the tone of the debate. President George W. Bush's administration is now discussing a national vaccine stockpile, and these discussions are not led by the Army. What is required is a different and proactive approach.

At the least, the Chemical Corps and Medical Corps must develop a strategy outlining why these vaccines are needed, what other efforts are being undertaken to defeat chemical and biological weapons, and what alternatives have been examined and rejected. OSD must engage the FDA to increase its interactions with the medical program and to identify methods to develop vaccines and medical countermeasures more quickly. The FDA took three years to develop and promote an option to use animal test data for efficacy of biological vaccines, while continuing other tests to ensure safety in their use. This was entirely too long and detrimental to the Army's efforts to develop safe vaccines in the face of nations such as Iraq and North Korea that have these weapons. Last, the Army leadership must help articulate this strategy to Congress as a major initiative, not from the Chemical Corps and not from the Medical Corps but from the Chief of Staff of the Army, his Vice, or the Deputy Chief of Staff for Operations and Plans.

This kind of engagement is absolutely mandatory not merely for vaccine programs, but for major DOD issues such as the Gulf War illness investigations and its planned response capability for chemical and biological terrorism within the United States. While both programs are handled explicitly by OSD offices, the potential impact on the Army and specifically on the Chemical Corps are so dramatic that they should not leave these programs to OSD policy makers to develop alone. The Gulf War illness findings on chemical and biological detection systems, for instance, could drive the Army and the Chemical Corps to develop overly sensitive and expensive devices that are ill-suited for combat situations. But this is the least of the potential bad news.

When the Central Intelligence Agency offered its services to assess the coalition bombing of chemical weapons production plants and the Khamisiyah depot destruction, it took the initiative away from DOD (not that DOD was trying to answer the question at first). The result was that the CIA set the standard for exposure to chemical agents by using the general population limit in its downwind predictions. This established an exposure level that, if a person were to be exposed to this agent concentration for the rest of his or her life, he or she would suffer no ill effects. This exposure standard was several orders of magnitude too conservative for determining the threat of chemical agent exposure to service members that were in a dangerous area for a few days, but more than 100,000 service members now believe they could have been exposed to nerve agents when in all likelihood, they were not exposed to any noticeable or medically significant extent. The resulting furor over whose model was correct and what assumptions were valid is well known and still debated years after the results were announced. DOD will probably use that same measure for future wars that feature the potential exposure of troops to chemical warfare agents, if nothing else because it has become a precedent. Thus, we will continue to hear about similar nerve agent exposure incidents in future conflicts, regardless of whether or not there was any real risk.

The Army National Guard is taking on the response to chemical and biological terrorism through the development and fielding of the Weapons of Mass Destruction Civil Support Teams (WMD CSTs). The Army leadership should become much more proactive in this area, not merely because Congress wants these teams but also because the Guard has the attitude that it can make its own destiny without the Chemical Corps' input. The Marine Corps has been more than willing to take kudos from Congress through the prestige of preparing to respond to chemical and biological terrorism incidents. While the Marines are well trained, they are not the appropriate force; they are too few to focus their chemical and biological experts in one force as they do, and they lack the infrastructure to invest and build upon chemical and biological defense programs. Yet they are the ones mentioned by name by Congress, by combatant commanders, and by the media when the DOD response to CB terrorism is mentioned.

Initially the plan was to deploy one 22-man WMD CST per EPA region, of which there are 10. When Congress saw where these ten teams were being stationed, they wanted more, not because there was a risk-based assessment that said there should be more, but rather for the prestige of being able to state that they were looking out for their constituents. The number of teams increased to 17, then 27, and now 32 WMD CSTs are "authorized" by Congress to be established by the National Guard. The common thought is that Congress will inevitably ask for up to 55 teams to cover all U.S. states and territories (maybe two each for California and Texas). The scarey thought is that the Defense Department will probably accommodate this request (if it is made) despite the absence of a CB terrorist threat in all these states and the lack of evidence that these teams actually can contribute to the emergency response to a CB terrorist incident. Great if they can, but is there really a CB terrorist threat in North Dakota or is that state's congressional legislation just trying to make sure they get their team?

There has been a great deal of focus on this strategy, questions as to their true capabilities in responding, the associated costs, and the National Guard's role in homeland security vice military operations overseas. Any response to chemical and biological terrorism would be very well covered by the media, so it is in the Army's best interests to ensure that the response is a correct one. The National Guard, however, is intent on running the program without interference from even other Army agencies, and it is very, very politically connected. Also in the mix are at least three OSD offices, the Air Force National Guard, the National Fire Protection Association, and several universities interested in starting up centers to train personnel to respond to chemical and biological terrorist incidents.

In all these issues, the mix of OSD, Joint Staff, other services, other government agencies, Congress, mass media, and the public's interests, there needs to be a public policy approach to develop the best strategy with the available resources. Currently, there is not any coherent strategy other than reacting to what some congressional representatives demand and what the media put out in the evening news report. It is inherent on the Army leadership to support the Chemical Corps in addressing these very important issues. The minimum that the Army leadership needs to do is to start increasing its legislative liaising on these and similar issues. The challenge to the Chemical Corps is to convince the Army leadership of the need to engage Congress in these discussions.

The Army leadership has been in the forefront of ignoring its own require-ments for chemical and biological defense, let alone public policy issues. Take the new "transformed" Army division envisioned by General Eric Shinseki, the current Army Chief of Staff, for instance. The Army moved its division chemical company to corps level, leaving three NBC reconnaissance vehicles in the cavalry squadron (half the company's former strength of six vehicles). Outside of the NBC reconnaissance vehicles, none of the Army's planned future light armored vehicles will have collective protection systems. Essentially, in an adversarial world increasingly armed with chemical and biological weapons, the new medium-strength division will have a minimal capability to protect itself. Convincing the Army leadership of the need to pay more attention to chemical and biological defense issues will be a challenge, let alone changing the course of how these issues are addressed in the public forum.

The Chemical Corps can not change how it does business without the Army's culture changing, and its military leaders move to other positions too quickly to adjust to how policy works in Washington without Army leadership support. The Army leadership should see the value of supporting what is surely the most misunderstood branch within its service, but it does not, for whatever reason, pay attention to the Chemical Corps' business. If nothing else, the Chemical Corps must realize that the successful completion of these issues can only be accomplished by addressing these issues as public policy challenges.

OSD leadership, as the group that deals with Congress the most on these issues, needs to reach out to the Army leadership and Chemical Corps as well. Instead of taking the hits for the Army's perceived lack of action on these important issues, OSD should partner with the Army leadership and Chemical Corps and proactively turn this business around. Developing these issues as public policy is the right thing for the Army, OSD, Congress, and inevitably the public. These are not tough issues, but they are tough to execute when Congress and the public are not on your side and you lack a strategy that can advance your cause. It is up to the public policy advocates to advise the Army leadership on the best way to be successful at executing its responsibilities in chemical demilitarization and other chemical and biological defense issues; now, if only the Army leadership is there to listen.

# Appendix A

## Life Cycle Costs of the Program

As a very short note to explain the next few pages, these numbers represent the funds allocated to the many projects within the chemical demilitarization program. All numbers are in millions of dollars, and are identified as research and development (R&D) funds, procurement (PROC) funds, operations and maintenance (O&M) funds, and military construction authority (MCA) funds. The R&D funds is self-explanatory, the procurement funds buy contractor support and equipment, O&M pays salaries. The Army spent its own MCA funds to build the facilities, so officially these should not be included in the total life cycle costs of the program.

At the bottom of the second, fourth and sixth pages, there is a running total of costs, the estimated total program costs that year, and the expected year of completion. The costs in each year reflect that current year's figures from the PMCD's annual report to Congress, and have not been adjusted to a constant rate. Also, the numbers from 2002 on are my estimated costs based on the PMCD's expected total cost numbers. I recognize that the program is expected to overrun the $15 billion mark and continue past 2007, but I did not have that data available by year to make even an educated guess. Spending an extra $9 billion between now and 2012 is awfully hard to imagine, but the budget experts say that is what projected costs look like. I will leave it to the reader's imagination how the funds are allocated, until we see those annual reports.

| | 1985 | 1986 | 1987 | 1988 | 1989 | 1990 | 1991 | 1992 | 1993 |
|---|---|---|---|---|---|---|---|---|---|
| **Program Mgmt** | | | | | | | | | |
| R&D | 0 | 0.5 | 0.5 | 0.5 | 0 | 0 | 0 | 0 | 0 |
| O&M | | 5 | 8.5 | 7.7 | 8 | 8 | 8.1 | 8.1 | 10.3 |
| **Technical Support** | | | | | | | | | |
| R&D | | | | 1.1 | 1.6 | 1.8 | | | 2.5 |
| PROC | | 0.4 | 0 | 0.1 | 0 | 4.9 | 23.4 | 32.2 | 17 |
| O&M | | 6.5 | 7.7 | 1.6 | 1.9 | 18.1 | 20.5 | 26.4 | 30.2 |
| **Cryofracture** | | | | | | | | | |
| R&D | | | | 3.8 | 16.3 | 6.1 | 5.3 | 13.9 | 4 |
| PROC | | | | 16.2 | 0 | 0 | 0 | 20 | 0 |
| **CAMDS** | | | | | | | | | |
| R&D | | 0 | 0 | 0 | | 0.9 | 1.3 | 0.9 | 0.5 |
| PROC | | 7.1 | 1 | 2.5 | 2.4 | | | | |
| O&M | | 18.1 | 17.6 | 18.4 | 19.6 | 23 | 20.4 | 20.2 | 21.3 |
| **DATS** | | | | | | | | | |
| O&M | | 3.5 | 1 | 0 | 0 | | | | |
| **JACADS** | | | | | | | | | |
| PROC | | 54 | 32 | 12.3 | 6.3 | 5.1 | 3.4 | 2.4 | 1.7 |
| O&M | | 10.4 | 10 | 19.4 | 36.9 | 66.8 | 79.3 | 100.1 | 104 |
| **BZ Disposal** | | | | | | | | | |
| PROC | | 15.8 | 13.4 | 0 | 0 | | | | |
| O&M | | 7.9 | 0 | 33.1 | 29.2 | 9.2 | | | |
| **European Retrograde** | | | | | | | | | |
| O&M | | | | | 1.1 | 27.3 | 13.2 | | |
| **CSDP** | | | | | | | | | |
| PROC | | 0 | 7 | 53.6 | 13.4 | 16.2 | 66.7 | 83.4 | 213.4 |
| O&M | | 13.8 | 12.2 | 13.6 | 16.1 | 3.5 | 5.9 | 22.5 | 41.6 |
| MCA | | | | | | 0 | 76.3 | 132.4 | 15 |

| | 1985 | 1986 | 1987 | 1988 | 1989 | 1990 | 1991 | 1992 | 1993 |
|---|---|---|---|---|---|---|---|---|---|
| **CDTF** | | | | | | | | | |
| PROC | | | | 11.2 | 2.5 | 7.2 | 6.4 | | |
| O&M | | | | | 1.1 | 4.1 | 2.9 | 1.8 | 1.5 |
| **CSEPP** | | | starts | | | | | | |
| PROC | | | | 0 | 8 | 37.9 | 13.9 | 12.9 | 12.1 |
| O&M | | | | 2.5 | 3.4 | 14.1 | 20 | 25.9 | 52.2 |
| **Nonstockpile** | | | | | | | | starts | |
| R&D | | | | | | | | 0 | 0 |
| PROC | | | | | | | | 0 | 0 |
| O&M | | | | | | | | 3.7 | 6.3 |
| **ATAP** | | | | | | | | | |
| R&D | | | | | | | | | |
| **ACWA** | | | | | | | | | |
| R&D | | | | | | | | | |
| **Other** | | | | | | | | | |
| R&D | Mun Overpack | 8.4 | 7.8 | 0 | 0 | | | | |
| PROC | | | | 0.2 | 2.6 | 0 | 2 | | |
| O&M | | | | 0.7 | 0 | 0 | | | |
| MCA | | | | | | | | | |
| Total R&D | | 8.9 | 8.3 | 5.4 | 17.9 | 7.9 | 5.3 | 13.9 | 6.5 |
| Total Proc | | 77.3 | 53.4 | 96.1 | 35.2 | 72.2 | | 151.8 | 244.7 |
| Total O&M | | 65.2 | 57 | 97 | 117.3 | 174.1 | 170.3 | 208.7 | 267.4 |
| End-of-year Cost | | 151.4 | 118.7 | 198.5 | 170.4 | 254.2 | 175.6 | 374.4 | 518.6 |
| Total MCA | 0 | 0 | 0 | 0 | 58 | 0 | 76.3 | 132.4 | 15 |
| Running Program Total | | 151.4 | 270.1 | 468.6 | 639 | 893.2 | 1068.8 | 1443.2 | 1961.8 |
| Total Estimated Costs | 1700 | 2000 | 2700 | 3400 | | 6500 | 6500 | 7900 | 8600 |
| **Completion Date** | | Sep-94 | | Apr-97 | | | Jul-99 | Dec-04 | |

|  | 1994 | 1995 | 1996 | 1997 | 1998 | 1999 | 2000 | 2001 | 2002 |
|---|---|---|---|---|---|---|---|---|---|
| **Program Mgmt** | | | | | | | | | |
| R&D | | | | | | | | | |
| O&M | 11.2 | 12.8 | 15.2 | 15.9 | 18.1 | 17.8 | 22.1 | 22 | 22 |
| **Technical Support** | | | | | | | | | |
| R&D | | | | | | | | | |
| PROC | 7.7 | 2.4 | 38.7 | 62.2 | 11 | 10 | 5.9 | 10 | 10 |
| O&M | 27.5 | 23.6 | 26.9 | 36.9 | 43.7 | 32.4 | 45.1 | 45 | 45 |
| **Cryofracture** | | | | | | | | | |
| R&D | 25 | | | | | | | | |
| PROC | | | | | | | | | |
| **CAMDS** | | | | | | | | | |
| R&D | | | | | | | | | |
| PROC | 3 | 0.9 | 1.1 | 0 | 0.9 | 0.5 | 0 | | |
| O&M | 21.4 | 21.7 | 24.4 | 24.2 | 25.6 | 19.8 | 25.2 | 24 | 24 |
| **DATS** | | | | | | | | | |
| O&M | | | | | | | | | |
| **JACADS** | | | | | | | | | |
| PROC | 0 | 1.6 | 3.5 | 0 | 3.2 | 13.6 | 1 | 0 | 0 |
| O&M | 106.5 | 114.5 | 118.3 | 158.9 | 84.1 | 126.5 | 127.6 | 80 | 60 |
| **BZ Disposal** | | | | | | | | | |
| PROC | | | | | | | | | |
| O&M | | | | | | | | | |
| **European Retrograde** | | | | | | | | | |
| O&M | | | | | | | | | |
| **CSDP** | | | | | | | | | |
| PROC | 6.5 | 131.7 | 164.2 | 82.1 | 30.2 | 72 | 141.4 | 300 | 644.8 |
| O&M | 53.4 | 104.9 | 81.5 | 121.6 | 121.8 | 160.9 | 218.4 | 400.2 | 400 |
| MCA | 112.4 | 24 | 0 | 110 | 77.3 | 71 | 171 | 180 | 200 |

| | 1994 | 1995 | 1996 | 1997 | 1998 | 1999 | 2000 | 2001 | 2002 |
|---|---|---|---|---|---|---|---|---|---|
| **CDTF** | | | | | | | | | |
| PROC | | | | | | | | | |
| O&M | 2.3 | 4.1 | 4.1 | 6.8 | 7.5 | 3.9 | 8.9 | 6 | 6 |
| **CSEPP** | | | | | | | | | |
| PROC | 31.6 | 1.4 | 26.1 | 21.7 | 26.7 | 14.2 | 35.5 | | |
| O&M | 47.7 | 54.2 | 57.8 | 56.6 | 63.3 | 57.4 | 58.6 | 71.3 | 69.5 |
| **Nonstockpile** | | | | | | | | | |
| R&D | 5.7 | 11.3 | 37.1 | 32.1 | 36.8 | 38.6 | 37.6 | 154.4 | 166.5 |
| PROC | 2.2 | 1.4 | 25.4 | 2.5 | 0.2 | 4.2 | 4.6 | | |
| O&M | 21.3 | 11.3 | 15.8 | 31.5 | 48.1 | 67 | 34.9 | | |
| **ATAP** | starts | | | | | | | | |
| R&D | | 9.4 | 15.9 | 23.5 | 25.5 | 8.5 | 9.4 | 10 | 36 |
| **ACWA** | | | | starts | | | | | |
| R&D | | | | 39.9 | 4 | 32.8 | 109 | 100 | 100 |
| **Other** | | | | | | | | | |
| R&D | | | | | | 0 | 0 | | |
| PROC | | 59.6 | | | | | | | |
| O&M | | 8.7 | | | 1 | 1 | 0.9 | | |
| MCA | 1.5 | | | 4.1 | 9.2 | 3.8 | 2 | | |
| **Total R&D** | 30.7 | 20.7 | 53 | 95.5 | 66.3 | 171 | 292.5 | 264.4 | 302.5 |
| **Total Proc** | 51 | 199 | 259 | 168.5 | 72.2 | 114.5 | 188.4 | 310 | 224.6 |
| **Total O&M** | 291.3 | 355.8 | 344 | 452.4 | 413.2 | 486.7 | 541.7 | 648.5 | 626.5 |
| **End-of-year Cost** | 373 | 575.5 | 656 | 716.4 | 551.7 | 772.2 | 1022.6 | 1222.9 | 1153.6 |
| **Total MCA** | 113.9 | 24 | 0 | 114.1 | 86.5 | 48.3 | 119.5 | 180 | 200 |
| **Running Program Total** | 2334.8 | 2910.3 | 3566.3 | 4282.7 | 4834.4 | 5606.6 | 6629.2 | 7852.1 | 9005.7 |
| **Total Estimated Costs** | 10200 | 11900 | 12400 | 14200 | 15000 | | | | 24000 |
| **Completion Date** | | | | Apr-07 | | | | | Apr-12 |

| (Estimated Costs) | 2003 | 2004 | 2005 | 2006 | 2007 | 2008 | 2009 | 2010 total |
|---|---|---|---|---|---|---|---|---|
| **Program Mgmt** | | | | | | | | |
| R&D | | | | | | | | |
| O&M | 22 | 20 | 20 | 10 | 5 | | | 299.3 |
| **Technical Support** | | | | | | | | 871.9 |
| R&D | | | | | | | | |
| PROC | 10 | 10 | 10 | 5 | 5 | | | |
| O&M | 45 | 45 | 30 | 20 | 10 | | | |
| **Cryofracture** | | | | | | | | |
| R&D | | | | | | | | |
| PROC | | | | | | | | |
| **CAMDS** | | | | | | | | 490.9 |
| R&D | | | | | | | | |
| PROC | | | | | | | | |
| O&M | 24 | 25 | 20 | 20 | 10 | | | |
| **DATS** | | | | | | | | 4.5 |
| O&M | | | | | | | | |
| **JACADS** | | | | | | | | 1563.4 |
| PROC | 0 | | | | | | | |
| O&M | 20 | | | | | | | |
| **BZ Disposal** | | | | | | | | 108.6 |
| PROC | | | | | | | | |
| O&M | | | | | | | | |
| **European Retrograde** | | | | | | | | 41.6 |
| O&M | | | | | | | | |
| **CSDP** | | | | | | | | 7135.6 |
| PROC | 203.3 | 338.9 | 100 | 70 | 50 | | | |
| O&M | 791 | 700.1 | 600 | 500 | 394 | | | |
| MCA | 100 | 0 | 0 | 0 | 0 | | | |

| (Estimated Costs) | 2003 | 2004 | 2005 | 2006 | 2007 | 2008 | 2009 | 2010 | total |
|---|---|---|---|---|---|---|---|---|---|
| **CDTF** | | | | | | | | | 110.3 |
| PROC | | | | | | | | | |
| O&M | 6 | 6 | 4 | 4 | 2 | | | | |
| **CSEPP** | | | | | | | | | 1173.5 |
| PROC | | | | | | | | | |
| O&M | 66.2 | 60.8 | 50 | 50 | 50 | | | | |
| **Nonstockpile** | | | | | | | | | 1300.5 |
| R&D | 100 | 100 | 100 | 100 | 100 | | | | |
| PROC | | | | | | | | | |
| O&M | | | | | | | | | |
| **ATAP** | | | | | | | | | 780.2 |
| R&D | 52 | 200 | 200 | 120 | 70 | | | | |
| **ACWA** | | | | | | | | | 735.7 |
| R&D | 150 | 100 | 100 | 0 | 0 | | | | |
| **Other** | | | | | | | | | 113.5 |
| R&D | | | | | | | | | |
| PROC | | | | | | | | | |
| O&M | | | | | | | | | |
| MCA | | | | | | | | | |
| Total R&D | 302 | 400 | 400 | 220 | 170 | 0 | 0 | 0 | 2862.7 |
| Total Proc | 213.3 | 348.9 | 110 | 75 | 55 | 0 | 0 | 0 | 3120.1 |
| Total O&M | 974.2 | 856.9 | 724 | 604 | 471 | 0 | 0 | 0 | 8947.2 |
| End-of-year Cost | 1489.5 | 1605.8 | 1234 | 899 | 696 | 0 | 0 | 0 | 14930 |
| Total MCA | 100 | 50 | 0 | 0 | 0 | | | | 1318 |
| Running Program Total | 10495.2 | 12101 | 13335 | 14234 | 14930 | 14930 | 14930 | 14930 | |
| Total Estimated Costs | | | | | | | | | 14930 |
| **Completion Date** | | | | | | | | | |

# Appendix B

## Congressional Views on Demilitarization

### PL 91-121, Armed Forces Appropriations for 1970, Title IV, sec. 409, November 19, 1969

- Directs submission of a semiannual report to Congress identifying funds spent during the preceding year for research, development, test, evaluation (RDT&E), and procurement of all lethal and nonlethal CB agents.
- Calls for involvement of HEW and the Surgeon General to review public/worker health and safety issues.
- Restricts all transportation and open-air testing of CBW agents without identification of national security interests, precautionary safety measures, and prior notice to congressional leaders and state governors where testing/transport takes place.
- Restricts future deployment and/or storage of CBW agents or delivery systems outside the United States without prior notice to host nation.

### PL 91-441, Armed Forces Appropriations for 1971, Title V, sec. 506, October 17, 1970

- Amends PL 91-121 to include disposal, prohibiting disposal of CB agents within or outside United States unless they have been detoxified, except in emergency cases, which would require an immediate report to Congress.
- Prohibits disposal of any munitions in international waters.
- Requires a NAS study of the use of herbicides in South Vietnam.

### PL 91-672, Foreign Military Sales Act, sec. 13, January 12, 1971

- Denies funding for the purpose of transporting chemical munitions from Okinawa to the United States.
- Permits funds for detoxification or destruction of chemical munitions only outside the United States.

## PL 92-532, Marine Protection, Research, and Sanctuaries Act, Title I, October 23, 1972

*Sec. 101, Prohibited Acts*
- Restricts transport from any location (to or from the United States) of any radiological, biological, or chemical warfare agent, or high level radioactive waste, for the purpose of ocean dumping, by any person or government agency.

## PL 93-608, Submission of Reports to Congress, sec. 2(4), January 2, 1975

- Changes requirement in PL 91-121, submission of a semiannual report to Congress setting forth the amounts spent during the preceding year for RDT&E of all lethal and nonlethal CB agents, to an annual requirement.

## PL 94-106, DOD Appropriation Authorization Act, 1976, Title VIII, October 7, 1975

*Sec. 818*
- Requires the president to certify to Congress that production of binary chemical munitions is essential to the national interest and submit a full report to the House and Senate leadership prior to appropriating any funds for production of binary chemical munitions.

## PL 94-251, March 29, 1976

- Authorizes the sale of approximately 2 million pounds of carbonyl chloride (phosgene) in 1,294 steel ton containers stored at Rocky Mountain Arsenal and the shipment of those containers.

## PL 95-79, Armed Forces Appropriation Authorization Act, Title VIII, July 30, 1977

*Sec. 808*
- Requires an annual report on all DOD experiments and studies involving the use of human subjects for testing of CBW agents and restricts both government agencies and DOD contractors from conducting tests and experiments involving the use of any CBW agents on civilian populations without prior notification of local civilian officials.

## PL 96-418, Military Construction Act for 1981, Title VII, October 10, 1980

*Sec. 809, Removal of Chemical Munitions, Rocky Mountain Arsenal*
- Requires the removal of all chemical munitions from RMA not later than one year after enactment of this act and a report to the Senate and House Armed Services Committees on proposed methods to carry out the move within 90 days of this report.

## PL 97-375, Congressional Reports Elimination Act of 1982, Title II, December 21, 1982

*Sec. 203, Reports by the Department of Defense*
- Moves requirement to submit an annual report on all DOD experiments and studies involving the use of human subjects for testing of CB agents from PL 95-79 to PL 91-121 (consolidates the annual reports on CBW agents).

## PL 98-94, DOD Authorization Act for 1984, Title XII, September 24, 1983

*Sec. 1233, Limitation on Procurement of Binary Chemical Weapons*
- Withholds obligation or expenditure of funds for the production of binary chemical munitions until the president certifies to Congress that for each 155-mm binary artillery shell or aircraft-delivered binary aerial bomb produced, a serviceable unitary artillery shell from the existing stockpile is rendered permanently useless for military purposes.

## PL 98-525, DOD Authorization Act for 1985, Title XV, Part B, October 19, 1984

*Sec. 1511, Chemical Warfare Review Commission*
- Directs the establishment of a "Chemical Warfare Review Commission" to review the overall adequacy of the chemical warfare posture of the United States, in particular to determine whether the U.S. government should produce binary chemical munitions.
- Requires the president to submit the commission's report findings and recommendations to Congress by April 1, 1985.

## PL 99-145, DOD Authorization Act for 1986, Title XIV, Part B - Chemical Weapons, November 8, 1985

*Sec. 1411, Conditions on Spending Funds for Binary Chemical Weapons*
- Limits FY 1986 funds not to be spent on procurement or assembly of binary chemical munitions or establishment of production facilities except in two cases (see following two bullets).
- Requires president to certify that the United States has developed a plan to deploy binary chemical munitions overseas in support of contingency plans to deter chemical weapons attacks against the United States and its NATO allies.
- Requires president to certify that binary chemical munitions are required as a national security interest, that it will be safe to handle and store the munitions, and that the Secretary of Defense plan to destroy existing stocks is ready for implementation.
- Requires the binary components to be built and stored in separate states and transported separately.
- Declares a sense of Congress that existing unitary chemical munitions should be replaced by modern, safer binary chemical munitions.
- Requires the president submit a report not later than October 1, 1986, on NATO chemical deterrent posture.

*Sec. 1412, Destruction of Existing Stockpile of Lethal Chemical Agents and Munitions*
- Directs the Secretary of Defense to carry out destruction of existing stockpile of lethal chemical agents and munitions that exists as of date of act, to be completed by

September 30, 1994 (or by the date established by a treaty banning possession of chemical weapons, if ratified by the United States).

- Directs provisions for maximum protection for the environment, the general public, and the personnel involved and adequate and safe facilities designed solely for the destruction of lethal chemical agents and munitions.
- Directs that the disposal facilities not be utilized for any purpose other than chemical demilitarization and, upon completion, dismantled and disposed of in accordance with applicable regulations.
- Calls for a plan to provide an evaluation of alternative destruction concepts, technical advances, a permanent written record, and description of methods and facilities to be used, schedule, and management organization, to be coordinated with HHS and EPA.
- Establishes a new Army management organization headed by a "qualified" general officer to be established not later than May 1, 1986, with funds set forth as a separate account not to be included in any other military account.
- Calls for an annual report on the U.S. stockpile and proposed demilitarization activities by site and related funding actions.
- Prohibits further development or procurement of unitary chemical agents or munitions for other than intelligence or defensive research analysis.
- Reaffirms the U.S. position on first use of chemical weapons as that set out in the Geneva Protocol of 1925, ratified with reservations in 1975 (CW does not include use of herbicides, riot control agents, smoke, or obscurants).

*Sec. 1413, Report concerning the Testing of Chemical Warfare Agents*
- Calls for a report within 90 days on all DOD sites that tested diluted or undiluted CW agents, the nature and extent of consultations with state and local officials, consideration of nearby residential and public facilities, need for an EIS, costs to assist companies to test in more isolated areas, and related testing issues for the site selection process.

## PL 99-661, DOD Authorization Act for FY 1987, Title I, Part E—Chemical Weapons, November 14, 1986

*Sec. 151, Authorization of Appropriations for Chemical Demilitarization Program*
- Authorizes $120.1 million for chemical disposal operations.

*Sec. 152, Limitation on the Expenditure of Funds for the Bigeye Binary Chemical Bomb*
- Prohibits expenditures of FY 1987 funds to procure or assemble the Bigeye bomb. Holds back authorization to spend FY 1986 funds until the president certifies that production of the binary bomb is in the United State's national security interests and that the design, planning, and environmental requirements for the production facility are satisfied.
- Directs GAO monitoring of the bomb's operational testing and a report from the Comptroller General on an assessment of that testing.
- Requires the Secretary of Defense to submit a report on the military requirements for long-range standoff chemical munitions not later than March 15, 1987.

*Sec. 153, Chemical Weapons, Agents, or Components at Lexington-Bluegrass Depot*
- Prohibits the shipment of any chemical weapons, agents, or components used in chemical weapons to Blue Grass Army Depot. After completing disposal of the depot's

current stockpile, prohibits any other assembly, construction, testing, storage, or disposal of any CB weapons.
- Permits the Secretary of Defense to waive this section in the interests of national security.

*Sec. 154, Report on Chemical Weapons Demilitarization Program*
- Requires the Secretary of Defense to submit a report to the House and Senate on the chemical demil program, outlining methods to optimize safety considerations and cost-effectiveness considerations not later than February 1, 1987, not considering a chemical weapons elimination deadline of September 1997.

*Sec. 155, Technical Amendment to PL 99-145 Relating to Binary Chemical Munitions*
- Amends PL 99-145 by replacing "North Atlantic Council" with "Defense Planning Committee of the North Atlantic Treaty Organization meeting in permanent session."

## PL 100-180, National Defense Authorization (NDA) Act for FY 1988–1989, Title I, December 4, 1987

*Sec. 125, Revision of Chemical Demilitarization Program*
- Calls for a final programmatic EIS on the chemical demil program not later than January 1, 1988. Withholds procurement and military construction funds until Secretary of Defense certifies to Congress that the plan includes an evaluation of alternative technologies, full-scale operational verification procedures for the approved disposal technology, and maximum protection for public health and the environment.
- Calls for an alternative concept plan for the demil program to include the above qualifications plus a revised schedule and funding requirements necessary to execute.

*Sec. 126, Withdrawal of European Chemical Stockpile*
- States that the U.S. unitary chemical munitions stored in Europe should not be removed until the munitions are replaced with an equal capability using binary chemical munitions stationed on the soil of at least one European NATO country (although not stated in the bill, this country was Germany).

## PL 100-456, NDA Act for FY 1989, September 29, 1988

*Sec. 118, Modifications in Chemical Demilitarization Program*
- Replaces the stockpile elimination date stated in PL 99-145 with the general term "stockpile elimination deadline," which for purposes of this section, means April 30, 1997.
- Requires the Secretary of the Army to successfully complete operational verification testing of the incineration technology at Johnston Island prior to conducting a system test of any equipment at any other chemical disposal facility (this does not apply to CAMDS at Tooele).
- Requires the Secretary of Defense to submit a report to the House and Senate certifying the completion of the successful operational testing of the Johnston Island's equipment and the facility.

**PL 101-165, DOD Appropriations Act for FY 1990, Title VI—Chemical Agents and Munitions Destruction, Defense, November 21, 1989**

- Authorizes expenses of $148.4 million for O&M, $73 million for procurement, and $8 million for research and development, of which $6.1 million is to be used for cryofracture operations. Of the FY89 funds, $16.3 million in R&D will be obligated on cryofracture operations not later than January 15, 1990.
- Authorizes the Secretary of Defense to delegate responsibility for all aspects of the chemical demil operations and retrograde movement of chemical agents and munitions to the Secretary of the Army (planning for movement of the European stockpile).
- Limits obligation or expenditure of retrograde funds to $10 million until the Secretary of Defense certifies to Congress that JACADS has successfully destroyed live chemical agent munitions, and that adequate storage capacity exists on Johnston Island.
- Denies any obligation of funds to construct additional chemical munitions storage facilities on Johnston Island.

**PL 101-189, NDA Act for FY 1990–1991, Title I, Part H, November 29, 1989**

*Sec. 171, Restriction on Obligation of Funds for Procurement of Binary Chemical Munitions*
- Restricts use of FY 1990 funds for the use of producing 155-mm binary chemical projectiles until the Secretary of the Army certifies that the incumbent contractor can keep up delivery rates of the components and rounds to schedule and that the rounds meet government specifications. Calls for a GAO audit of the monthly production rates starting in February 1990 until the contractor can demonstrate consistent success.

*Sec. 172, Chemical Munitions European Retrograde Program*
- Restricts use of FY 1990 funds for the purpose of retrograding the European chemical stocks until Secretary of Defense certifies that an adequate binary chemical munition stockpile will exist, and that the retrograde program is based on minimum technical and operational risk and maximum safety to the public.
- Directs the Secretary of Defense to deliver a report on the full budgetary impact of the program and the potential effect of the retrograde program on the chemical demil program.

*Sec. 173, Chemical Demilitarization Cryofracture Program*
- Calls for development of an operational cryofracture facility at Tooele Army Depot, Utah, as expeditiously as possible, designating $16.3 million of FY 1989 chemical demil funds for research and development in this area

*Sec. 243, Restoration of Certain Reporting Requirements Relating to Chemical and Biological Warfare Agents*
- Amends Goldwater–Nichols DOD Reorganization Act of 1986 to require continued annual reports on chemical demil as per PL 91-121, PL 91-441, and PL 95-79.

**PL 101-510, NDA Act for FY 1991, Title I, Part G—Chemical Munitions, November 5, 1990**

*Sec. 171, Annual Report on Safety of Chemical Weapons Stockpile*
- Adds requirement for an assessment of the safety status and integrity of the stockpile to include an estimate of how much longer the stockpile can be safely stored, a site-by-

site safety assessment, and steps taken to monitor the stockpile's safety and to mitigate further deterioration.

*Sec. 172, Funding Clarification for Chemical Weapons Stockpile Disposal Program*
- Permits Secretary of Defense to make CSEPP grants to state and local governments directly or through FEMA.

*Sec. 173, Chemical Weapons Stockpile Safety Contingency Plan*
- Requires Secretary of Defense to develop a plan for DOD to take actions if the stockpile began an accelerated rate of deterioration not later than 180 days after date of act.

*Sec. 364, Report on Transportation of Chemical Weapons from Federal Republic of Germany to Johnston Island*
- Requires Secretary of the Army to prepare a report analyzing safety aspects of the project to remove and transport chemical weapons from Federal Republic of Germany to Johnston Island, due not later than 60 days after completion of move.
- Report will be used in site-specific EIS studies to assist in determination of validity of programmatic on-site disposal decisions.

## PL 102-95, FY 1992 Defense Appropriations Act, Title VI, June 7, 1991

- Prohibits obligation or expenditure of funds for the procurement of equipment for chemical weapon disposal facilities (other than Tooele) until the Secretary of Defense certifies that (1) operational verification testing at the JACADS Facility is complete, (2) a report on the results of the tests has been submitted to the Congress, (3) plant design has been verified, and (4) necessary environmental permits have been secured for the sites for which the equipment is to be procured.

## PL 102-190, NDA Act for FY 1992–1993, Title I, December 5, 1991

*Sec. 151, Chemical Weapons Stockpile Elimination Deadline*
- Changes demilitarization deadline from April 30, 1997, to July 31, 1999, and permits the Secretary of Defense to provide funds through cooperative agreements with state and local governments for the purpose of assisting them in processing and approving permits and licenses necessary to construct and operate the chemical demil facilities.

## PL 102-484, NDA Act for FY 1993, Title I, Subtitle G—Chemical Demilitarization Program, October 23, 1992

*Sec. 171, Change in Chemical Weapons Stockpile Elimination Deadline*
- Changes demilitarization deadline from July 31, 1999 to December 31, 2004

*Sec. 172, Chemical Demil Citizen Advisory Commissions (CACs)*
- Establishes a citizens' commission for each state in which there is a "low-volume" site (i.e., less than 5 percent of the total stockpile) and for other states with a chemical stockpile if the governor requests such a commission.
- Directs ASA(IL&E) to send a representative to meet with each commission.

*Sec. 173, Evaluation of Alternative Technologies*
- Directs submission of a report to Congress not later than December 31, 1993, on alternatives to chemical demil, including analysis of the NAS report on alternative chemical demil technologies, comparisons of each alternative technology to incineration on safety, environmental protection, and cost effectiveness, examination of Russian technology approaches, and consideration of appropriate CAC concerns.
- Stops site preparation and construction of chemical demil sites (but not project planning, obtaining permits, etc.) unless it started previous to this Act's date (means Pueblo and Blue Grass depots).

*Sec. 174, Alternative Disposal Process for Low-Volume Sites*
- Commits the Army to use alternative disposal technology if it is proven to be significantly safer and equally or more cost-effective than incineration process.

*Sec. 175, Revised Chemical Weapons Disposal Concept Plan*
- Commits Army to submit a revised plan if an alternative technology is proven out and consider revisions to program and schedule that might result in reduced cost and decreased program risk.

*Sec. 176, Report on Destruction of Non-stockpile Chemical Material*
- Requires submission of report not later than February 1, 1993, on plans for destruction of all chemical warfare material not covered by 1986 NDA Act (everything outside of the stockpiles).
- Identifies materiel to be covered as binary chemical munitions, buried chemical munitions, chemical munitions recovered from ranges, chemical weapons production facilities, and all other chemical warfare material outside of the stockpiles.
- Report to include list of suspected locations, estimates of numbers, inventory of former production facilities, inventory of binary chemical munitions, use of CAMDS, if any, in destroying these materials, estimate of costs, and time to complete destruction effort.

*Sec. 177, Physical and Chemical Integrity of the Chemical Weapons Stockpile*
- Calls for a report not later than May 1, 1993, on the status of the physical security and safety of the stockpile, focusing on leak incidents and associated risks and actions that could be taken to minimize/eliminate the risks.

*Sec. 178, Sense of Congress concerning International Consultation and Exchange Program*
- Recommends that the Secretary of Defense establish a program to exchange disposal technology with other nations participating in chemical weapons treaties.

*Sec. 179, Technical Amendments to Section 1412*
- Amends PL 99-145 by eliminating requirement to destroy unitary chemical munitions in conjunction with procuring binary chemical munitions and eliminating the requirement to account for all lethal chemical agents and munitions in the stockpile as of November 1985 in annual reports.

*Sec. 180, Definition of Low-Volume Sites*
- Defines a "low-volume site" as one of the three chemical weapons storage sites in the United States at which there is stored less than 5 percent of the total U.S. stockpile of unitary munitions (Blue Grass, Newport, and Aberdeen).

## PL 103-139, DOD Appropriations Act for 1994, November 11, 1993

*Sec. 8075A*
- Prohibits use of funds for the preparation of studies on the feasibility of removal or transportation of unitary chemical weapons from the eight chemical storage sites within CONUS (exception: nonstockpile munitions).
- Prohibits use of funds for the preparation of studies on the potential future uses of the nine disposal facilities for purposes other than the destruction of stockpile chemical munitions (exception: CAMDS).

## PL 103-160, NDA Act for FY 1994, Title I, November 30, 1993

*Sec. 107, Chemical Demilitarization Program*
- Authorizes the obligation and expenditure of funds for destruction of chemical warfare material not covered by PL 99-145 (nonstockpile).

*Sec. 155, Administration of Chemical Demilitarization Program*
- Amends PL 102-484 to permit submission of comments by CACs on the Army's alternative technology report to the Senate and House Armed Services Committees.

*Sec 156, Chemical Munitions Disposal Facilities, Tooele Army Depot, Utah*
- Holds back funds for systemization of Tooele disposal facility until Secretary of Defense certifies to Congress that the facility will not jeopardize the health, safety, or welfare of the surrounding community and that adequate base support, management, oversight, and security personnel are present to ensure the public safety during operations.

*Sec. 2106, Construction of Chemical Munitions Disposal Facilities (a.k.a. the Browder Amendment)*
- Suspends obligation of funds for building a new chemical munitions disposal facility at Anniston Army Depot until the Secretary of Defense certifies to Congress that JACADS has operated successfully for six months, meeting all required environmental and safety standards, and is proven operationally effective.
- Requires the Secretary of the Army to schedule the award of another chemical munitions disposal facility at another non-low-volume chemical weapons storage site within 12 months of the award of a construction contract for the disposal facility at Anniston Army Depot.

## PL 103-337, NDA Act for FY 1995, Title I, October 5, 1994

*Sec. 142, Identification in Budget of Funds for Chemical Demil Military Construction Projects*
- Amends PL 99-145, Sec. 1412(f), to add "including funds for military construction projects necessary to carry out this section."

*Sec. 143, Transportation of Chemical Munitions*
- Prohibits the transportation of any chemical munition of the chemical stockpiles out of the state in which the munition is located on date of act and prohibits the entry of any chemical munition not located in a state into that state.
- Permits the transportation of discovered chemical munitions not previously part of the stockpile to the nearest chemical stockpile storage facility as long as Secretary of

Defense considers the transportation as necessary and the transportation can be accomplished while protecting public health and safety.

## PL 104-106, NDA Act for FY 1996, Title I, Subtitle E—Chemical Demilitarization Program, February 10, 1996

*Sec. 151, Repeal of Requirement to Proceed Expeditiously with Development of Chemical Demil Cryofracture Facility at Tooele Army Depot, Utah*

- Repeals PL 101-189, sec. 173, requirement to proceed expeditiously with development of cryofracture facility at Tooele Army Depot.

*Sec 152, Destruction of Existing Stockpile of Lethal Chemical Agents and Munitions*

- Directs the Army to proceed with the program for destruction of the chemical munitions stockpile, while maintaining maximum protection of the environment, the general public, and the personnel involved.
- Ensure that support measures required by Army chemical surety and security regulations, general and site chemical demil plans specific to that site, and Solid Waste Disposal Act and Clean Air Act are in place.
- Conduct an analysis of alternatives assessing the current status of the demil program and identify measures to significantly reduce the total cost of the program while ensuring maximum protection and submit an interim report on the current status of the program by March 1, 1996.
- Review and evaluate impact of base closures caused by chemical demil effort on local community within 90 days of act.

*Sec 153, Administration of Chemical Demil Program*

- Amends PL 102-484, sec. 172(g) to identify that members of the CACs receive no pay for their involvement but will cover travel costs.
- Requires quarterly reports on such funding.
- Amends PL 99-145, sec. 1412(e) by stating that a civilian equivalent to a general officer can be the Program Manager for Chemical Demilitarization.

*Sec. 1061(k), Reports and Notifications Relating to Chemical and Biological Agents*

- Repeals sec. 409(a) of PL 99-121, requiring an annual report on research, development, test, evaluation, and procurement of all lethal and nonlethal CBW agents.

## PL 104-201, NDA Act for FY 1997, Title I, September 23, 1996

*Sec. 142, Destruction of Existing Stockpile of Lethal Chemical Agents and Munitions*

- Amends PL 104-106 by adding requirement for an assessment of the chemical demil program for destruction of assembled chemical munitions and of the alternative technologies and processes required (other than incineration) that could be used, while ensuring "maximum protection" for the general public, to be completed not later than December 31, 1997.
- Requires the assessment to be conducted in coordination with the NRC and must evaluate the costs of alternative technologies against incineration.
- Identifies $25 million for construction of a pilot plant for demilitarization of chemical agents for assembled munitions if the Secretary of Defense makes the decision to continue development of an alternative technology or process.

*Sec. 1073(d), Chemical Demilitarization Citizens Advisory Commissions*
- Amends PL 102-484 to require the ASA(RDA) to meet with the CACs instead of the ASA(IL&E).

*Sec. 1074(d)(2), Technical and Clerical Amendments*
- Amends PL 99-145 requirement for a period report by making technical changes to the U.S. Code's language.

*Sec. 1076, Chemical Stockpile Emergency Preparedness Program*
- Calls for a report from the Secretary of the Army on implementation and success of establishing Integrated Product/Process Teams between the states, FEMA, and the Army as a management tool for CSEPP not later than 120 days after date of act. Failing this action, the Secretary of the Army assumes full control and responsibility for CSEPP.

## PL 104-208, DOD Appropriations Act for 1997, Title VIII, September 30, 1996

*Sec. 8038*
- Restricts federally funded R&D centers from preparing studies on removing or transporting chemical weapons or agents from the eight stockpile sites to Johnston Island (exception: GAO) or studies on the potential future uses of the nine chemical disposal facilities for purposes other than for chemical munitions (exception: CAMDS).

*Sec. 8065*
- Identifies $40 million from the chemical demil program for conduct of a pilot program to identify and demonstrate alternative destruction technologies for assembled chemical munitions (ACWA), with the requirement that the USD(A&T) (later USD[AT&L]) designate a project manager not associated with the demil program and an annual report to Congress on activities within the ACWA program.
- Requires the USD(A&T) to evaluate the effectiveness of the alternative technologies identified in their ability to demil munitions within all applicable federal and state environmental and safety regulations.
- Repeals sec. 142(f)(3) of PL 104-201 requiring the pilot program to be conducted at the selected chemical agent stockpile site for which the process is recommended.
- Suspends the obligation of any construction funds for a chemical disposal facility at Blue Grass or Pueblo Army Depots until 180 days after the Secretary of Defense submits a report to Congress on the alternative technologies' effectiveness and safety.
- Prohibits the obligation of funds for the preparation of studies, assessments, or planning of the removal and transportation of stockpile assembled unitary chemical weapons or neutralized chemical agent to any of the eight stockpile sites within the United States.

## Senate Resolution 75, April 24, 1997

- The Senate advises and consents to the ratification of the Chemical Weapons Convention, meaning that the chemical weapons stockpile must be destroyed by April 29, 2007.

## PL 105-85, NDA Act for FY98, Title X, November 18, 1997

*Sec. 1041, Repeal of Miscellaneous Reporting Requirements*

- Eliminates quarterly report on travel funding for chemical demil CACs established by PL 104-106.

*Sec. 1078, Restrictions on the Use of Human Subjects for Testing of CB Agents*

- Repeals sec. 808 of PL 95-79, restates prohibition of conducting (directly or by contract) any test or experiment involving the use of CBW agents on a civilian population or human subjects

- Identifies exceptions to preceding statement, to include if the test or experiment carried out was for peaceful purposes related to various research activities, any purpose directly related to protection against CB weapons and agents, or law enforcement purposes to include those related to riot control.

- Requires informed consent from human subjects and submission of a report from Secretary of Defense to the Senate and House Armed Services Committees 30 days prior to the beginning of such tests.

## PL 105-261, NDA Act for FY99, Title I, Subtitle E—Other Matters, October 17, 1998

*Sec. 141, Chemical Stockpile Emergency Preparedness Program*

- Amends PL 99-145 by defining director of FEMA responsibilities, to carry out a program to provide assistance to state and local governments in developing emergency capabilities to respond to stockpile and disposal facility incidents.

- Establishes that no funding is to be provided past the completion of a site's destruction of its stockpile. Requires an annual report on funding these actions.

*Sec. 142, Alternative Technologies for Destruction of Assembled Chemical Weapons*

- Directs PM ACWA to continue development and testing of alternative technologies to incineration, independent of PM CD and reporting to USD(A&T). Report due to Congress not later than September 30, 1999.

- Upon successful demonstration of a technology and USD(A&T) approval, take actions to prepare appropriate documentation and award a contract for development of a pilot facility for the technology.

- Requires USD(A&T) certify to Congress that alternative technology is as safe and cost-effective for disposal operations as incineration and is capable of meeting CWC deadline and can meet federal and state environmental and safety laws. Requires NRC consultations on this certification.

## PL 105-277, Chemical Weapons Convention Implementation Act of 1998, Div I—Chemical Weapons Convention, Title VI, October 21, 1998

*Sec. 601, Repeal*

- Repeals sec. 808 of PL 95-79, requiring an annual report of the use of human subjects for the testing of CBW agents.

*Sec. 602, Prohibition*

- Prohibits the Secretary of Defense or employee of the U.S. government, directly or by contract, to conduct any test or experiment involving the use of any CBW agent on a civilian population or use of human subjects for the testing of CBW agents.

- Defines a biological warfare agent as any microorganism or component of any microorganism that is capable of causing death, disease, or other biological malfunction in a human, animal, plant, or another living organism; deterioration of food, water, equipment, supplies or materials, or deleterious alteration of the environment.

## PL 106-52, Military Construction Appropriations Act for 2000, August 17, 1999

*Sec. 131*

- Prohibits the obligation or expenditure of funds for any purpose relating to the construction at Blue Grass Army Depot or any facility employing a specific technology for demilitarization of assembled chemical munitions until the Secretary of Defense certifies to Congress that DOD has completed a demonstration of six alternative technologies as identified by the ACWA program (three additional technologies).

## PL 106-65, NDA Act for FY 2000, Div A, Title I, Subtitle E—Chemical Stockpile Destruction Program, October 5, 1999

*Sec. 141, Destruction of Existing Stockpile of Lethal Chemical Agents and Munitions*

- Calls for the Secretary of Defense to conduct an assessment of the chemical demil program, including ACWA, for the purpose of significantly reducing the cost of the program while ensuring completion of the program under the CWC, "while maintaining maximum protection of the general public, the personnel involved in the demil program, and the environment."

- Requires a report from the Secretary of Defense on actions to be taken and any recommendations for additional legislation that may be required to effect cost reductions within said parameters.

- Amends PL 99-145 by requiring all disposal facilities to be disposed of when no longer needed for the purpose of chemical demil and forbids use of the facilities for any purpose other than disposing of chemical agents and munitions that existed on November 8, 1985.

- Exception to preceding bullet agents and munitions created after 1985, if the state issues appropriate permits and licenses for a disposal facility to destroy these agents and munitions.
- Directs the U.S. Comptroller General to review and assess the entire chemical demil program not later than March 1, 2000, to include the disposal program, non-stockpile project, CSEPP, ATAP, and ACWA programs.

*Sec. 142, Comptroller General Report on Anticipated Effects of Proposed Changes in the Operation of Storage Sites for Lethal Chemical Agents and Munitions*

- Requires the Comptroller General to submit a report to the Senate and House not later than March 31, 2000 on the proposal to reduce the federal civilian workforce involved in the operation of the eight stockpile sites. Workforce would be converted to contractor operation and be effectuated by FY 2002. Report will focus on each site separately.
- Directs the report to focus on associated programmatic and safety risks of changing workforce, effects on environmental protection, ability to perform industrial missions, and recommendations to mitigate risks and adverse effects identified in the report.

## PL 106-79, DOD Appropriations for 2000, October 25, 1999

*Sec. 8077*

- Prohibits the use of funds to transport chemical munitions to Johnston Island for the purposes of storage or demilitarization, excluding former U.S. obsolete World War II munitions found in the Pacific Theater of Operations.
- Permits the president to suspend the above prohibition in times of war.

*Sec. 8159*

- Directs the Secretary of Defense to add a description and assessment of the management of the ACWA program to the annual report to Congress on the chemical demil program.

## PL 106-398, NDA Act for 2001, Subtitle F, October 30, 2000

*Sec. 151, Pueblo Chemical Depot Chemical Agent and Munitions Destruction Technologies*

- Directs the Secretary of Defense to consider, for purposes of disposal of chemical munitions at Pueblo, incineration or any technology demonstrated under ACWA on or before May 1, 2000.

*Sec. 152, Report on Assessment of Need for Federal Economic Assistance for Communities Impacted by Chemical Demilitarization Activities*

- Requires the Secretary of Defense to report to Congress on the impact of the DOD chemical demil program on the communities in the vicinity of the eight stockpile storage sites and associated activities.

- Report is to include the assessment of whether federal economic assistance is needed and appropriate.

*Sec. 153, Prohibition Against Disposal of Non-Stockpile Chemical Warfare Material at Anniston Chemical Stockpile Disposal Facility*

- Prohibits the use of funds to facilitate the disposal of any non-stockpile munitions or material at Anniston Army Depot unless it is already stored at the depot.

## PL 107-117, DOD and Emergency Supplemental Appropriations for Recovery from and Response to Terrorist Attacks on the United States Act, January 10, 2002

*Sec. 8075*

- Prohibits the appropriation of funds to transport or provide for transportation of chemical munitions or agents to Johnston Island for the purpose of storing or demilitarizing such munitions or agents, except in the case of obsolete World War II-era U.S. chemical munitions or agents found in the Pacific Theater of Operations.

*Sec. 8164*

- Requires the Secretary of the Army to submit a report to Congress assessing the current risks under and alternatives to the current Army plan for destruction of chemical weapons. The plan must address risks of terrorist attacks on the stockpile sites, continued storage of the weapons, and recommendations on eliminating or reducing the risks.

# Notes

## PREFACE

1. Grant T. Hammond, *The Mind of War: John Boyd and American Security* (Smithsonian Institution: Washington, DC, 2001), p. 158.

## CHAPTER 1: NO MORE CHEMICAL ARMS

1. Katherine Bouma, "Governor Vows He'll Sue To Stop Army Incinerator," *Birmingham News*, February 2, 2002.

2. Lane Harvey Brown, "Army Speeds Up APG Plans," *Baltimore Sun*, January 10, 2002.

3. The U.S. Senate ratified the Geneva Protocol of 1925 in 1975, following international concerns raised over the use of tear gases and herbicides in Vietnam.

4. Craig E. Colten and Peter N. Skinner, *The Road to Love Canal: Managing Industrial Waste before EPA* (Austin: University of Texas Press, 1996), pp. 148–51.

5. Ibid., pp. 56–57; also see company web sites of Northern Disposal Services: (http://www.northerndisposal.co.uk/services/dwinjection.htm) and of L. Sims and Associates: (http://www.simsenv.com/deepwell.htm).

6. Sterling Seagrave, *Yellow Rain: A Journey through the Terror of Chemical Warfare* (New York: M. Evans & Co., 1978), pp. 258–61.

7. I do not believe that the Army was responsible for the alleged sheep deaths at Dugway Proving Ground in 1968, a statement that is contrary to public perception but supported by a review of the facts. I more thoroughly address this in my book, *America's Struggle with Chemical-Biological Warfare* (Westport, CT: Praeger, 2000). However, the timing and resulting public reaction were unfortunate and created incredibly bad press for the Chemical Corps, affecting its future in chemical demilitarization, offensive weapon development, and even defensive equipment development.

8. There were more than 40 major movements of chemical agents and munitions from Rocky Mountain Arsenal to Tooele Army Depot in the summer and fall of 1968 and nearly 20 movements to Tooele in 1969. William R. Brankowitz, "Chemical Stockpile Disposal Program: Chemical Weapons Movement History Compilation," Aberdeen Proving Ground, MD: PEO-PM for Chemical Demilitarization, 1987.

9. There was one final CHASE dump on August 18, 1970. CHASE X had been stopped from dumping in 1968, but the Army requested an exception due to a large number of obsolete M55 rockets and no acceptable demilitarization options available. The Liberty ship SS *Le Baron Russell Briggs* was towed under escort 250 miles east of Cape Kennedy, Florida, and scuttled.

10. Charles O. Jones, *An Introduction to the Study of Public Policy, 3rd ed.* (Monterey, CA: Brooks/Cole, 1984), p. 26. The original quote came from Heinz Eulau and Kenneth Prewitt, *Labyrinths of Democracy* (Indianapolis: Bobbs-Merrill, 1973), p. 465.

11. Jones, *An Introduction to the Study of Public Policy*, p. 38.

12. Thomas R. Dye, *Understanding Public Policy, 9th ed.* (Englewood Cliffs, NJ: Prentice Hall, 1998), p. 2–3.

13. Stephen K. Scroggs, *Army Relations with Congress: Thick Armor, Dull Sword, Slow Horse* (Westport, CT: Praeger, 2000), pp. 175–203.

14. I should make a point that, as I talk about Army leadership, I mean the Army two-, three- and four-star general officers outside the Chemical Corps. Similar to Scroggs' discussion about Army patterns with other issues, the Army often sends one-star general officers or colonels to state its issues to Congress and the other services for chemical warfare issues, as the upper leadership does not see the need to get involved. Often Chemical Corps officers are sent into policy/program discussions without strong endorsement from its higher (non-chemical) leaders.

15. In fairness, the late 1960s was a different culture—the public trust (and to an extent, Congressional trust) in the Army was low, and perhaps the Army leadership knew they couldn't win this one.

16. Steve Vogel, "EPA Urges Quicker Pace in NW Probe for Arsenic," *Washington Post*, February 15, 2001, p. B3.

17. It was Dr. Ted Prociv's observation that while Army general officers supported making chemical weapons, they thought the huge investment in destroying them was a complete waste of resources. Ironically, the chemical demilitarization program cost more than many major weapon systems.

## CHAPTER 2: A LEGACY OF CHEMICAL WEAPONS

1. The various forms of mustard are HD—distilled mustard (more pure), HT—mustard plus an additive to lower the freezing point, HN—nitrogen mustards (eliminates the odor but less persistent). TGA and TGB are thickened versions of GA and GB, designed to increase the persistency of these semi-volatile liquids.

2. PM Chemical Demilitarization, *Department of Defense's Status Assessment for the Chemical Demilitarization Program* (Aberdeen Proving Ground, Program Manager for Chemical Demilitarization, 1997), pp. 2-11 and 2-12. This annual report has all the leaker incidents identified by munition type from 1983 to 1996. Approximately 1,708 leakers were noted prior to 1983, with 2,249 leakers noted between 1983 and 1996.

3. Contrary to the plot of Michael Bay's 1996 movie *The Rock*, M55 rockets are not guided missiles, nor can they be disassembled.

4. Six bomblets were found in a scrap yard within Rocky Mountain Arsenal in mid-October 2000. This issue was detailed in the first chapter. After careful assessment and development of a disposal capability, the Army detonated the bomblets safely within an explosives disposal system. In May 2001, a continued investigation of the scrap yard led to the discovery of four more bomblets. The same cautious state-approved process of carefully moving the bomblets to the explosives disposal system was successfully carried out on July 20.

5. The 20-odd Army specialists were painting the ammunition bunkers when exposed to low levels of nerve agent. They reported to the medics and were released within 24 hours. The news that there were U.S. chemical weapons on a Japanese-owned island without the

Japanese government's knowledge lasted much longer. Operation Red Hat had moved the chemical weapons from the Army depot on Okinawa to Johnston Island in 1971. Operation Steel Box moved U.S. chemical weapons stored in Germany to Johnston Island in November 1990. Both operations were carried out without incident and without casualties.

6.  Raytheon Engineers and Construction and Westinghouse Electric's demilitarization activities were acquired by Morrison Knudsen Corporation, which created Washington Group International in July 2000. Washington Demilitarization, one of its divisions, runs the chemical disposal operations.

7.  Given the lack of explosives in ton containers and the relative persistence of the agent, Army safety regulations permit the storage of mustard ton containers outside without cover. Aberdeen, Tooele, and Pine Bluff Arsenal all store their mustard ton containers outdoors. Anniston stores its containers in igloos, and Umatilla stores its containers inside a warehouse. U.S. Army Program Manager for Chemical Demilitarization, *Chemical Stockpile Disposal Program Final Programmatic Environmental Impact Statement* (hereafter referred to as the CSDP FPEIS), Aberdeen Proving Ground, January 1988, p. 2-9.

8.  Prior to 1969, the Army could move chemical weapons across state lines with minimal oversight. In this case, Congress demanded, under Public Law 96-418, that the Army move all chemical munitions from Rocky Mountain Arsenal in response to public concerns about the location of the chemical weapons storage near the airport. They were flown to Dugway Proving Ground and trucked to Tooele, Utah. Utahn groups challenged the move in federal court, but the court ruled against them. The total cost of the move was approximately $6 million. National Research Council (NRC), *Disposal of Chemical Munitions and Agents* (Washington, DC: National Academy Press, 1984), p. 134.

## CHAPTER 3: DEATH AND BIRTH OF A PROGRAM

1.  Albert J. Mauroni, *America's Struggle with Chemical-Biological Warfare* (Westport, CT: Praeger, 2000), pp. 29–43. In short, a great deal of circumstantial evidence, compounded by political ambitions and media speculation, forced the Army leadership to settle out of court with Utahn ranchers for an alleged nerve gas exposure. The media have since incorrectly stated that the Army "killed 6,000 sheep." Actually, the official claim was that 4,372 sheep had been "killed by nerve gas" and that 1,877 were disabled and shot by ranchers. In fact, many of the sheep were weakened but alive, and most were killed by ranchers rather than nerve agent. I make the case in this previous work that it was dubious at best that VX agent affected the sheep and that the Army made a huge mistake by settling out of court on an issue based on circumstantial evidence. This event resulted in the loss of open-air chemical agent testing for the Army, caused increased and unjustified fears about the chemical storage sites, and was the basis for many misinterpretations of the Gulf War illnesses.

2.  Kevin Flamm, "Chemical Agent and Munition Disposal: Summary of the U.S. Army's Experience," Aberdeen Proving Ground: Program Executive Officer-Program Manager for Chemical Demilitarization, September 1987, p. 2-9; and National Research Council, "Disposal of Chemical Munitions and Agents," Washington, DC: National Academy Press, 1984, p. 21.

3.  This option was removed entirely by Congress in 1972, in passage of the Marine Protection, Research, and Sanctuaries Act (PL 92-532).

4.  This relatively simple fact of science ("the solution to pollution is dilution") evades many people when they discuss chemical agent toxicity. One reason experts do not see

poisoning of city reservoirs as a real threat is the same issue—it takes an enormous amount of contaminant, be it biological or chemical warfare agents, to create a hazard to the water supply and its treatment capability. Certainly, the often-quoted movie scenario of terrorists dropping a bottle of cholera or arsenic in the city water supply is not seen as a credible threat.

5. National Research Council, *"Recommendations for the Disposal of Chemical Agents and Munitions* (Washington, DC: National Academy Press, 1994), p. 23.

6. While President Nixon did not call for the end of development of chemical weapons, many in Congress assumed that, as he had called for the end of biological warfare, the end of chemical warfare was part of that philosophy. When the Congress slashed the funding for the Army's CB program (to ensure that the funds supporting offensive munitions development were reinvested), it accidentally crippled the CB defense program. Of course, when General Creighton Abrams recommended disestablishing the Chemical Corps in 1972 (making them a special weapons asset of the Ordnance Corps), the CB defense program tanked.

7. Department of State memorandum from Ronald Spiers to the Secretary of State, subject: US Policy on Chemical and Biological Warfare, dated November 17, 1969.

8. Respectively, these laws were Public Laws 91-121 (November 19, 1969), 91-441 (October 17, 1970), 91-672 (January 12, 1971), and 92-532 (October 23, 1972). See Appendix B for more details.

9. Program Manager Charter, Demilitarization of Chemical Materiel, U.S. Army Munitions Command, 1974, from the records of the U.S. Army Environmental Center.

10. These were the newly arrived stocks from the Chibana Army Depot, Okinawa, about 1,600 tons of various chemical munitions. These were delivered between January and September 1971 under Operation Red Hat. There were 19 chemical-filled M55 rockets (18–GB, 1–VX) that were leaking, which required demilling and disposal in October-November 1973.

11. The bulk phosgene was eventually sold to industry rather than destroyed as part of Project Eagle–Phase III. The commercial chemical industry used (and continues to use) phosgene, also known as carbonyl chloride, as a commercial component in manufacturing isocynates, polyurethanes, polycarbonate resins, pesticides, and dyes. The movement of 3,865 tons of phosgene in gas cylinders from Colorado to other states was not without public and political controversy, if only because the gas had been procured and packaged as a war materiel. The Department of Transportation had stopped the rail shipments in September 1969 to ensure that the Army had adequate packaging and safety precautions prior to moving the phosgene. Not until 1975 did Congress approve the Army's sale of the last 1,294 tons. There were no accidents in the Army's movements of phosgene from Rocky Mountain Arsenal.

12. Flamm, "Chemical Agent"; pp. 4-5–4-8, 4-22. As a point of notice, the Resource Conservation and Recovery Act (RCRA) was enacted in 1976 as a result of Public Law 94-580. The Clean Air Act and Clean Water Act followed in 1977. As such, at this time, the demilitarization program was liable only to follow existing standards laid out by the EPA on disposal operations.

13. Ibid., pp. 3-8, 3-75. The Army had never tried neutralization of VX agent on an industrial scale for many of the same challenges as in the mustard agent neutralization, although it was evaluated in the laboratory. VX neutralization by acid chlorinolysis was potentially explosive. It was also very difficult to verify the low-level safety standards set

by the government at the end of neutralization (VX standards, because of its lethality, had lower required end concentrations than GB or H).

14. Memorandum from Deputy Secretary of Defense to Secretary of the Army, subject: Elimination of Risk Associated with Chemical Agent Storage—Rocky Mountain Arsenal (RMA), Colorado, dated October 13, 1973. This memorandum, in addition to encouraging the Army to quickly resolve the situation, offered the support of approving the sale of the remaining phosgene (subject to legislative conditions set up by Congress) and a reassessment by the Joint Chiefs of Staff that the chemical agents stored at RMA were no longer required (the National Security Council had concurred as well).

15. There were 10 10,000-gallon underground tanks intended as a temporary holding site for newly manufactured GB agent. From these tanks, agent would be pumped and transferred to a building for filling munitions. The Honest John warheads and cluster bombs were considered obsolete. Colonel Gerald Watson, later to become the Chief of Chemical in the 1980s, oversaw the execution of Project Eagle Phase II as the commander of RMA.

16. GAO/NSIAD-86-1FS, *Chemical Munitions: Cost Estimates for Demilitarization and Production* (Washington, DC: GAO, October 31, 1985), p. 8.

17. First Lieutenant Ted Prociv, then stationed at Dugway, designed and built a transportable chemical laboratory to accompany the DATS. This was his first, but not last, role in chemical weapons disposal efforts.

18. National Research Council, *Disposal of Chemical Agent Identification Sets* (Washington, DC: National Academy Press, 1999), p. 19.

19. This work was done in part by Jack Scott when he was working for the Army. He is now the president of Parsons, which is responsible for several of the demilitarization facilities.

20. Flamm, "Chemical Agent," 4-27–4-28.

21. Data taken from table in Flamm, Table 4-15, p. 4-48.

22. The full details on the comparison of technologies is in Flamm, pp. 3-75 through 3-82.

23. This evaluation had been initiated as a result of General John Guthrie (commander, AMC) commenting to General Ed Myer (Chief of Staff of the Army) that there were concerns about the condition of the chemical munitions on Johnston Island at the 1979 Army Commanders Conference. In June 1980, Colonel John Mason, commander of USATHAMA, completed the study with the final report and recommendations on how to deal with the Johnston Island stockpile (and other sites) being sent to HQ DA in September. HQ AMC, *Annual Historical Review for FY80*, p. 41.

24. NRC, *Disposal of Chemical Munitions and Agents*, p. 24.

25. NRC, *Recommendations for the Disposal of Chemical Agents and Munitions*, pp. 185–88.

26. Stockholm International Peace Research Institute (SIPRI), *Chemical Weapons: Destruction and Conversion* (London: Taylor and Francis, 1980), pp. 103–4.

27. These standards were developed and approved over time, 1971 for GB, 1985 for HD, and 1987 for VX. In 1988, a working group convened to consider the potential adverse health effects of long-term exposure to low doses of lethal chemical agents. The group reexamined the standards for GB, VX, and HD. Subsequently, the PHS accepted Army recommendations for maximum permissible exposures for workers and for the general population. These standards were published by the PHS in the *Federal Register*. Source: http://www.pmcd.army.mil/.

## CHAPTER 4: PUBLIC AND CONGRESSIONAL INTERESTS

1. Jones, *An Introduction to the Study of Public Policy*, pp. 30–32.

2. These offices changed names to ASA(IL&E) and ASA(ALT), respectively, in the 1990s.

3. Chemical Study Group, memorandum for the Chief of Staff of the Army, "Consolidation of Chemical Corps Functions," December 15, 1972.

4. House of Representatives Committee on Foreign Affairs, Subcommittee on National Security Policy and Scientific Development, *U.S. Chemical Warfare Policy* (Washington, DC: GPO, 1974), pp. 147–50.

5. Charles Bay, *The Other Gas Crisis: Chemical Weapons* (Carlisle Barracks, PA: Strategic Studies Institute, 1979), pp. 5–6.

6. Senate Committee on Labor and Public Welfare, *Chemical and Biological Weapons: Some Possible Approaches for Lessening the Threat and Danger* (Washington, DC: GPO, 1969), p. 47.

7. U.S. Army, *U.S. Army Activity in the U.S. Biological Warfare Programs*, Vol. I, February 24, 1977, pp. 4-2 through 5-2.

8. House of Representatives Committee on Foreign Affairs, *U.S. Chemical Warfare Policy*, pp. 147–48.

9. Ibid., p. 20.

10. J. Perry Robinson, "Binary Nerve-Gas Weapons," in SIPRI, *Chemical Disarmament: New Weapons for Old* (New York: Humanities Press, 1975), p. 24.

11. Ibid., p. 23.

12. The use of chemicals that simulate physical properties of chemical warfare agents is fraught with conditions and compromises. There is no way to simulate all the properties of a chemical warfare agent, to include its volatility, droplet size, dispersion pattern, persistence, and the way that they interact with chemical agent detectors, so often there are a number of simulants to choose from, depending on the test under way. While one simulant could show how effectively binary munitions dispersed agent, for instance, the same simulant would not be used to test how well the two components mixed prior to being dispersed. The bottom line is that while laboratory tests can document how well simulants imitate chemical warfare agent behavior, there is no substitute for observing the real thing. Unfortunately, the Army was severely limited from testing binary munitions with binary chemical agents in the open. It begs the question how the Army intended to develop chemical weapons targeting data for the munitions, which all chemical and artillery specialists using special weapons would require to actually employ the agents.

13. This was included in Public Law 95-79, DOD Appropriation Act of 1976, October 7, 1975.

14. Bay, *The Other Gas Crisis*, p. 9.

15. Project Manager for Binary Munitions, "Binary Chemical Munitions Fact Sheet," September 1989, p. 1.

16. Senate Committee on Armed Services, *Chemical Warfare* (Washington, DC: GPO, September 4, 1980), pp. 2–21.

17. Mauroni, *America's Struggle*, pp. 138–39.

18. This meant that U.S. forces could use riot control agents and herbicides with presidential approval in defensive military modes.

19. Patrick Glynn, *Closing Pandora's Box: Arms Races, Arms Control, and the History of the Cold War* (New York: Basic Books, 1992), p. 290.

20. Bay, *The Other Gas Crisis*, p. 5.

21. Matthew Meselson, ed., *Chemical Weapons and Chemical Arms Control* (New York: Carnegie Endowment for International Peace, 1978), p. 78.

22. Glynn, *Closing Pandora's Box*, pp. 275–80.

23. During a weekend radio announcement, President Reagan was asked to test the microphones. He stated, "Today, my fellow Americans, I am pleased to tell you that I've signed legislation that will outlaw Russia forever. We begin bombing in five minutes." Unfortunately, the mikes were hot, and the world heard this live.

24. Brigadier General (ret.) Walt Busbee gives full credit for developing this philosophy to Brigadier General Bobby Robinson, a Chemical Corps general in the Army's Office of the Deputy Chief of Staff for Operations and Plans. Brigadier General Robinson, working with Amie Hoeber (Deputy Under Secretary of the Army) and OSD staff, was instrumental in convincing Congress that Public Law 99-145, linking the two efforts, was necessary.

## CHAPTER 5: DEVELOPING A DISPOSAL PROGRAM

1. Sean Murphy, Alastair Hay, and Steven Rose, *No Fire, No Thunder: The Threat of Chemical and Biological Weapons* (New York: Monthly Review Press, 1984), p. 5. "In the US [sic] at least, Reagan's pressure to vote the money for the binary nerve gas programme is coming from a powerful Chemical Corps lobby. . . . And behind the US [sic] Chemical Corps, and hungry for orders, stands the giant US [sic] chemical industry looking for a way out of a recession. To some of that industry, $8 billion spent on [a] new plant to make the binary weapons, and on inactivating old stock, is money worth playing for." This was really too incredible to believe given the lack of support that the Army gave the Chemical Corps, and a very skeptical industry did not rise to support the chemical defensive or offensive program until the later 1980s.

2. Brigadier General (ret) Hidalgo recalls two companies that lobbied the Army leadership to demonstrate how they could take on the entire responsibility of disposal more efficiently than the PMCD, but the Army leadership was not convinced that private industry should take control of this sensitive area.

3. U.S. Army Toxic and Hazardous Materiels Agency (USATHAMA), *Construction and Operation of the Proposed BZ Demilitarization Facility at Pine Bluff Arsenal, Pine Bluff, Arkansas* (Aberdeen Proving Ground, MD: U.S. Army, August 1983), p. 115.

4. In November 1978, the President's Council on Environmental Quality had issued specific regulations to implement NEPA. The purposes of these regulations were to ensure that public officials and citizens had environmental information available before the federal government took actions that might adversely impact the environment; that the EIS would focus on significant issues vice numerous and mind-numbing small details; and to help public officials make decisions based on understanding environmental consequences rather than on proponency science and take actions that would protect, restore, and enhance the environment. After a government agency drafted its initial EIS, it would have to request comments from any federal agency that was authorized to develop and enforce environmental standards: any federal, state, local agencies, Indian tribes, or other agencies that requested involvement; and public citizens and organizations that might be interested or affected. The final EIS would then be completed to include addressing all comments received.

5. NRC, *Disposal of Chemical Munitions and Agents*, pp. x–xi. The recommendations following the paragraph are from the executive summary.

6. Ibid., p. 92.

7. Headquarters, Department of the Army, *Collected Works of the 30ᵗʰ Chief of Staff, USA: John A. Wickham, Jr., General, USA, Chief of Staff of the Army, June 1983–June 1987* (Washington, DC: HQ DA, 1987), p. 86.

8. GAO/NSIAD-86-1FS, *Chemical Munitions: Cost Estimates for Demilitarization and Production* (Washington, DC: GAO, 1985), p. 1.

9. Ibid., p. 7.

10. Chemical Warfare Review Commission, "Report of the Chemical Warfare Review Commission" (Washington, DC: GPO, 1985), p. 35.

11. In risk management terms, this required the Army to demonstrate an order of magnitude increase in safety over the DOE's nuclear program, which operated under the directive of "reasonable assurance."

12. Statement of Henry W. Connor before the Subcommittee on Investigations, House Armed Services Committee, on Demilitarization of the Chemical Munitions Stockpile, Washington, DC: GPO, July 25, 1986, p. 2–3. The regulations permitted either a site-specific or programmatic option in building an EIS. A site-specific EIS would focus on environmental impacts on each specific area. A programmatic EIS covers environmental matters in a broader statement with subsequent statements concentrating on location-specific concerns. The EPA encourages use of the programmatic EIS when considering programs of national scope.

13. Officially, the PMCD was authorized 12 military and 130 civilians. About 60 would come from USATHAMA and about 40 from CRDEC. Originally, all the bodies were to come from USATHAMA, which complained to HQ AMC that it could not accomplish its own mission (albeit reduced) with such a transfer.

14. At this particular time, the Army was reforming its acquisition program through the establishment of program executive officers (PEOs) and program/project Managers to focus on specific research, development, and acquisition goals. The Army's revitalized nuclear, biological, and chemical (NBC) defense program was no exception, and the Army had designated a PEO for Chemical and Nuclear Matters, Dr. Billy Richardson. The PEO was to oversee a PM for Smoke and Obscurants, a PM for NBC Defense Systems, and the PMCD and PM Binary Munitions. The PEO was disestablished in 1989, in part because a program manager scrub task force decided that the PEO was not necessary for oversight of the (relatively) limited funding and programs associated with the subordinate offices.

## CHAPTER 6: RISK MANAGEMENT

1. National Research Council, *Recommendations for the Disposal of Chemical Agents and Munitions*, p. 81.

2. The definitions and illustrative sidewalk example are from the National Research Council report, *Risk Assessment and Management at Deseret Chemical Depot and the Tooele Chemical Agent Disposal Facility* (Washington, DC: National Academy Press, 1997), pp. 59–74.

3. Colten and Skinner, *The Road to Love Canal*, p. 17.

4. Marquita K. Hill, *Understanding Environmental Pollution* (Cambridge: Cambridge University Press, 1997), p. 57.

5. Ibid., p. 66.

6. Colten and Skinner, *The Road to Love Canal*, pp. 18, 47.

7. Ibid., pp. 136–37.

8. Ibid., p. 86–87, 137–38.

9. The Army's computer model D2PC is designed to simulate the aerosolization, evaporation, transport, diffusion, deposition, and inhalation of chemical agents. The model is a general Gaussian diffusion model used in the dispersion analysis of many risk assessments. The Army has specifically calibrated the D2PC model for chemical agents and has included field data from agent tests to help set the model parameters. It has since been replaced by D2-Puff.

10. The partial relocation option came about during the public comments on the draft PEIS, in which the citizens around Aberdeen and Blue Grass were more vocal than others about seeking alternatives other than incineration on-site. These concerns were largely articulated in response to the fact that the two stockpiles had the largest surrounding populations of the eight CONUS sites. In response, the Army evaluated this concept and included it in the final PEIS.

11. Reprinted with permission from Dr. Gregory Benford, "Risks and Realities," *Fantasy and Science Fiction* (September 2000), p. 114.

12. Ibid., p. 118.

13. Amy Smithson, *The U.S. Chemical Weapons Destruction Program: Views, Analysis, and Recommendations* (Washington, DC: Henry L. Stimson Center, 1994), p. 54.

## CHAPTER 7: LEGITIMATING INCINERATION

1. This past experience included safe demilitarization at Rocky Mountain Arsenal in the 1970s (some 3,100 agent tons of mustard agent by incineration and 4,088 tons of nerve agent by chemical neutralization) and the CAMDS experience up to 1985 (105.3 agent tons of nerve agent neutralized and 18.8 tons of nerve agent incinerated).

2. All of these quotes are detailed in volume 2 of the Army's PEIS, along with the Army's response to these concerns.

3. The Sierra Club had always been opposed to incineration, focusing more on the larger national issue of incineration for disposal of municipal waste. Some felt that the Sierra Club saw the Army's chemical disposal program as a way to get national attention to the risks of incineration and win the war on incineration efforts. Certainly the Sierra Club made frequent references to municipal and private incineration efforts in cities when they discussed the potential challenges of the Army's effort.

4. Smithson, *The U.S. Chemical Weapons Destruction Program*, p. 35.

5. HQ AMC, *Annual Historical Report for FY87*, September 1989, p. 73.

6. Interview with Brigadier General (ret.) Dave Nydam.

7. GAO/PEMD-88-26, *Bigeye Bomb: 1988 Status Report* (Washington, DC: GAO, May 1998); GAO/PEMD-89-27, *Bigeye Bomb: Unresolved Developmental Issues* (Washington, DC: GAO, August 1989); and GAO/PEMD-89-29, *Bigeye Bomb: Evaluation of Operational Tests* (Washington, DC: GAO, August 1989).

8. Consider President George Bush's recent declaration that Yucca Mountain would be the national nuclear waste facility and the storm of controversy that it has created. On the one hand, it directly ensures that the many states with nuclear waste can eliminate a local hazard. On the other hand, it has caused numerous accusations that the administration had not adequately addressed environmental and safety issues for the duration of storage (hundreds or even thousands of years). Yet others noted that the EPA was forcing nuclear safety standards that tried to impose standards far below those that the public might receive from normal radiation exposure. Another fascinating public policy parallel.

## CHAPTER 8: IMPLEMENTING THE DISPOSAL PROGRAM

1. Raytheon won an eight-year contract to test and operate the facility in 1988, which was expected to cover the entire disposal process and tear down the facility following the end of operations.

2. The Army and FEMA signed a memorandum of understanding outlining their roles and responsibilities for supervision and management of the program. They created an Emergency Response Steering Committee composed of several federal agency representatives, that the two would co-chair. The Army would allocate funds to FEMA for off-post projects. Congress would pass language in 1990 (PL 101-510, NDA Act for FY 1991) giving the Secretary of Defense license to either give money directly to the states or give the money to FEMA for allocation as appropriate.

3. CSEPP Policy Paper Number 1, from the CSEPP Internet site.

4. GAO/NSIAD-90-222, *Chemical Weapons: Stockpile Destruction Delayed at the Army's Prototype Disposal Facility* (Washington, DC: GAO, July 1990), pp. 15–21.

5. NRC, *Recommendations for the Disposal of Chemical Agents and Munitions*, 1994, pp. 93–94.

6. In an effort to ensure impartiality, the Army chose Argonne National Laboratory as an independent contractor to develop detailed, site-specific data and analyze the data to determine if the Final PEIS findings had to be changed for each site. If there were no significant differences between findings and the final PEIS analysis, the PM's office would develop the site-specific EIS.

7. Edward M. Spiers, *Chemical and Biological Weapons: A Study in Proliferation* (New York, NY: St. Martin's Press, 1994), p. 96.

8. The Bilateral Destruction Agreement allowed each side to retain 5,000 tons of chemical weapons, reducing the stockpile to a sixth of its current size but allowing the U.S. military to retain a retaliatory capability.

9. Mauroni, *America's Struggle*, pp. 142–46, and Spiers, *Chemical and Biological Weapons*, pp. 90–95. Of interest is the fact that while the Soviet Union signed the bilateral agreement, they have never ratified the agreement, and the Russian government has never committed to the agreement's measures for the start of destruction of its stocks or the call for inspections. The Russian government has claimed that this is due to technical and environmental challenges that it has yet to overcome.

10. The best account of this operation is narrated in GAO/NSIAD-91-105, *Chemical Warfare: DOD's Successful Effort to Remove U.S. Chemical Weapons from Germany* (Washington, DC: GAO, February 1991).

11. Smithson, *The U.S. Chemical Weapons Destruction Program*, pp. 87–88.

## CHAPTER 9: MANAGING THE DISPOSAL PROGRAM

1. Because Anniston Army Depot was right outside the gates of Fort McClellan, the training center of the Chemical Corps, this town had been more sympathetic to the Chemical Corps. The increasing media focus and actions by the CWWG resulted in more controversy about the disposal facility planned at Anniston, especially given the relatively large population near the depot. Representative Glen Browder, once a proponent for the chemical demilitarization, became more polarized against the plans as his constituents made their fears known.

2. This statement is based on public surveys conducted by Science Applications International Corporation (SAIC) for the PMCD office around the stockpile sites in the 1990s.

3. The Army's 1992 annual report called for a one-year slip to December 2000, an 18-month extension in the deadline. This would take into account the delays encountered getting TOCDF operational (the JACAD OVTs and court challenges being the major delays) and changing the contract award dates for Umatilla and Pine Bluff based on funding slips.

4. To further clarify, the CWC treaty specified that countries did not have to dig up suspected or known chemical weapons burial sites if the weapons were buried prior to 1975. This was to the benefit of a number of nations that had tested or employed chemical weapons, either on the battlefield or on testing grounds, not merely the United States.

5. House Appropriations Report 101-822.

6. GAO/NSIAD-93-50, *Chemical Weapons Destruction: Issues Affecting Program Cost, Schedule, and Performance* (Washington, DC: GAO, January 1993), pp. 18–20.

7. Another good-news, bad-news story. While the TOCDF disposal process would be greatly improved over JACADS, the concrete had already been poured for much of the Tooele facility. Redesigned equipment meant that the Army would have to tear up much of its work to ensure that the new equipment would fit correctly in the newly designed facility.

8. National Research Council, *Recommendations for the Disposal of Chemical Agents and Munition*, p. 96.

9. Brigadier General (ret.) Walt Busbee credited Colonel Lou Jackson, USATHAMA commander, for leading the research. The report listed 224 burial sites at 96 total locations, located in 38 states plus the U.S. Virgin Islands and the District of Columbia.

10. Again, for clarity, many of the munitions were not chemical-agent filled but rather were smoke projectiles with a similar hollow interior. The Army Corps of Engineers, overseeing the project and interfacing with the nervous homeowners, would call in the Technical Escort Unit every time that it hit a munition to assess its nature. The few chemical-filled munitions were transported back to Aberdeen Proving Ground. The Corps of Engineers also had to deal with the chemical materiels such as arsenic that had been buried by the World War I scientists. While the majority of chemical materiels were below EPA hazard limits, the implication of chemical warfare agents would cause a continuous public outcry for absolute minimal risk by calling for the Army to evacuate the contaminated soil and to test every residence in the area. American University threatened to sue the Army based on the reduced property values and disrupted academic schedule, which is ironic since it was the American University that begged the Army's Gas Service to fund its chemical warfare research in 1918 in the first place.

11. Committee on Alternative Chemical Demilitarization Technologies, *Alternative Technologies for the Destruction of Chemical Agents and Munitions* (Washington, DC: National Academy Press, 1993), pp. 92–93. This report has a very thorough explanation of the baseline incineration process and chemical disposal efforts by other nations, in addition to its thorough examination of the alternative technologies.

12. From the 1994 NRC report, pp. 130–31. The findings included the following:
- Proceed expeditiously with technology that minimizes total risk to the public.
- Conduct new risk analyses that explicitly account for latent health risks.
- Update the risk assessments of storage, handling, and disposal activities.
- Conduct site-specific risk assessments and reconsider schedule of construction and operation of disposal facilities to reduce the total cumulative risk to the public.

- Continue research on alternative technologies and reexamine potential risk reduction efforts at each site, but do not delay the disposal program pending completion of this research.
- Proactively seek out greater community involvement in decisions regarding the technology selection process, oversight of operations, and decommissioning plans.
- Design disposal systems to separately process agents, energetics, metal parts, and so on.
- Continue with mechanical methods to disassemble the munitions and to separate materiel streams.
- Research means to extract, handle, and process gelled (due to age) CW agents.
- Dispose of energetic materiels by incineration.
- Use incineration (or other high-temperature treatment) for metal parts.
- Identify and demonstrate those improvements to the baseline system that are proven to be safer, less costly, or more rapidly implementable for future facilities.
- Evaluate the application of activated charcoal filter beds to the incineration discharge.
- Accelerate and expand neutralization research to include field-grade and gelled materiels.
- Continue to monitor research developments in pertinent alternative technology areas.
- Examine neutralization followed by transport for final treatment as an alternative for Aberdeen and Newport chemical stockpile sites.
- Consider other proven alternative technologies on the basis of site-specific assessments.
- Maintain the facility and staff at CAMDS facility for future experimentation.
- Demonstrate any alternative technologies at CAMDS and not at the storage sites.
- Continue research into the stability of the M55 rockets and increase stockpile surveillance of potential leakers.
- Establish a program to incrementally hire personnel to ensure that staff growth is consistent with the workload and technical and operational challenges.

13.    GAO/NSIAD-94-123, *Chemical Weapons Destruction: Advantages and Disadvantages of Alternatives to Incineration* (Washington, DC: GAO, 1994), p. 3.

14. In February 1994, DOD changed the Assistant to the Secretary of Defense for Atomic Energy (ATSD(AE)) to become the Assistant to the Secretary of Defense for Nuclear and Chemical and Biological Matters (ATSD(NCB)). The DATSD(Chem Demil) was Dr. Ted Prociv, who served from 1994 through 1998.

15. The ATSD(NCB) position was codified in the National Defense Authorization Act for FY96, Title IX - DOD Organization and Management, Section 901, "Redesignation of the Position of the Assistant to the Secretary of Defense for Atomic Energy."

16. Michael Vigh, "Incinerator Gets Judge's Go-Ahead," *Tooele Transcript-Bulletin* (August 15, 1996), p. 1.

17. OSD and the Army agreed to pay $12 million to Tooele County as an "impact fee," a decision that would later cause problems at the other stockpile sites when the local politicians realized they had a precedent to demand more funds from the Army.

## CHAPTER 10: THE IMPACT OF PUBLIC OUTREACH

1. Most states, especially Arkansas, Alabama, Colorado, and Utah, were very hospitable with the exception of some hecklers. In Oregon, the locals around Umatilla were generally good with the Army, but the big-city officials were less than friendly. Kentucky and Maryland meetings often hosted hostile crowds. Kentucky's state and congressional

representatives in particular often reflected that hostility to the Army's representatives with a strong lack of cooperation.

2. Brigadier General Nydam actually started the paperwork to declassify the stockpile in 1991, following the Bush administration's decision to eliminate most of the stockpile but 5,000 tons (as per the bilateral agreement with the Soviet Union). This information had always been sought by the community activists and environmentalists as necessary information to base the health hazard assessments and risk assessments.

3. Bryan L. Williams, et al., "A Hierarchal Linear Model of Factors Associated with Public Participation among Residents Living Near the U.S. Army's Chemical Weapons Stockpile Sites" (Aberdeen Proving Ground, MD: U.S. Army, 1999), p. 4.

4. Alan Rosenthal, "What's Wrong with the Political System, and How Can It Be Fixed?" *Public Affairs Review* (2001): pp. 2–7.

5. Ibid., p. 3.

6. Innovative Emergency Management and Rowan & Blewitt, Inc, "Chemical Demilitarization Public Outreach: Anniston Baseline Public Opinion Survey," December 1995.

7. Dr. Ted Prociv noted that the CWWG once remarked to him that it would stop monitoring the program and stop going to Congress if the Army committed to not using incineration. In fact, he said, they would have supported transportation as long as the chemical munitions and materiels were not transported to an incinerator. They were very one-dimensional, focusing on the "evils" of incineration and not how well the Army did its job.

8. NRC, *Review and Evaluation of Alternative Chemical Disposal Technologies* (National Academy Press: Washington, DC, September 1996), pp. 4–5.

9. There have been constant discussions on who would take over ACWA and when. No final decisions have been made as of the release of this book.

10. I personally observed this exchange at an early ACWA meeting. The Army engineers, used to working with hard numbers, came to discuss screening criteria, one of which was "no thermal technologies." When it came to measuring efficiencies, the CWWG representative was not prepared to come in with good advice but was rather making the point that the Army engineers had to convince him directly if they wanted to meet the public's trust.

11. The tests were conducted at Aberdeen Proving Ground, Dugway Proving Ground, and CAMDS. The companies participating included Burns and Roe, General Atomics, and Parsons/Allied Signal. Teledyne-Commodore dropped out of the competition. While the Burns and Roe plasma arc technology had promise, its thermal nature reminded the ACWA group of incineration, which essentially doomed it.

12. Recall that had the Army started an incineration-based disposal facility on time, it had estimated completing operations by 1993. The ACWA efforts were adding years and millions of dollars onto a program to address two sites amounting to about 10 percent of the chemical weapons stockpile. Add to this that the ACWA effort really only repeated the same search for technologies that ATAP had proven out.

13. The CTR efforts also built on the U.S.–Soviet Bilateral Chemical Weapons Destruction Agreement, with both countries sharing technical and safety information on destruction technologies. The U.S. government contributed funds to initiate the design and renovation of the Moscow central analytical laboratory, as well as providing analytical equipment worth $4.7 million.

14. OSD divested itself of five other programs to the services. Since then, Congress has directed that all the programs moved by the Defense Reform Initiative be returned to OSD oversight. So much for governmental reform.

15. GAO/NSIAD-97-91, *Chemical Weapons Stockpile: Changes Needed in the Management of the Emergency Preparedness Program* (Washington, DC: GAO, June 1997).

16. In 1994, the Army and FEMA had developed benchmarks to assess the measure of success of their efforts. The GAO used these benchmarks in 1997 to note that the majority of sites had not been completely outfitted. FEMA noted that, while it was correct that no stockpile site was 100 percent prepared, there was measured progress in improving that capability at all eight stockpile sites.

17. GAO-01-850, *Chemical Weapons: FEMA and Army Must Be Proactive in Preparing States for Emergencies* (Washington, DC: GAO, August 2001). The Army noted that the four states that had not yet been certified as meeting the national benchmark level would have done so prior to the start-up of disposal operations. They are continuing to actively work with the remaining three states.

18. This was the result of legislation created by Senator Daniel Inouye (D-HI), who decided to stop any chance of transporting chemical munitions and materiels from one of the CONUS stockpile sites to Johnston Island.

19. These events included (1) a faulty release of agent into the liquid incinerator when it was not functioning; (2) two instances of low agent levels detected in the unpacking area; (3) agent detected in a toxic maintenance area; and (4) agent detected in the corridors and airlocks surrounding a toxic area following a power failure. In all cases, personnel were using protective equipment and were not exposed to the agent. Also, at no time did the agent leave the facility.

20. Testimonies about the event can be found at http://www.house.gov/hasc/schedules/2000.html.

## CHAPTER 11: EVALUATING AND TERMINATING THE DISPOSAL PROGRAM

1. Matthew Creamer, "Army Reorganizes Chemical Weapons Disposal Oversight," *Anniston Star*, December 14, 2001. There is some debate as to whether the Army was being chastised for its execution of the chemical demilitarization program or if the Army was being accused of a general lack of leadership in the chemical and biological defense program and consequence management (fielding WMD Civil Support Teams), and if the demil program was just thrown in along with these two issues. In any event, the decision was made at the top levels of DOD.

2. "Army Ambush," *Anniston Star*, September 24, 2002. http://www.annistonstar.com/opinion/2002/as-editorials-0924-editorial-2i23q1850.htm.

3. Part of this reorganization is an internal Army move to create a research and development command, consolidating SBCCOM and other major commands. The operations elements of SBCCOM responsible for managing the stockpile sites would move into this new agency with the PMCD, causing a consolidated management effort of the entire chemical weapons and disposal program for the first time in history.

4. *Federal Evaluation Policy* (Washington, DC: GAO, 1989).

5. Dye, *Understanding Public Policy*, pp. 349–50. Dye quotes Wilson as denying this is a cynical viewpoint. Groups that are evaluating the policy by law #1 accept the agency's own data, adopt a long-term time frame that maximizes the chance to observe effects, and

don't look for other variables that might be influencing the program. Groups that are evaluating the policy by law #2 (such as the GAO) gather data independently of the agency, adopt a short-term time frame that minimizes the chance to observe effects, and often search for other variables that might explain the program's success other than the agency's own efforts.

6.   See their web page at http://www.cwwg.org for their official positions and commentaries on the program.

7.   Dye, *Understanding Public Policy,* pp. 338–39.

8.   Roseann Mauroni, interview with author. Universal rule number one: everything leaks. Two-liter soda bottles leak, food storage containers leak, tires leak, everything not in a perfect vacuum leaks. The key is whether the leaks are hazardous and to whom; the chemical weapons leaks in and of themselves were hazardous to the workers, not the off-base population.  The potential accidents releasing a large amount of agent were greater hazards.

9.   Neely Tucker and Michael Grunwald, "U.S. Court Upholds Pollution Standards," *Washington Post*, March 27, 2002, pp. A-1, A-4.

10.   Arthur Santana, "First Suit Filed over Chemicals in NW Soil," *Washington Post*, January 29, 2002, p. B-3.

11.   Personally, I have real difficulty believing that other countries will stop manufacturing CB weapons merely because we wear white hats, but that's what the arms control community believes. There will always be those countries that recognize that chemical and biological weapons are very efficient at keeping military conflicts short by attacking an adversary's weakness (poor to nonexistent CB defense equipment and methods).

12.   Gregg Kakesako, "Army Finishes Up Chemical Arms Cleanup at Atoll," *Honolulu Star-Bulletin*, November 30, 2000. The EPA is pushing the DOD to completely restore a pristine environment to the island, meaning the removal of all buildings and dredging up plutonium contamination in the lagoon. Estimates are that it would cost $1.5 billion to restore the island, so that ocean-faring birds could crap on it. Many have joked that the military should just let the ocean reclaim the island, as three-quarters of it would go underwater if the seawalls were not maintained.

13.   Alan C. Miller and Myron Levin, "Disposal of Chemical Arms in U.S. Lags as Costs Mount," *Los Angeles Times*, September 28, 2001.

14.   Source: http://www.whitehouse.gov/omb/budget/fy2003/bud12.html.

15.   GAO/NSIAD-97-18, *Chemical Weapons and Materiel: Key Factors Affecting Disposal Costs and Schedule* (Washington, DC: GAO, February 10, 1997), pp. 6–7.

16.   See http://www.cagw.org/site/PageServer?pagename=news_NewsRelease _04 092002.

17.   Roseann Mauroni, interview with author. Universal rule number two: every time you do something good, something unexpected happens. One could also say that no good deed goes unpunished.

18.   Derek Bok, *The Trouble with Government* (Cambridge, MA: Harvard University Press, 2001), p. 38. Dr. Prociv left the DASA(Chem Demil) position in 1999 after controversy erupted about the amount of funds that the PMCD claimed was actually expended and accounted for. While the bad bookkeeping was eventually corrected, the CWWG and other critics called for Dr. Prociv's removal.

19.   Roseann Mauroni, interview with author: Universal rule number three: nothing's free. Enough said.

20. See http://www.cdc.gov/ncipc for more details.

## CHAPTER 12: REFLECTING ON PUBLIC POLICY

1. Joe Stephens, "Bush 2000 Advisor Offered to Use Clout to Help Enron," *Washington Post*, February 17, 2002, p. A1.

2. Scroggs, *Army Relations with Congress*, pp. 215–24.

3. Ibid., p. 226.

4. Bok, *The Trouble with Government*, pp. 294–95.

5. James R. Carroll, "Chemical Weapons: The Long Goodbye," *Louisville Courier-Journal*, May 21, 2001, p. 1. Quotes from the article attributed to Senator McConnell: "The potential of harm to the public is enormous"; "There's significant doubt that the deadlines will be met because the program has been mismanaged for so long. It doesn't lead you to have much confidence in anything they tell you"; "What we would like is sound science applied to this review [of the chemical demil program], and we'd like attention to this whole matter at the highest possible levels at the Department of Defense."

6. Bok, *The Trouble with Government*, p. 353.

7. Ibid., p. 397.

8. Dye, *Understanding Public Policy*, pp. 323–24.

9. Bok, *The Trouble with Government*, pp. 77–80.

# Selected Bibliography

## BOOKS

Bay, Charles. *The Other Gas Crisis: Chemical Weapons*. Carlisle Barracks, PA: Strategic Studies Institute, 1979.

Bok, Derek. *The Trouble with Government*. Cambridge, MA: Harvard University Press, 2001.

Colten, Craig E., and Peter N. Skinner. *The Road to Love Canal: Managing Industrial Waste before EPA*. Austin: University of Texas Press, 1996.

Dye, Thomas R. *Understanding Public Policy, 9th edition*. Englewood Cliffs, NJ: Prentice Hall, 1998.

Glynn, Patrick. *Closing Pandora's Box: Arms Races, Arms Control, and the History of the Cold War*. New York, NY: Basic Books, 1992.

Hill, Marquita K. *Understanding Environmental Pollution*. Cambridge: Cambridge University Press, 1997.

Jones, Charles O. *An Introduction to the Study of Public Policy, 3rd edition*. Monterey, CA: Brooks/Cole, 1984.

Mauroni, Albert J. *America's Struggle with Chemical-Biological Warfare*. Westport, CT: Praeger, 2000.

Scroggs, Stephen K. *Army Relations with Congress: Thick Armor, Dull Sword, Slow Horse*. Westport, CT: Praeger, 2000.

Seagrave, Sterling. *Yellow Rain: A Journey through the Terror of Chemical Warfare*. New York: M. Evans, 1978.

Spiers, Edward M. *Chemical and Biological Weapons: A Study in Proliferation*. New York, NY: St. Martin's Press, 1994.

Stockholm International Peace Research Institute (SIPRI). *Chemical Weapons: Destruction and Conversion*. London: Taylor and Francis, 1980.

## GOVERNMENT REPORTS

Brankowitz, William R. "Chemical Stockpile Disposal Program: Chemical Weapons Movement History Compilation." Aberdeen Proving Ground, MD: PEO-PM for Chemical Demilitarization, 1987.

Chemical Warfare Review Commission. "Report of the Chemical Warfare Review Commission." Washington, DC: GPO, 1985.

Flamm, Kevin. "Chemical Agent and Munition Disposal: Summary of the U.S. Army's Experience." Aberdeen Proving Ground: PEO-PM for Chemical Demilitarization, September 1987.

General Accounting Office. *Bigeye Bomb: 1988 Status Report*. Washington, DC: GAO, 1998.

———. *Bigeye Bomb: Unresolved Developmental Issues*. Washington, DC: GAO, 1989.

———. *Bigeye Bomb: Evaluation of Operational Tests*. Washington, DC: GAO, 1989.

———. *Chemical Munitions: Cost Estimates for Demilitarization and Production*. Washington, DC: GAO, 1985

———. *Chemical Warfare: DOD's Successful Effort to Remove U.S. Chemical Weapons from Germany*. Washington, DC: GAO, 1991

———. *Chemical Weapons and Materiel: Key Factors Affecting Disposal Costs and Schedule*. Washington, DC: GAO, 1997.

———. *Chemical Weapons: FEMA and Army Must Be Proactive in Preparing States for Emergencies*. Washington, DC: GAO, 2001.

———. *Chemical Weapons: Stockpile Destruction Delayed at the Army's Prototype Disposal Facility*. Washington, DC: GAO, 1990.

———. *Chemical Weapons Destruction: Advantages and Disadvantages of Alternatives to Incineration*. Washington, DC: GAO, 1994.

———. *Chemical Weapons Destruction: Issues Affecting Program Cost, Schedule, and Performance*. Washington, DC: GAO, 1993.

———. *Chemical Weapons Stockpile: Changes Needed in the Management of the Emergency Preparedness Program*. Washington, DC: GAO, 1997.

House of Representatives Committee on Foreign Affairs, Subcommittee on National Security Policy and Scientific Development. *U.S. Chemical Warfare Policy*. Washington, DC: GPO, 1974.

National Research Council. *Disposal of Chemical Agent Identification Sets*. Washington, DC: National Academy Press, 1999.

———. *Disposal of Chemical Munitions and Agents*. Washington, DC: National Academy Press, 1984.

———. *Recommendations for the Disposal of Chemical Agents and Munitions*. Washington, DC: National Academy Press, 1994.

———. *Risk Assessment and Management at Deseret Chemical Depot and the Tooele Chemical Agent Disposal Facility*. Washington, DC: National Academy Press, 1997.

———. *Review and Evaluation of Alternative Chemical Disposal Technologies*. Washington, DC: National Academy Press, 1996.

Senate Committee on Armed Services. *Chemical Warfare*. Washington, DC: GPO, September 4, 1980.

Senate Committee on Labor and Public Welfare. *Chemical and Biological Weapons: Some Possible Approaches for Lessening the Threat and Danger*. Washington, DC: GPO, 1969.

U.S. Army Program Manager for Chemical Demilitarization. *U.S. Army Activity in the U.S. Biological Warfare Programs, Volumes I–II*. Aberdeen Proving Ground: U.S. Army, February 24, 1977.

———. *Chemical Stockpile Disposal Program Final Programmatic Environmental Impact Statement, Volumes I–III*. Aberdeen Proving Ground: U.S. Army, January 1988.

U.S. Army Toxic and Hazardous Agents Materials Agency. *Construction and Operation of the Proposed BZ Demilitarization Facility at Pine Bluff Arsenal, Pine Bluff, Arkansas*. Aberdeen Proving Ground: U.S. Army, August 1983.

## JOURNAL ARTICLES AND INDEPENDENT REPORTS

Rosenthal, Alan. "What's Wrong with the Political System, and How Can It Be Fixed?" *Public Affairs Review* (2001).

Smithson, Amy. *The U.S. Chemical Weapons Destruction Program: Views, Analysis, and Recommendations.* Washington, DC: Henry L. Stimson Center, 1994.

Williams, Bryan L., et al. "A Hierarchal Linear Model of Factors Associated with Public Participation among Residents Living Near the U.S. Army's Chemical Weapons Stockpile Sites." Aberdeen Proving Ground: U.S. Army, 1999.

# Index

## About the Author

**AL MAURONI** is Senior Policy Analyst with Analytic Services Inc. His previous works include *Chemical-Biological Defense: U.S. Military Policies and Decisions in the Gulf War* (Praeger, 1998) and *America's Struggle with Chemical- Biological Warfare* (Praeger, 2000).